THE POLITICS OF WOMEN'S RIGHTS

THE POLITICS
OF WOMEN'S RIGHTS

PARTIES, POSITIONS,
AND CHANGE

Christina Wolbrecht

PRINCETON UNIVERSITY PRESS   PRINCETON, NEW JERSEY

Library of Congress Cataloging-in-Publication Data
Wolbrecht, Christina.
The politics of women's rights :
parties, positions, and change / Christina Wolbrecht.
p. cm.
Includes bibliographical references and index.
ISBN 0-691-04856-8 (cloth: alk. paper) — ISBN 0-691-04857-6
(pbk.: alk. paper)
1. Women's rights—United States. 2. Political parties—United States.
3. United States—Politics and government—1945–1989.
4. United States—Politics and government—1989–1993. I. Title.
HQ1236.5.U6 W63 2000
305.42'0973—dc21   99-048918

This book has been composed in Galliard typeface

The paper used in this publication meets the minimum requirements
of ANSI / NISO Z39.48-1992 (R1997) (*Permanence of Paper*)

http://pup.princeton.edu

Printed in the United States of America

1   3   5   7   9   10   8   6   4   2

_____ **For My Parents** _____

TOM AND CHERYL WOLBRECHT

Contents

Illustrations

Tables

Acronyms

AAUW	American Association of University Women
AFL-CIO	American Federation of Labor-Congress of Industrial Organizations
BPW	National Federation of Business and Professional Women's Clubs
EEOC	Equal Employment Opportunity Commission
ERA	Equal Rights Amendment
GOP	Republican party ("Grand Old Party")
NARAL	National Abortion Rights Action League
NOW	National Organization for Women
NWP	National Women's Party
NWPC	National Women's Political Caucus
NYT	*The New York Times*
RWTF	Republican Women's Task Force
UAW	Union of Auto Workers
WCF	Women's Campaign Fund
WEAL	Women's Equity Action League

Acknowledgments

I ALWAYS peruse the acknowledgments first when I pick up a book, even one I have no intention of reading. I would like to think this practice reflects the natural inquisitiveness of a social scientist, but my motivations are probably less noble. As I now sit down to compose my own acknowledgments, I am overwhelmed by the task of adequately expressing my gratitude to those who have contributed to this work along the way. I accept full responsibility for all remaining errors, but given the quality of guidance and advice I have received, any commendation is necessarily shared.

This project began as my dissertation at Washington University in St. Louis, where I enjoyed an unusually challenging, stimulating, and, dare I say, pleasurable graduate school experience. My committee deserves particular recognition for their role in setting me on this course. Lee Epstein provided, and continues to provide, invaluable advice and input not only on the substance of my research, but also on all aspects of my academic career. I am most grateful. Bob Salisbury's knowledge of history, politics, and social science never cease to amaze me; I hope this work reflects in just a small way the richness of his understanding of these times, events, and processes. Finally, I am convinced that to understand what it means to be one of John Sprague's students you must experience it for yourself; it cannot adequately be described. Luckily, more than a few of us have been so blessed. For the rest of you, I can only say that John's insight, generosity, and energy know no bounds. His sage counsel, conviction that this project was worth doing and that I was the person who should and could do it, and persistent admonition (which sometimes took the form of e-mails from vessels docked off the eastern seaboard) that I *write* made this project not only possible, but—within reason—enjoyable.

Sadly, I am unable to express my gratitude directly to one of my most important mentors. Bob Durr signed off on my original dissertation proposal, and he and I had many conversations about this research in its earliest stages. He died in August 1996 when the project was still in its infancy. Yet as a teacher, example, co-author, and friend, Bob's influence is reflected throughout this work. This research would have been improved by his presence, but his instruction and encouragement nonetheless inspired and guided me throughout. I regret that Bob will not see this work in its final form. I regret far more the loss of a dear friend.

I benefited from other input as well. Conversations with Kevin Quinn, Andy Whitford, Kevin Corder, Bill Lowry, and Carol Kohfeld on topics from substantive interpretation to statistical modeling challenged and focused my thinking. Kathy Corder introduced me to the wonderful world of data and taught me much about negotiating academia. I owe a special debt to Andrew Martin, who read drafts, suggested approaches, accessed data, supplied Stata code, and otherwise served as an invaluable critic, sounding board, and friend. Lee Ann Banaszak offered thoughtful insights and advice, while the willingness of both Anne Costain and Barbara Burrell to share data and sources serve as models of the scholarly ideal. Some of the data employed in this research were made available through the Inter-University Consortium for Political and Social Research (ICPSR). Other data were available because Keith Poole and Howard Rosenthal set high standards of scholarship by sharing their Congressional NOMINATE scores via the Internet. None of these individuals or institutions bear any responsibility for the interpretations or analyses offered here.

The University of Notre Dame provided a conducive academic home for the completion of this research. I am grateful to Jim McAdams, Sam Best, and Ben Radcliff for their input and advice and to the Institute for Scholarship in the Liberal Arts in the College of Arts and Letters for valuable research support. Finally, the careful critiques offered by the anonymous reviewers greatly improved the final version of this manuscript. I thank the editorial staff at Princeton University Press, particularly editor Malcolm Litchfield, for making the arduous process of bringing this work to its present form as pleasant as possible.

My family and friends, especially Tim and Venessa Wrye, Stephanie Martin, Kim and Derek Enz, Nicole Brackman, Bethany Wolbrecht, and Eric Wolbrecht, made the journey bearable. This book is dedicated to my parents, Tom and Cheryl Wolbrecht, with love and gratitude for their sense of humor and perspective and for their unshakable faith in and unceasing support of all my endeavors. Finally, I thank my husband, Matt Doppke, who truly makes it possible for me to enjoy both a professional and personal life and fills the latter with so much meaning and joy.

THE POLITICS OF WOMEN'S RIGHTS

CHAPTER ONE

Women's Rights and the American Parties

AT ITS 1980 convention, the Republican party refused to endorse the Equal Rights Amendment (ERA) in its platform, reversing a pattern of nearly forty years of official party support. In convention that same year, the Democratic party not only retained a pro-ERA plank but also pledged to provide financial support only to those candidates who backed the amendment. Just as the Republicans' move signaled a historic break, the Democratic party's action represented the culmination of an important shift; Democrats had traditionally been ambivalent, if not hostile, to the ERA. Four years later, feminists wielded enough power within the Democratic party that their central demand—a woman on the party's presidential ticket—was met. Moreover, by 1984 the parties had so diverged over women's rights that the women's movement's preeminent organization, the National Organization for Women (NOW), abandoned its traditional nonpartisanship and endorsed the Democratic ticket.

For women's rights and the American political parties, the lines are now drawn with considerable clarity. The Republican party has largely adopted an opposing position, distancing itself from feminism and siding with those who prefer more traditional women's roles. The Democratic party has placed itself at the other end of the women's rights spectrum, generally supporting public policies that assist in the expansion of social, political, and economic roles for women. In short, the two American parties have become polarized over the issue of women's rights, when once there was at the least consensus and, prior to that, perhaps even the opposite alignment.

These developments present a compelling empirical puzzle: Why did the parties adopt the positions they did on women's rights issues, and how and why have they changed? Party history vis-à-vis women's rights prior to the 1970s does not anticipate the present alignment; if anything, it suggests a tendency toward the very opposite arrangement. This work addresses this puzzle by developing a theoretically grounded explanation for the adoption and change of party issue positions and by applying that model to the specific case of the parties' relative positions on women's rights from 1952 to 1992.

While this research examines a particular empirical puzzle, it speaks to our understanding of American politics generally, particularly the American party system. Understanding how and why political parties adopt positions on issues has occupied theorists at least since Downs (1957), and has been of interest to scholars concerned with a wide range of related phenomena ranging from voting behavior and party identification to public policy development and implementation. Questions of change with regard to issues and alignments have been central to the study of American elections, particularly in Key's work (1959, 1955) on critical realignment and in the extensive literature that has followed (cf. Shafer 1991; Sundquist 1973; Burnham 1970). Congressional realignments have also attracted considerable attention (cf. Sinclair 1982; Asher and Weisberg 1978). These issues are brought into sharper focus by the issue evolution model proposed by Carmines and Stimson (1989). This research also draws from agenda-setting literature that offers relevant insights into the role of issue definition and agenda setting in shaping political alignments (cf. Baumgartner and Jones 1993; Kingdon 1984; Cobb and Elder 1983).

Moreover, I am concerned with a phenomenon—party change on women's rights—that has largely gone without comment, much less serious analysis, from social scientists (for exceptions, see Freeman 1987 and Costain 1991). Gender politics, unilaterally and as part of a larger cultural politics, has occupied a central place in twentieth-century American political discourse for some thirty years. At the same time, polarization over women's rights has emerged as one of the most readily identifiable, if not defining, distinctions between the parties. This polarization has had important consequences for the shape of debate and for the outcome of the public policy processes regarding issues of women's rights. Systematic examination and explanation of the evolution of the parties' positions on women's rights thus address a meaningful "real world" phenomenon as well as fill a scholarly void.

THE PUZZLE: A VERY BRIEF HISTORY

In 1952, the two parties' positions on women's rights were largely as they had been since World War II. The Democratic party stood on the side of the protectionist status quo, preferring public policy that provided special protections for women and opposing, for the most part, legal sex equality. Republicans, on the other hand, generally favored proposals for greater legal equality for women. In 1940, the GOP became the first party to endorse the ERA and since that time had been relatively more supportive of the amendment. The Democrats added the ERA to their platform in 1944, but generally emphasized their commitment to protecting the health and welfare of working women by siding with the protectionists (Costain 1991; Evans 1989).

Despite these differences, neither party actively championed women's rights. Presidents from both parties made occasional weak statements in support of women's rights, but their appeals to women as an electoral constituency largely took the form of symbolic actions, such as speeches and appointments. Support for women's rights legislation was lukewarm on both sides of the Congressional aisle. The ERA did pass the Senate in 1953, with greater support from Republicans than from Democrats, but it was blocked from floor consideration in the House by Democratic Judiciary Committee chair and ERA foe Emanuel Celler. Women's rights issues attracted little public note or press coverage (Costain 1992, 1991; Harrison 1988).

As women's rights became increasingly salient in the 1960s and early 1970s, a gradual convergence of the Democratic and Republican positions occurred (Costain 1991). Democratic President John F. Kennedy initiated the President's Commission on the Status of Women (in part, to counter growing support for the ERA), which provided evidence of and suggested policy solutions to counter discrimination against women. His successor, Lyndon Johnson, issued a number of executive orders in response to emergent feminist demands. Republican Richard Nixon publicly supported the ERA, but otherwise largely ignored feminist requests, even those coming from within his own party (Freeman 1975). In Congress, the parties' delegations became less differentiated by their positions on women's rights through the 1960s, and in the early 1970s, a historic number of women's rights–related bills and provisions were passed into law. By 1972, feminist concerns occupied the attention of both parties' conventions as never before, with Republican and Democratic platforms pledging similar action on women's rights (Freeman 1987; Tolchin and Tolchin 1973).

When efforts for Congressional enactment of the ERA began in earnest in 1970, both parties were active in the alliance organized to seek its passage (Freeman 1975). That goal was achieved by a similarly bipartisan voting coalition in March 1972. Yet what was originally a bipartisan effort became an increasingly partisan debate as the battle for ratification by the states dragged on through the decade. The ERA dominated the national discourse over women's rights at the same time that the "mood of bipartisan consensus on ERA in the 1970s began to show stress cracks" (Costain 1992, 125). Bipartisanship still seemed possible at mid-decade. Republican President Gerald Ford favored the amendment, and his wife Betty campaigned extensively for its passage. Republican feminists fought successfully to retain the pro-ERA plank in the party's platform at its 1976 convention (Hartmann 1989). Democratic President Jimmy Carter was likewise an ERA supporter, campaigning for the ERA and supporting other feminist positions (Costain 1991).

As the 1970s came to a close, however, the parties became increasingly polarized on the ERA and other women's rights issues. In 1980, the Republican party removed the ERA from its platform, while Democrats solidified and strengthened their support for the ERA and other feminist concerns. On other issues, such as abortion, the parties' positions diverged sharply as well. By the early 1980s, the two parties stood on opposing sides of the debate over women's rights (Costain 1992). Party actions since that time have only reinforced and deepened this alignment, as both parties' official platforms continued to reflect the differences that emerged in 1980. By 1992, convention observers identified differences on women's rights as among the most striking distinctions between the two parties (Freeman 1993).

The lines have thus been drawn with considerable clarity since 1980. The Democratic party stands as the party of women's rights, aligned with feminist organizations and most likely to support feminist policy initiatives. The Republican party, on the other hand, has generally staked out an opposing position, distancing itself from feminism and siding with those who prefer more traditional women's roles and responsibilities. As I have suggested, a different alignment characterized the parties' positions on women's rights prior to the 1970s. The women's rights agenda was quite small and attracted little public attention, but on that small agenda, Republicans were more active. As we will see, it is overstating the case to suggest that Republicans were once great supporters of women's rights, while Democrats were opponents. In truth, the majority of elites in both parties—indeed, the entire political system—did little to promote gender equality or address women's needs through public policy during the 1950s and early 1960s. In the early 1970s, however, the parties held strikingly similar positions on women's rights, as represented by their platforms and the behavior of their members of Congress and presidents. Thus, the puzzle is why the parties have moved apart on women's rights since that time and why the resultant alignment is so different than what party positioning in the 1950s might have predicted.

PREVIOUS EXPLANATIONS

Political parties have been called the "missing variable" in women and politics research (Baer 1993). The past thirty years have witnessed an explosion of social science research on women and politics, a topic long ignored or considered irrelevant. Yet, while much of this literature touches on issues of partisanship—particularly the considerable body of work on the partisan gender gap (cf. Clark and Clark 1999; Carroll 1988; Conover 1988; Erie and Rein 1988; Miller 1988; Mansbridge 1985)—few have focused specifically on the realignment of the parties over women's rights, even when that realignment is an implicit assumption of many explanations of said gender gap. Studies of the modern women's movement (cf. Costain 1992; Davis 1991; Freeman 1975), the rise and fall of the ERA (cf. Mathews and De Hart 1990; Mansbridge 1986; Boles 1979), and the evolving role of women in politics (cf. Hartmann 1989) note increasing party polarization over women's rights, but few seek to explain this phenomenon or examine its consequences. A few practitioners of politics—activists, pundits, and the press—have commented on this development, but the emphasis is on description rather than explanation, and where explanation is attempted, it is not consciously theoretical or derived from any scholarly tradition (cf. Blumenthal 1996; Melich 1996; Burkett 1996). When scholars have addressed realignment on women's rights, the focus has generally been on one institutional form of party, such as party conventions (Freeman 1987) or presidents (Costain 1991). Work examining other gender-related phenomenon has often treated the present party alignment as natural or preordained. Costain and Costain (1987), for example, describe the changing strategies of the women's movement, including the shift to party and electoral politics in the 1980s. Yet they make little note of the fact that when the movement began to emphasize party politics, it was almost exclusively *Democratic* party politics.

Students of the political parties as organizations or within the institutions of government have also been unlikely to take note of the transformation and polarization of party positions on women's rights. Studies of Congressional realignment and polarization in the twentieth century, for example, give little attention to women's issues (cf. Rohde 1991; Sinclair 1982). Those interested in the emergence and impact of cultural or social, as opposed to economic, political cleavages either ignore women's issues (Miller and Levitin 1984) or lump them together with family, cultural, or general social issues (Shafer and Claggett 1995; but see Leege and Wald n.d. for an exception). Generally, when women's rights are mentioned, it is in the context of discussions of the emergence of the New Right and social conservatism (cf. Himmelstein 1990; Baer and Bositis 1988) or more general rights-based politics (cf. Edsall and Edsall 1991) and the party system. As I argue, the development of the link between social conservatism and feminism is crucial to understanding the polarization of the party's positions on women's rights. Likewise, the association of women's rights with a more general rights agenda, especially civil rights for racial minorities, was an important development that helps explain the positions adopted by party elites across this time period. These developments merit closer examination.

Despite the general lack of attention to the emergence of a party cleavage on women's rights, a few hypotheses can be identified. In a rare explicit attempt to explain this outcome vis-à-vis the parties' organizations,

Freeman (1987; also 1986) argues that the Democratic party is generally more responsive to organized interests that can claim to represent recognized party constituencies. Those seeking power in the Republican party, she asserts, do better to build alliances with powerful individuals within the party and conduct bargaining in a less public and contentious manner. She suggests that the structure and political culture of the respective parties make the Democratic party more receptive to organized groups, particularly those on the periphery of society. For Republicans, the party itself is expected to be the primary loyalty, and conflicting alliances are viewed with suspicion. Describing the efforts of both Democratic and Republican feminists for influence within their national party organizations in the 1970s and 1980s, she provides a framework for understanding why the former were so much more successful than the latter.

Freeman identifies a number of important differences between the Democratic and Republican parties that we might expect to affect their positions on women's rights. Her explanation is not entirely satisfactory, however. Freeman overstates the resistance of the Republican party to demands based on representation of an important constituency. Arguing that power in the Republican party can only be gained through personal connections to powerful party elites disregards the sway the religious right (in its various incarnations) has obtained within the GOP over the last twenty years and the influence that other electoral constituencies boast within the party. Women's groups also attempted to pressure the Republican party on the merits of their numbers and resources. The GOP responded with appeals to certain demographic groups of women (Witt 1985; Mueller 1988a; Bonk 1988), but demands for feminist planks have been almost uniformly rebuffed since 1980 (Hartmann 1989). As Freeman concedes, there have been feminists with affiliations to the various power centers within the GOP, but "the personal connections of Republican feminists have not been to the winners of intraparty political struggles" (1987, 215). The coalition politics Freeman alludes to are crucial to understanding the fate of women's rights in the Republican party.

While not the focus of their research, others have suggested explanations for the transformation and polarization of party positions. Fading opposition to the ERA on behalf of organized labor and the invalidation of protective legislation via the implementation of Title VII of the 1964 Civil Rights Act are oft-cited reasons for the Democratic side of the shift (Costain 1992; Hartmann 1989; Freeman 1975). The labor movement opposed the ERA historically, as they expected it to eliminate the special protections they had fought to obtain for women workers. Not coincidentally, protective legislation also had the effect of discouraging employers from hiring women and thus reducing competition for jobs. Yet by 1970, both the Equal Employment Opportunity Commission (EEOC) and the federal judiciary were interpreting Title VII to invalidate protective legislation, usually by extending those privileges to men (Mansbridge 1986). As a result, labor's—and thus the Democratic party's—main grounds for opposition were eliminated.

The role of labor unions and the declining relevance of protective legislation are important factors in explaining the Democratic party's changing position on the ERA and women's rights in general. There is evidence, however, that the Democratic party was moving toward what was then the GOP position in support of the ERA *before*, or at the very least *as*, it was becoming clear that Title VII would invalidate protective legislation for women, and *before* labor officially endorsed the amendment. Costain (1992) shows that in the early 1960s sponsorship of the ERA was negatively correlated with support for labor unions. Yet "by the mid-sixties, when labor opposition remained firm, new sponsors of the ERA were disproportionately pro-labor and liberal" (60). Something more complex than a simple causal link between the union's official stance and the Democratic party's position appears to be at work.

Others have emphasized the rise of conservatism, and the consequent near elimination of moderates, in the Republican party's coalition as a factor in explaining the GOP's historic reversal in 1980 and its subsequent positions on women's rights (Melich 1996). Hartmann writes, "Feminism gave its last gasp within the Republican party in 1976. By 1980, conservatives had wrested control of the party and, although women were well represented as delegates, feminist concerns were not" (1989, 84). Costain echoes the sentiment: "The growing power of the conservative wing of the Republican party seems to have virtually silenced GOP presidential support for women's rights" (1991, 121).

There can be little doubt that the rise of conservatism in the Republican party played a major role in reversing that party's position on the ERA and on women's rights in general. Yet such an explanation should not be oversimplified. First, a distinction needs to be clearly drawn between libertarian or economic conservatives and religious or social conservatives (Klatch 1987). The conservative movement within the Republican party in the 1950s and 1960s was largely of the libertarian type, although traditionalists were part of that coalition (Brennan 1995). When the conservative wing gained power within the GOP in the 1970s, however, social conservatives were at the forefront. This distinction is important because while laissez-faire conservatives are not particularly opposed to women's rights and have, in fact, supported parts of the feminist agenda, social conservatives have evaluated, and as a result opposed, women's rights from a very different perspective. Second, while social conservatives used their influence to shape the Republican party's stance on women's rights, they gained that influence initially because women's rights (particularly the ERA and abortion) were such powerful mobilizing issues in the 1970s (Himmelstein 1990). An understanding of the effect of the religious right on elite party polarization over women's rights in the 1970s must carefully consider the changing meaning of that issue to those already participating and those drawn into the debate.

As this discussion suggests, attempts to explain the evolution of the parties' positions on women's rights thus far have been largely ad hoc and descriptive. Very few authors have made elucidation of this phenomenon a focus of their work, and others have simply assumed causality in broad strokes. The purpose of this research is to provide a more theoretically satisfying and empirically supported explanation.

EXPLAINING PARTY ISSUE REALIGNMENT

I adopt as a first principle the assumption that the primary goal of parties is electoral success. While clearly parties can and do pursue other goals, the necessity of winning elections to achieve most of those objectives gives the electoral goal primacy. Policy issues are thus primarily a means for electoral success (Downs 1957). This is not to say that party elites do not have preferences with regards to many, or most, important policy issues, nor that such elites do not at times insist upon those positions despite negative electoral repercussions. Yet a party that repeatedly goes against the policy preferences of the majority of the electorate on every issue (particularly those most salient) will eventually fail to win any elections, and a party that does not win elections ceases to exist (Schlesinger 1984). Considerable debate wages over the question of whether parties are office-seeking or benefit-seeking (cf. Wittman 1990; Schlesinger 1975). I take the position I believe is most consistent with reality: Parties are, by necessity if not by definition, primarily office-seeking, but the centrality of that goal does not rule out neither the existence nor the consequences of secondary objectives, including public policy goals (Schlesinger 1975; Aranson and Ordeshook 1972).

My thesis is that party positions are determined by the perceived utility of specific issue positions for maintaining and expanding the party's base of support. Position on any issue at any one time is thus determined by three factors: the party elites, the party coalitions, and the issue itself. A shift in a party's position can result from a change in any one of these three factors. Party elites determine which stances will best achieve the goal of maximizing votes and seats. A change in the membership of that elite may introduce new preferences or understandings of the link between an issue position and the party coalition. The party's coalition of interests shapes the decision calculus of those elites by informing their expectations vis-à-vis the relationship between a given issue stance and support from the party's base. The parties' coalitions are likewise open to shifts and changes, which can contribute to an evolution of issue positions on the part of one or both of the parties as elites seek to respond to the changing coalition. Finally, the nature and meaning of the issue in terms of its real and perceived advantages and disadvantages vis-à-vis the party's coalition shape the response of party elites. Issues can vary across time in the meaning and consequences associated with them in ways that are important for the interest cleavages that form around them and, as a result, for the calculations of elites concerning the relationship between issue position and the party coalition.

The stability and salience of the issue provide the fourth important ingredient for explaining change in the relative issue positions adopted by the parties. Most issues are characterized by stability of participation, understanding, and alliances most of the time (Carmines and Stimson 1989). Under such conditions—what Baumgartner and Jones (1993) describe as issue equilibrium—the issue is largely absent from the broader political debate, and participation is limited to a small number of interested activists, members of Congress, and bureaucrats. The parties' positions, if they adopt them at all, are largely fixed. From time to time, however, this equilibrium is disturbed and the issue moves on to the larger political agenda, becoming the grist for the more public mill of presidents, Congress, and parties. Issue redefinition is likely, and the alignments of the interests around the issue shift and develop. It is under these conditions that shifts in either party's position on the issue as a result of changes in the factors identified here become most likely, in part because it is those very sorts of changes that are likely to contribute to a disruption in issue equilibrium and in part because the attendant public salience, and thus greater electoral relevancy, forces party elites to examine and reevaluate their previous positions.

My argument is that the way women's rights were defined, framed, and understood changed across this period. In the 1950s and early 1960s, the debate over women's rights was largely understood as a choice between protection, the status quo, and equality. Women's rights mapped only weakly on to the general left–right spectrum, if at all. For various reasons consistent with both their basic ideological predispositions and the preferences of their constituencies, Republicans favored equality and Democrats favored protection. As a result of various legal, political, and social developments, the equality versus protection debate generally dissipated in the late 1960s and early 1970s. As women's rights grew increasingly salient, the debate became defined in very different terms. Women's rights were viewed through the lens of the counterculture politics of the 1960s and were linked in policy and approach to social movement politics, particularly the struggle for civil rights. Rather than equality versus protection, the women's rights debate became framed in terms of tradition versus liberation and was associated with controversy over the relationship between the political sphere and the family, sexuality, religion, and morality. The women's rights agenda expanded and diversified. Women's rights issues took on a sharp dimensionality, mapping onto the left–right political spectrum.

As a result of these changes in the meaning associated with women's rights, and compounded by shifts in the composition of their coalitions, Democrats emerged as the party far more supportive of women's rights policy initiatives, while Republicans generally staked out positions in opposition. For Democrats, women's rights fit well with that party's tradition of favoring government intervention on behalf of the marginalized and oppressed. The association of women's demands with those of racial minorities encouraged the Democratic party, considered the party of civil rights (Carmines and Stimson 1989), to support women's rights. Women's rights were attractive to important elements of the party's coalition, particularly the various social movement–related, rights-oriented groups that had come to identify with the Democratic party in the 1960s and 1970s, as well as to the growing number of working women who were an increasingly important part of the party's electoral strategy. For Republicans, on the other hand, the emerging dimensionality of women's rights was anathema to the party's conservative small government philosophy. The identification of feminism with a radical counterculture and threats to traditional sexual and familial arrangements alienated the social conservatives who were becoming a larger and more important portion of the GOP's coalition. Traditional business interests, long the province of the Republican party, opposed the interference into economic practices that many feminist policies were viewed as requiring. The result was a realignment and polarization of the parties on women's rights.

This investigation into the transformation of the parties' relative positions on women's rights issues thus highlights the importance of issues themselves—the context, conditions, meanings, and frames associated with them—in determining the positions adopted by political parties. Even when many actual policy proposals remain unchanged, how an issue is viewed and understood can change dramatically. The women's rights revolution transformed the politics of women's rights and coincided with, as well as contributed to, significant shifts in the composition of the parties' coalitions. Together, these factors led Democratic and Republican elites, both new and old, to view the electoral utility of various positions on women's rights with very different cognitive frames and expectations in the 1990s than they had in the 1950s, with significant consequences for the parties' relative positions.

POLITICAL PARTIES AND THE REPRESENTATION
OF INTERESTS

"Democracy," E. E. Schattschneider claims in his classic text *Party Government*, "is unthinkable save in terms of parties" (1942, 1). An examination of the changing stands of the Democratic and Republican parties on the specific issue of women's rights necessarily entails an investigation into the functioning of the American party system, and thus of American democracy. The United States is not characterized by a responsible party system where political parties put forward specific platforms that are translated directly into public policy by the party that controls the government. Nevertheless, as the central link between citizens and government, political parties play a crucial role in the functioning of American democracy (cf. Eldersveld 1981). In the words of V. O. Key, "political parties are the basic institutions for the translation of mass preferences into public policy" (1967, 432).

Political parties contribute to the operation of democracy in the United States in a number of ways. As mobilizing agents, parties stimulate, manage, and organize the political participation of citizens, an important condition of a functioning democracy (cf. Wielhouwer and Lockerbie 1994; Huckfeldt and Sprague 1992). For citizens of various levels of sophistication and education, parties provide a vital source of the assimilation, socialization, and information necessary for negotiating a complex and multilayered political system (cf. Beck 1997; Erie 1988; Ranney 1968; Ranney and Kendall 1956). Parties contribute to the stability of the polity by managing conflict and promoting the peaceful transition of power (cf. Eldersveld 1981; Key 1964).

Such contributions, however, are incidental to the central purpose of political parties: the contesting of elections for the purpose of attaining control of the levers of government. Other organizations may mobilize, socialize, or unify, but the unique and defining functions of political parties are the selection, promotion, and organization of candidates for elective office. Thus, electoral competition, the principal mechanism in a representative democracy, defines the central characteristic of political parties. Moreover, while much research of the past twenty years has focused on the decline of American parties, parties' role in structuring electoral choice remains unchallenged. Americans still go to the polls to elect—almost exclusively—Democrats and Republicans to national, state, and, in many cases, local offices. While the ties between individual citizens and the parties, as reflected in reported party identification, appear to have weakened across the twentieth century, the two major parties nevertheless continue to dominate electoral competition (Schlesinger 1985, 1984; Winters 1976).

Parties thus determine the alternatives available to voters. As such, parties control both the candidates and the public policy alternatives from which citizens select (Ranney and Kendall 1956). In a representative democracy, voting is the primary mechanism for the expression of the preferences of the people, and that mechanism is fundamentally influenced by the options the parties choose to put forward. Said another way, "the effects of voting behavior are conditioned by the alternative policy positions represented by opposing candidates and parties" (Ginsberg 1976, 41).

For this reason, parties have long been viewed as mediating linkages between citizens and government (cf. Brown 1995; Eldersveld 1981; Key 1967). Early theorists expressed concern that the multitude of choices and messages with which citizens would have to contend made democracy unwieldy and impractical; by organizing elections, parties have long been lauded as making democracy workable (Ranney and Kendall 1956; Schattschneider 1942). Indeed, theorists, social scientists, and political practitioners alike often describe parties as uniquely suited to provide this vital link between the people and their government. As broad-based organizations, American parties are praised for their ability to negotiate consensus and cooperation among wide-ranging interests and groups. As established institutions, parties boast the resources, experience, and skills necessary to undertake the complex task of putting forth slates of candidates and policy positions. Party elites have a vested interest in protecting and upholding the party's reputation, be it for particular standards of conduct, candidate quality, or stands on issues (Wittman 1990; Alesina 1988; Bernhardt and Ingberman 1985). Thus, the longevity of the American parties contributes to an accountability that extends beyond particular electoral contests, times, and places. "In short, only political parties can provide us with the cohesion, continuity and accountability necessary to make democracy work" (California Committee on Party Renewal, quoted in Polsby and Wildavsky 1991, xiv; see also Budge and Hofferbert 1990; Eldersveld 1981; Key 1964; Ranney and Kendall 1956).

If political parties provide crucial mediation between citizens and government, then the quality of that linkage is of central interest for what it reveals about the quality of our democracy. Several concerns are relevant here. First is the degree of choice offered by the parties. A functioning democracy requires that citizens encounter real options at the ballot box. If the parties offer candidates and platforms that are not greatly distinguished from each other, then the voters' decision contains no potential for affecting the functioning of government, and the democratic linkage is meaningless. Clearly, the degree of choice offered by the two major American parties pales in comparison to that within the party systems in many other advanced industrial democracies (Beck 1997; Erikson, Wright, and McIver 1989; Hibbs 1977). Yet, despite the Downsian prediction of two indistinguishable parties concentrated at the median of public opinion (Downs 1957), research suggests that considerable differences do exist between the policy positions presented by the two parties (cf. Monroe 1983; Pomper and Lederman 1980; Page 1978; Ginsburg 1976). Thus, while circumscribed relative to other party systems, the American parties generally appear to fulfill at least the minimum requirement of providing actual electoral choice.

Yet, to say the parties present divergent choices is not to say that all interests are equally represented, or represented at all, by the alternatives offered. Political equality is a fundamental principal of democratic rule, so to the extent that parties function to structure democratic choice, the degree to which the parties do, and do not, represent the diversity of mass preference is of interest (see Ranney and Kendall 1956). Here, the success of the American parties in contributing to the functioning of representative democracy is less clear. On one hand, the parties do appear to represent differing groups and cleavages within society; indeed, parties often are characterized as coalitions of interests and are lauded for their ability to bring together a wide range of concerns (cf. Brown 1995; Monroe 1983; Petrocik 1981; Key 1964). Yet the representation of interests within both parties appears biased toward those groups and classes with greater access to resources and the associated higher levels of electoral participation and other characteristics valued by parties in their pursuit of votes and seats (cf. Hill and Leighley 1996; Reiter 1993). In addition to class bias, the degree to which various interests are voiced by one or both of the parties appears to vary considerably over time, at least in part based on the interests' relative political power and strategic electoral value (cf. McAdam 1982). Thus, an understanding of the parties' policy positions reveals a great deal about who is represented within the system and which voices are heard. Given their role as crucial linkage institutions, questions of issue representation by parties speak directly to how well our democracy functions vis-à-vis political equality and full representation (see Brown 1995).

A final link between citizens and government provided by parties has yet to be considered. The level of choice and quality of representation provided by parties are meaningless if no connection exists between the parties' policy positions and policy outputs. Parties may provide every possible policy choice and represent every existing interest, but if parties' and candidates' behavior once elected does not reflect those policies or interests, then the electoral lever is devoid of meaning or consequence. Representative democracy depends on some connection between the voters' choices and the behavior of their representatives, as well as the outcome of public policy. In the American system, such connections are complicated by federalism, separation of powers, and checks and balances, making direct accountability difficult. Yet an evaluation of the role of political parties in American democracy necessitates an investigation into what difference party control—of one seat, one chamber, or the entire government—makes (Ginsberg 1976).

Considerable evidence suggests partisanship does make a difference vis-à-vis public policy making. In the U.S. Congress, party structures the workings of the body (Cox and McCubbins 1993) and is one of (if not *the*) most powerful predictors of roll call behavior; Republicans vote differently than Democrats *ceteris paribus* (Poole and Rosenthal 1997, 1991; Grofman, Griffin, and Glazer 1990; Brady and Lynn 1973; Fiorina 1974; Clausen 1973). Party appears to structure policy making in state legislatures as well (Jewell and Olson 1988; Hedlund and Hamm 1996; Jewell 1955). Research indicates that presidential administrations implement a substantial portion of their party's platforms (Budge and Hofferbert 1990; Krukones 1984; Pomper and Lederman 1980). Party control of the presidency leads to differing economic policy outcomes (Hibbs 1977) and budget allocations (Budge and Hofferbert 1990), although the relationships and links are complicated, as extensions of these literatures suggest (Beck 1982; King and Laver 1993). At the state level, a rich literature connects party control (variously conceived) with public policy outcomes, although again, the conditions and causal links are rarely straightforward (Smith 1997; Brown 1995; Erikson, Wright, and McIver 1989; Jennings 1979; Morehouse 1973; Erikson 1971; but see Winters 1976). In short, while the relationships are complex, considerable evidence suggests that party matters both for the behavior of those in office and for the public policy produced.

Political parties define the alternatives for democratic choice and structure public policy making by decision makers. An understanding of how and why parties develop and modify the policy alternatives they offer thus intersects directly with questions of the quality of the democratic linkage parties provide. While this study is limited to a specific set of issues— women's rights—it proposes a more general model of the role of issues, constituency groups, and elites in the formation of party positions. As the major institutional linkage between citizens and government, the choices parties make vis-à-vis public policy issues reveal a great deal about the representation of interests in American democracy.

DEFINITIONS

The central objects of this book—parties, positions, and women's rights— hold out the possibility of myriad interpretations and definitions. When we speak of a political party, for example, do we simply mean the national party organization? What of the state party organizations, the party's delegation in Congress, presidential candidates, and presidents? Clearly, it is crucial to begin with a delineation of the major terms employed here so that author and reader are of at least a similar mind as to what actors, events, and behaviors are being analyzed and discussed.

Parties and Positions

Political parties are notoriously difficult to define (cf. Miller and Jennings 1986; Schlesinger 1984; Ranney 1968). This is particularly true in the case of the United States, where the party in the electorate is defined by self-identification rather than by membership, where party organizations have comparatively little control over the selection of the candidates who bear their label, and where the party in government is loosely organized compared to most democratic systems. In the development of Western political thought, *party* was synonymous with interest and faction; in Edmund Burke's oft-quoted construction, a party is "a body of men [sic] united, for promoting by their joint endeavours the national interest, upon some particular principle in which they are agreed" (quoted in Ranney 1968, 146). The contemporary approach to parties is narrower; while real points of contention exist, most scholars agree to a definition of parties as organizations that seek to control the levers of political power through electoral means (cf. Schlesinger 1985, 1984; Downs 1957; Ranney and Kendall 1956). The activities of nominating candidates and contesting elections are fundamental to this definition, distinguishing political parties from other organizations such as interest groups (Beck 1997).

A major component of the debate over defining parties concerns the question of membership: Who or what exactly comprises the political party? In his well-known delineation, Key (1964) identifies three main components: the party-in-the-electorate, the party organization, and the party-in-the-government. In this work, the party-in-the-electorate is specifically excluded. If parties are organizations constituted for the purpose of contesting elections, the voters are the choosers among the competing parties, not the parties themselves (Schlesinger 1984; Schattschneider 1942). This is not to say that voters are not central to an understanding of parties or party systems; rather, I distinguish between the parties as organizations and actors who compete in elections and participate in governance and the voters who, with various degrees of allegiance to specific parties, choose between them. What the parties do, both in elections and from the seats of political power, is of direct consequence for the workings of democracy, a system of government in which the people are presumed to have considerable voice, but in the simplest terms, the parties are not the people; the two are distinct. My definition of political party is thus limited to *party elites*—the leaders, elected and otherwise, who represent and comprise the party organization and the party-in-the-government. Unlike mass identifiers, party elites have significant influence over party concerns, including the forging of issue positions, raising and spending of funds, directing of campaign strategy, and so on (Ranney 1968).

Narrowing the population further, I am specifically interested in the various elites that make up a *national* political party: national party officials and leaders; each party's presidents, presidential candidates, and members of Congress; and well-known and recognized partisans (Burns 1997). In the American federal system, considerable variation exists in the party systems and in the characteristics of parties bearing the same name across geopolitical boundaries. For the most part, this work is not particularly concerned with the diversity of state and local parties. Yet all politics, as we know, are local, and the varying local constituency influences on national party elites should be remembered in any attempt to understand those elites' actions and policy positions. In general, however, my concern is with the policies and behavior of the parties at the national level.

When we turn to the parties' issue positions, we are once again confronted with the peculiar nature of the American political system. The very term *party issue position* is necessarily loosely employed in the American case. American parties are generally, and correctly, described as neither disciplined nor responsible, in the sense of putting forward candidates who are uniformly committed to an explicit platform that the party will follow through on if elected (Beck 1997). While failing to fulfill the responsible party model, American party elites are strikingly coherent and cohesive in their policy preferences. Causes of intraparty issue cohesion include the relative homogeneity of interests and constituencies that support each party's officeholders and candidates, the incentive to create and maintain an identifiable party image, and the similar personal issue preferences that may have contributed to an individual's initial selection of party label.

Yet unlike parties in other representative democracies, Democratic and Republican party elites are not bound to any platform, are not required to agree to any principles or specific policy positions in order to represent the party, and, partly as a result of the federal structure of the system, exhibit a great deal of intraparty diversity in positions. Thus, when we speak of the parties' positions, we are largely referring to *tendencies*. For example, recent Republican elites generally oppose abortion on demand, while Democratic elites tend to favor abortion choice. These tendencies are indeed so great within both parties that they are reflected in the parties' respective platforms and in the votes cast by each party's delegation to Congress (Adams 1997). Yet, a few pro-choice Republican elites and pro-life Democratic elites do exist. These individual elites are generally viewed as exceptions to the rule, however, thus suggesting we can indeed identify a rule, or general issue position, for each party.

The process of identifying the parties' positions necessarily varies by institution and form. In some cases, policy positions can be ascertained from formal statements, such as the platforms adopted by the national parties in convention every four years or the position papers issued by the parties' candidates. Positions also can be inferred from actions. Members of Congress cast roll call votes and cosponsor legislation, both reflecting to a certain degree their stance individually and, when aggregated, their party's stance collectively. The bills that a president, as his party's leader and most visible spokesperson, chooses to sign or veto or the executive orders he issues might also be thought of as indicators of his party's position on related policy questions.[1] Finally, party elites can simply be taken at their word, and positions inferred from their statements and other public remarks. This research takes into account a wide variety of forms from which party positions can be inferred, with some given more attention than others, in part because they are particularly appropriate for systematic analysis.

Unless a particular facet or form is noted, I mean by *party* the party writ large, as represented by all of its current elites in and out of office. Similarly, unless otherwise noted, the terms *party position* or *party issue position* are intended to refer to the issue positions of the party broadly and generally, without reference to the specific form or action by which that position might be observed. This is not to suggest that all party elites are in agreement as to this position or reflect the position in their actions or statements, but that enough consensus can be inferred from the available evidence to identify a partywide position, mindful of the vagaries of the undisciplined and irresponsible American party system.

Women's Rights Issues

I define *women's rights issues* broadly as that set of policies that concern women *as women*. This definition includes questions of women's political, economic, and social rights and opportunities, as well as policies that are otherwise directed specifically toward women. This conception of women's rights issues is consistent with Carroll's oft-used definition: "those issues where policy consequences are likely to have a more immediate and direct impact on significantly larger numbers of women than of men" (1985, 15). I have added, or have been more purposeful in emphasizing, the presence

---

[1] Neustadt's admonition is worth noting: "Throughout, the male gender is justified historically but not prospectively when referring to a President. When used as a synonym for human beings it is outmoded" (1990, 3).

of intention: *Women's rights issues are those for which women are the intended beneficiary, constituency, or object.*

Such a definition distinguishes women's rights from several related issues. First, women's rights as defined here are distinct from the numerous policies where women have traditionally been expected to have greater interest, such as those pertaining to the family, children, and other private or domestic sphere concerns (Sapiro 1981). Education, for example, is often perceived as a women's issue because of the association of women with motherhood and children. Education policy, however, is only included in the definition of women's rights employed here when it is specifically directed toward women, as in the case of prohibitions against sex discrimination in education. This is not to say that the role of some women as mothers and primary child care providers is not considered in the determination of women's rights issues. Policies that recognize the special interests of women, such as motherhood, and seek to provide women greater equality or opportunity, such as by furnishing child care services, are indeed included in this definition, as women are the intended beneficiaries of the policy (men, of course, are also parents and thus may benefit from such policy, yet women clearly continue to be the primary caregivers and are more likely to consider that responsibility in personal employment decisions [McGlen and O'Connor 1998]). A bill that provides more funding for public schools, on the other hand, is of direct benefit to students and only indirectly of benefit to women as mothers.

Second, feminist lobbyists have argued that women's interests should be considered in policy making on virtually all issues because women's unique position in the social and economic structure means that, while perhaps unintentional, most policies have a differential impact on women (Carroll 1985). As a result, feminists have been active in debates over a range of issues, including, for example, welfare, foreign affairs, and agriculture policies. Regardless of the validity of such an assertion, the conception of women's rights issues adopted here is more narrow and includes only those policies specifically directed toward women (some of which are related to welfare, foreign affairs, and agriculture), and not the myriad of policies that might be expected to have an *indirect* differential effect on women.

Pro–women's rights policies are those that have greater equality and opportunity for women as their goal (Mezey 1994). The definition of the pro–women's rights position employed here represents a modern, liberal feminist conception, meaning that it favors equality for women but also recognizes women's unique interests and the need to have those differences addressed in the shape of public policy. This definition is not without controversy. Debates over whether women should be treated with perfect equality under the law or whether the law should treat women differently in recognition of women's particular position in society have divided feminists since before suffrage. The decline in organized women's rights activity following suffrage is often partly attributed to the failure of feminist organizations to come to an agreement on this very point (Costain 1992). Those who adopted the special needs position in the early twentieth century favored protective legislation that took into account the unique social position and needs of women. Equality feminists of the period, on the other hand, argued that such legislation reinforced stereotypes about female abilities and kept women from enjoying their full rights and responsibilities as citizens; instead, they favored full legal equality for women.

The mainstream second wave women's movement is the ideological descendent of equality, not special needs, feminism (Costain 1988). Yet modern, liberal feminism combines the equality position with a preference for policies that acknowledge women's differences. While the original conception of special needs assumed more traditional roles and abilities for women (i.e., the need to *protect* women), the new conception, adopted here, builds from the premise of providing women greater equality and opportunity, including in nontraditional roles, by addressing their particular needs.

While controversial in the past, there is a general consensus within the gender politics literature as to the definition of pro–women's rights public policies: those that expand women's roles and opportunities, either through legal equality or some form of acknowledgment of women's special needs. The policies that others have included under that rubric are consistent with those examined here and include such issues as the ERA, pay equity, domestic violence, women's health, child care, reproductive rights, and pregnancy discrimination (cf. Burrell 1994; Mezey 1994).

Two additional notations are in order. First, throughout this document, the words *feminism* or *feminist* are considered synonymous with a pro–women's rights position. I recognize that the many individuals and organizations that embrace the feminist label do not always agree on goals or means. Unless otherwise noted, my use of the word *feminism* in this research simply means support for women's rights as defined here, while *feminist* signifies an active advocate for those rights. Second, while I speak of the issue of women's rights, the definition of that issue employed here includes a myriad number of public policies. The *issue of women's rights* is thus singular, as in a group of policies, while *women's rights* are plural.

OUTLINE OF THIS VOLUME

This research begins with a delineation of the substantive puzzle motivating this research: the evolution of the parties' positions on women's rights. While various aspects and periods of this development have been noted and described elsewhere, a major purpose of this book is to combine various primary and secondary sources to provide a comprehensive picture of the positions adopted by the parties with regards to women's rights from the early 1950s to the early 1990s. Chapter 2 examines the national party organizations, conventions and platforms, and presidents and presidential candidates. This chapter relies mainly on qualitative materials—accounts of party convention proceedings, party platforms, and the statements and actions of presidential candidates and presidents themselves—supplemented by systematic analysis of party platforms.

In chapter 3, I examine the parties' delegations in Congress. To the extent that this transformation has been noted, description and explanation have focused almost exclusively on presidents, presidential candidates, and party organizations. The central goal of this chapter is to determine if and to what extent this partisan shift has characterized the parties in Congress as well. The main data consist of all of the women's rights bills introduced into the House and Senate and all of their cosponsors across this time period. This analysis is supplemented with an examination of available roll call data and interest group ratings. These data allow for a full investigation into the evolution of the parties' positions on women's rights in Congress.

I then turn to the central analytic task of this work: explaining the adoption and change of party positions on issues generally and in the case of women's rights specifically. In chapter 4, I build from a number of scholarly traditions to construct a model of party issue position adoption and change. Chapters 5 and 6 apply that model to the specific case of the transformation and polarization of elite party positions on women's rights. Chapter 5 focuses on equilibrium disruption and the redefinition of the issue of women's rights, while chapter 6 examines the relevant changes in the parties' coalitions and in the party elites themselves. Finally, in chapter 7, the consequences of both the specific empirical phenomenon described here and the model developed to explain it are considered. More generally, the implications for our understanding of the quality and condition of American parties, and thus for American democracy, are discussed.

CHAPTER TWO

Of Presidents and Platforms

AN EXAMINATION of party positioning on women's rights from 1952 to 1992 suggests that both parties have shifted their positions over time. Republicans sided with the equality feminists in the 1950s and early 1960s, while Democrats generally opposed the equality position in favor of the status quo, protective policy for women. The parties' positions converged to a considerable degree in the late 1960s and early 1970s with both parties contributing to an unprecedented level of political activity and accomplishment on women's rights. Yet Democratic and Republican elites soon diverged again. In the resulting alignment, Democrats stood on the side of women's rights, while Republicans distanced themselves from feminism and pro–women's rights policy. Not only were the parties on different sides than might have been predicted prior to 1970, but by 1992, they were also far more polarized on women's rights than ever before.

This chapter provides a detailed description of this history, focusing on presidents, presidential candidates, party organizations, and party platforms. The purposes of this chapter are twofold. My primary goal is to provide a systematic account of the transformation and polarization of the parties' positions on women's rights over this time period. These phenomenon have not received much scholarly attention, and an aim of this chapter is to fill that void. Second, while the emphasis is on description, the narrative is provided with an eye toward the explanatory framework presented in chapter 4. This chapter thus lays the empirical groundwork for the application of that model to the case of women's rights in chapters 5 and 6.

The materials providing the evidentiary base for this chapter are speeches, statements, platforms, and actions of presidents, presidential candidates, and party organizations from the early 1950s to the early 1990s. As the de facto leaders of their parties, presidents and presidential candidates frame debate, influence platform and other party choices, and represent the parties' issue positions to the public. As such, they have been both the focus of pressure from those concerned with women's rights and actors in shaping the course of debate. National party organizations are examined concurrently, as the two—presidential candidates and national party organizations—are so interrelated in political history. The discussion of national party organizations centers on national conventions during presidential election years. Even as parties have developed permanent bureaucracies and presidential nominations are decided during the primary season rather than at the conventions, these events have remained important as the centers of debate over the parties' policy positions and as the focus of demands by party constituencies (Shafer 1988; Miller and Jennings 1986). The resultant party platforms are given particular attention as they provide a concrete statement of each party's official position on issues, at least until the next convention. While few citizens read the actual documents, platforms can be viewed as a means by which elites and the public can determine the interests and positions associated with each party. As a result, platforms have been of great interest to both party activists and interest groups (Sanbonmatsu 1996; Freeman 1993). Moreover, administrations do tend to implement a sizable portion of their party's platform, connecting party position to governance (Budge and Hofferbert 1990; Krukones 1984; Pomper and Lederman 1980). The actions of Congress are noted from time to time as they relate to the discussion of presidents and platforms, but the parties' Congressional delegations are largely left to chapter 3, where they are the focus of inquiry. Finally, attention is given to social and political developments related to women's rights as they shape the context in which party positions are forged.

This chapter proceeds as follows. First, a background for understanding women's rights and the American parties during the period of this study is provided through a brief discussion of the relationship between the parties and women's rights prior to 1952. I then examine the positions of the parties as represented by their presidents, candidates, party conventions, and platforms from 1952 to 1992 by way of historical narrative. Various accounts of the parties, presidential administrations, and gender politics are utilized, as are the parties' platforms and press coverage of the period. In the third section, content analysis of the parties' official platforms is employed to examine the level of attention and priority afforded women's rights by each party.

SETTING THE STAGE: WOMEN'S RIGHTS AND THE AMERICAN PARTIES BEFORE 1952

The issue of women's rights in American politics was first raised at the country's founding, when Abigail Adams famously reprimanded her husband John, a delegate to the 1776 Continental Congress, to "Remember the Ladies" (see Rossi 1973). Abigail Adams's supplication went unheeded. Suffrage and other rights were not granted to women in the original Constitution or Bill of Rights. Moreover, the legal structure adopted from British common law provided almost no legal rights for women. Under the principle of coverture, married women were not recognized by the law but were considered "covered" by their husbands. A married women had no legal standing, could not inherit property, and had no control over even her own earnings (McGlen and O'Connor 1998).

The origins of the first wave of the American women's movement can be traced to the Seneca Falls Women's Rights Conference of 1848. The Declaration of Sentiments drafted by Elizabeth Cady Stanton for the convention's consideration listed women's grievances and demands, focusing on such issues as control of property and earnings, guardianship of children, divorce, opportunities for education and employment, legal status, religion, and the general concept of female inferiority. The only resolution to which participants did not unanimously agree was that calling for female suffrage; Stanton's own husband refused to attend the convention if women's suffrage was to be proposed, but Stanton retained the plank at the urging of abolitionist leader Frederick Douglass, who pledged his support (Flexner 1959). Some of the original concerns expressed at Seneca Falls were eventually addressed by such reforms as the Married Women's Laws, passed by many states to provide basic legal rights to married women. Yet despite the initially lukewarm reception to women's right to vote, the first women's movement ultimately coalesced around suffrage as a primary goal to which various organizations and activists, often at odds over other policy questions, could agree (McGlen and O'Connor 1998; O'Neill 1969).

Because of their links to the abolition movement, many early feminists developed ties to the Republican party, which emerged in the 1850s as a coalition of former Whigs, Free-Soilers, Know-Nothings, and antislavery Democrats. Feminism made few inroads into the South, and most feminists favored the Union during the Civil War, in part because they expected that rights for women would follow from rights for blacks. Yet when the war ended, most abolitionists, Republicans, and some women's rights activists argued that women's claims should wait, as "this hour belongs to the negro" (Evans 1989, 122). The Fourteenth through Sixteenth Amendments, as passed by the Republican majority in Congress, extended the franchise and other rights to blacks. In doing so, however, Congress placed the word "male" in reference to suffrage in the Constitution for the first time (Melich 1986; Evans 1989).

This conflict led to a split in the women's rights movement, manifested in the creation of two separate women's suffrage organizations in the late 1860s. The National Woman Suffrage Association (NWSA), founded by Stanton and Susan B. Anthony, represented those who considered the Republican party's post–Civil War actions a betrayal, while the American Woman Suffrage Association (AWSA) supported the priority given to blacks' claims and continued to believe the Republican party was an appropriate venue for advancing women's rights. The two organizations functioned separately for more than twenty years. In response to AWSA pressure, Republicans included women's suffrage in their 1872 platform, but the mention was so brief it was referred to as a "splinter," as opposed to a plank. In subsequent years NWSA's distrust of parties was vindicated; women's suffrage was not so much as a splinter in either parties' platforms again until 1916. The two groups merged to form the National American Woman Suffrage Association (NAWSA) in 1890 (Evans 1989).

Both parties variously controlled the White House and Congress between the Civil War and 1920, but both resisted growing demands for women's suffrage for almost fifty years. In 1912, Theodore Roosevelt's Progressive party, a splinter off the Republican party, included women's suffrage in its platform, a position Roosevelt had failed to champion during his presidency. The decision was motivated by the support for women's suffrage among Progressives generally and by a desire to bolster Roosevelt's chances in the western states where women had already been granted the vote. Reunified in 1916, the Republican party included a women's suffrage plank in its platform, as did Democrats for the first time. Both conventions witnessed enormous demonstrations on behalf of the amendment outside their proceedings. Incumbent Democratic President Woodrow Wilson appeared before a NAWSA convention to declare he would now support women's suffrage. Yet Wilson insisted that women must be patient, and the Democratic majority in Congress—dependent on a coalition that included some of the strongest opponents of women's suffrage—continued to vote down women's suffrage (Melich 1996; Evans 1989).

New and old conflicts continued to divide feminists, even as the suffrage goal neared achievement. Many of the controversies were over tactics and strategy, including vis-à-vis the parties. While most feminists favored a bipartisan approach, the Congressional Union (led by Alice Paul) advocated imitating the British model of holding the party in power responsible. Beginning in 1914, the Union actively campaigned against Democratic candidates for Congress and opposed Wilson's reelection in 1916. Paul and others continued to view the Democratic party as opponents of women's rights long after suffrage was achieved (Evans 1989; Cott 1987; Flexner 1959).

The new Republican majority elected in 1918 easily passed the Nineteenth Amendment in 1919. By 1920 the necessary states had ratified. The attainment of the suffrage goal initially led to an impressive degree of responsiveness to women's interests from both parties. Both undertook organizational efforts designed to mobilize women voters and give women ostensibly equal roles in party leadership. Fifty-fifty rules, requiring equal representation of men and women on party committees, were disseminated throughout the national and state levels of both parties, although they were often only weakly enforced. The representation of women as delegates to the parties' conventions increased noticeably, but women remained a very small minority. Even where women were given leadership positions, their actual power was quite minimal. Moreover, male party elites continued to control women's appointments both to general positions within the parties and to the parties' women's organizations, so loyalty to the party, not women's interests, was clearly the prerequisite for party service (Harvey 1998; Andersen 1996; Blair 1929).

The Republican Congress passed a number of pieces of legislation considered responsive to women's concerns, most notably the 1921 Sheppard-Towner Act, which provided for maternal and infant health education. By the end of the decade, however, the women's vote was generally perceived as failing to materialize as a real political force, and while women voters were still courted, both parties' actions on women's issues declined. It is often noted, for example, that Congress failed to renew Sheppard-Towner in 1929. Attention to women's issues continued to fade with the onset of the Great Depression and World War II (Harvey 1998; Andersen 1996; Melich 1996; Evans 1989).

The record of both parties on women's rights was generally one of benign neglect during the 1930s and 1940s. In an effort to expand the party's electoral base in the face of the emergent Democratic New Deal majority, Republicans created the National Federation of Republican Women in 1938 (anticipating the need to mobilize women voters, Democrats had created a Women's Division in 1916). Franklin Roosevelt appointed the first woman to a cabinet post—Frances Perkins as Secretary of Labor—and during his administration Democrats showed some responsiveness to women's interests, largely as a result of pressure from Eleanor Roosevelt and Mollie Dewson, the women's rights activist that Roosevelt had appointed to head the Women's Division (Melich 1996; Evans 1989).

Two developments prior to 1952 warrant particular attention. In 1940, the Republican party formally mandated that women and men be equally represented on the party's national and executive committees. Democrats would not require similar representation of women on their committees until the McGovern-Fraser Commission reforms of 1972. In doing so, Republicans recognized and encouraged women's activism within the Republican party. At the same time, male party leaders continued to control women's appointments, so party loyalty rather than advocacy for women's interests determined selection for party office (Harvey 1998). Throughout this period, the volunteer activities of women often comprised the grassroots backbone of both parties, but despite their dedication, women were largely relegated to supportive, rather than leadership, roles (Melich 1996; Tolchin and Tolchin 1976).

The second development was the adoption of formal party positions on the Equal Rights Amendment (ERA). Feminists had been divided over the question of equality before suffrage, but opposing sides had been able to coalesce around the suffrage goal. When suffrage was achieved, the divisions could no longer be ignored or downplayed. On one side were social feminists who believed women's interests were best served by laws that took into account the unique qualities of women. On the other side were equality feminists who argued that protective legislation harmed women more than it helped them by advancing and reinforcing stereotypes about women's abilities and appropriate roles. Alice Paul, an outspoken advocate of the equality view, drafted the ERA in 1921, believing it was the necessary next step for women's rights. Support or opposition to an ERA soon became the "touchstone for joining one camp or the other" (Costain 1991, 115; see also O'Neill 1969).

Feminists on each side leaned disproportionately toward opposing parties in the postwar period. (Paul's National Women's Party [NWP], the organizational successor of the Congressional Union, was intended to provide an alternative to the traditional parties, but had only very limited support). Protection feminists were rooted in the reform and labor movements. Their Progressive heritage favored the Republican party, but after the New Deal, those movements were inclined to favor the Democratic party. Equality feminists were primarily professional and upper-class women represented by such groups as the National Federation of Business and Professional Women's Clubs (BPW). These women tended to identify with and were more active in the GOP (Costain 1991; Mansbridge 1986). Moreover, the positions of each side were in keeping with the basic approaches of the two parties. Support for the protection position was consistent with the New Deal Democratic stance in favor of government activism on behalf of the oppressed. The equality position, on the other hand, meshed well with Republican distaste for government interference and support for free markets.

In 1940 (the same year as it established a formal Women's Division), the Republican party became the first party to endorse the ERA in its platform. Democrats followed suit four years later. While neither party made the ERA or any other women's rights issue a priority during this period, Republicans were generally more supportive, while Democrats downplayed the ERA as a women's issue. In 1950, the Senate passed the ERA with comparatively greater support from Republicans. Yet for the most part, both parties continued to offer token appointments and occasional public statements as their rare concessions to women. As Costain writes, "Both parties, despite having staked out very different grounds on these issues, did little programmatically to advance them" (1991, 116).

WOMEN'S RIGHTS AND THE AMERICAN PARTIES, 1952–1992

The 1950s: Stable Alliances and Alignments

What few advances women made immediately following suffrage, in the heady days of New Deal activism, and as a result of extensive female work force activity during World War II were largely stalled during the 1950s. The Cold War and unprecedented prosperity formed the background for the dominance of an ideology, famously termed the "feminine mystique" by Betty Friedan, that emphasized women's sanctioned role at the center of the suburban, nuclear family.

The 1950s were a period of mixed messages for women's rights vis-à-vis the American parties. On one hand, neither party emphasized women's concerns, organizational changes actually decreased the power and influence of women within the parties, and elites generally treated the question of expanded women's rights with bemusement. Women's rights were almost entirely absent from political debate. Yet the Senate acted on the ERA, women's rights and votes received attention from politicians in ways they had not previously, and pressure for greater responsiveness to women's concerns from the political system generally, and the political parties specifically, slowly began to emerge, as women's experiences diverged from the feminine ideal espoused in the press, advertising, media, and popular culture.

In 1952, the Democratic party abolished its Women's Division, providing "a powerful manifestation of the disassociation of women and private life from politics" (Evans 1989, 247). Party elites claimed the reorganization would integrate women and women's concerns into the party structure, but the action eliminated the limited autonomy and influence the Women's Division had afforded women's activists. The Democratic platform that year included support for equal pay for equal work, the ERA, and, acknowledging the "several million mothers" in the work force, "adequately financed" day care facilities.[1] Despite the lip service the party gave to both equal pay and the ERA in their platform, it was widely recognized that the Democratic party was not committed to either, largely because of opposition from organized labor. Some Democratic party elites were beginning to shift their position, however. Most notably, Eleanor Roosevelt had dropped her opposition to the ERA as part of her advocacy of the United Nations charter, which included "equal rights for men and women" (Mansbridge 1986).

---

[1] Information regarding specific platform content is drawn from the documents themselves. Sources: 1952–1972, Johnson (1973); 1976–1992, *Congressional Quarterly Almanac* (various years).

Republicans underwent a similar structural reorganization in 1952, also reducing the autonomy and influence of women in their ranks.[2] The Republican platform mirrored that of the Democratic party, with the exception of a child care plank. The Eisenhower administration showed some signs of supporting women's rights, but did not make them a priority. The Republican businesswoman Eisenhower chose to head the Women's Bureau of the Department of Labor moved the Bureau from the active opposition to the ERA advocated by her unionist predecessor to a more neutral position (Mansbridge 1986). This was significant, since what little women's rights debate and policy making occurred in the 1950s was centered on a small network of activists that had the Women's Bureau at its center (Costain 1992; Evans 1989; Harrison 1988). In addition, Eisenhower appointed a woman to head the newly created Department of Health, Education, and Welfare and named a female U.S. Treasurer (Melich 1996). At the same time, Eisenhower's few public statements on women's rights during his first administration reflect the paternalistic and discriminatory attitudes of the time (as did the press coverage of those comments) and suggest that elites generally did not take women's rights seriously. The *New York Times*, for example, reported that President Eisenhower responded with "gallantry and diplomacy" when asked if he thought a woman could be president. "[A]mid much laughter," Eisenhower provided an "eloquent tribute to the attributes of women," concluding that while qualified, it was a job that women had the good sense not to want (*NYT* 1/14/54[3]).

Women's rights fared somewhat better in Congress during Eisenhower's first administration. The Senate passed the ERA again in 1954, with (again) greater support from Republicans than Democrats. Pro-ERA activists opposed the final version of the bill, however, as it included the Hayden rider, which exempted protective legislation, both already in place and passed in the future, from the application of the amendment. In the House, staunch ERA opponent Emanuel Celler (D-NY) chaired the Judiciary Committee, virtually guaranteeing that the amendment would fail to see the House floor (Melich 1996; Mansbridge 1985).

Support and interest in women's rights grew slightly across the decade. The 1956 Democratic platform included the three planks from 1952 (equal pay, ERA, and child care), but also noted (in passing) support for lowering the retirement age for women, a Social Security reform that took into account women's differential patterns of wage work. The Democratic

[2] Harvey (1998), on the other hand, argues that the elimination of the party divisions eventually provided an opportunity for women's rights advocates to form autonomous organizations to mobilize women's votes for substantive policy gains.

[3] *New York Times* stories for which no author is given are cited as *NYT* with the item date and are listed separately in the References.

party's ambivalence on the ERA, however, was reflected in criticism from amendment supporters at platform hearings. The president of the pro-ERA BPW, Hazel Palmer, protested that the party had supported the amendment in its platform in the past, but refused to take action. If this was to be the case again, she argued, the party should leave the amendment out. The ERA plank stayed in, but Palmer's comments suggest that knowledgeable elites recognized the lack of support within the Democratic party (*NYT* 8/12/56).

Republicans, on the other hand, maintained their support for equal pay and the ERA and added a plank in support of the elimination of sex discrimination in employment. In his State of the Union address the January following his reelection, Eisenhower became the first president to mention the ERA in a message to Congress, stating his support for the measure that had the formal endorsement of both parties for more than ten years (*NYT* 1/17/57). Yet as I have suggested, it is clear that Eisenhower shared the general skepticism of most Americans during the 1950s concerning the need for an expansion of women's rights. When asked the following August why he had not given the same attention to discrimination against women as he had given to other forms of discrimination, he replied facetiously that it was "hard for a mere man to believe that woman doesn't have equal rights" (*NYT* 8/8/57), and he later dismissed the idea that women had unique interests that are politically relevant (*NYT* 6/19/58). For the most part, both political elites and the general public considered women's rights a nonissue.

The 1960s: The Roots of Change

The 1960s would see the emergence of the second wave of the women's movement and the passage of some of the most significant women's rights legislation in U.S. history, but few would have predicted those events based on the level of attention given women's rights at the 1960 party conventions. The Republican platform continued the GOP's support for the ERA and equal pay and added an endorsement of what we might now consider an affirmative action program to assist women (among others) in the attainment of workplace skills and training. Nominee Richard Nixon addressed the NWP during the general election, reaffirming his and his party's support for the ERA (*NYT* 9/3/60).

Democrat John Kennedy, on the other hand, gave women's rights concerns virtually no attention as a candidate; when invited to address the National Council of Women on the topic during the primaries, Kennedy, unlike his opponent, Henry Cabot Lodge, ignored the conference theme and spoke on foreign policy (Dales 1960). The 1960 Democratic platform did *not* endorse the ERA per se. The party affirmed its support of equality of rights under law, including equal pay for equal work, and added a plank in opposition to sex discrimination in employment. Child care and Social Security reform were not mentioned. While Kennedy's election raised the hopes of liberal activists, his failure to address women's concerns led one columnist to comment that "it appears for women the New Frontiers are the old frontiers" (quoted in Hartmann 1989, 50).

Yet following his very narrow victory, Kennedy sought to reach out to various voting constituencies, including women (Costain 1992). As pressure from both sides of the ERA divide mounted, Kennedy's head of the Women's Bureau, Esther Peterson, a long-time labor lobbyist and ERA opponent, drafted a memo in June 1961 proposing that a committee to study the status of women might "substitute constructive recommendations for the present troublesome and futile agitation about the 'equal rights amendment'" (quoted in Davis 1991, 34). Kennedy's advisors viewed the commission favorably as a means for appealing to female voters (Harvey 1998). The President's Commission on the Status of Women (known as the Kennedy Commission) was established in December 1961. Peterson handpicked the members, almost all of whom were known to oppose the ERA. The Commission's final report, issued in October 1963, contained twenty-four specific recommendations that covered such topics as comparable worth, child care, maternity benefits, and sex discrimination in pensions, Social Security, jury duty, and property rights. Significantly, the Commission recommended that "a constitutional amendment need not now be sought"; the inclusion of the word "now" was all the Commission would allow despite extensive lobbying by feminist lawyer Marguerite Rawalt, one of the few ERA supporters on the Commission. While the Kennedy Commission was established to placate women's rights advocates, the effect was to broaden and stimulate debate. The Commission's report (published the same year as Betty Friedan's *The Feminine Mystique*) included not only recommendations but also extensive evidence of sex discrimination; 64,000 copies were sold. By unearthing "ample evidence of women's unequal status," the Kennedy Commission report "created a climate of expectations that something would be done" (Freeman 1975, 52). All fifty states established their own commissions in the aftermath of the national commission's report, and it was at a conference of state commissions in 1967 that the National Organization for Women (NOW) was founded (Davis 1991; Evans 1989; Hartmann 1989; Hunter 1963).

Kennedy responded to the Commission's recommendations by issuing an executive order prohibiting sex discrimination in civil service employment, establishing citizens' advisory and interdepartmental cabinet committees on women's status, and throwing his support behind the Equal Pay Act, leading to its passage in 1963 after many years of consideration. While the final form of the bill required equal pay for *equal* work, rather than the equal pay for *comparable* work that the Commission and women's rights supporters advocated, it was a significant legislative achievement (Costain 1992; Davis 1991; Evans 1989; Hartmann 1989).

The civil rights legislation championed by Lyndon Johnson following Kennedy's death included the most important legislative achievement thus far (and perhaps since) for women. Representative Howard W. Smith (D-VA) proposed the inclusion of sex in Title VII of the 1964 Civil Rights Act, which prohibited discrimination in all aspects of employment. Smith did so at the urging of members of the NWP (Smith was pro-ERA largely because he was anti-union), who wanted the provision considered but who also suggested to Smith, a segregationist, that the inclusion of sex might sink the entire bill. Representative Martha Griffiths (D-MI) had considered offering the amendment, but upon learning of Smith's plans she withdrew, knowing that Smith's sponsorship would encourage other conservatives and Southerners to lend their support. Smith later admitted to introducing the amendment as a joke, and it was largely greeted as such in chambers. Yet with the encouragement of most congresswomen, many Republicans and some Northern Democrats joined the Southern Democrats in passing the amendment. When it was considered in the Senate, several members, led by Republican Everett Dirksen (IL), attempted to remove the word sex, but Johnson came out in support of the sex provision in April 1964, and sex remained in the version that he signed into law the following summer (Davis 1991). Forcing the agency charged with carrying out Title VII, the Equal Employment Opportunity Commission (EEOC), to enforce the sex provision became a major mobilizing issue for the women's movement in the latter half of the 1960s (Freeman 1975).

The 1964 campaign is considered one of the most ideological in the postwar period. The coalition that engineered Barry Goldwater's nomination by the Republican party contained the seeds of the traditionalist, social conservative movement that would be so influential in the GOP in the 1970s and 1980s; Phyllis Schlafly, who would lead the charge against feminism, was one of Goldwater's most vocal supporters. Still, Goldwater's conservatism was more of the laissez-faire, states' rights, anti-communist variety (as was Schlafly's at the time), and the 1964 Republican platform reflected his and the GOP's focus on issues other than women's rights. The only mention of gender-specific policy is a statement of "opposition to discrimination based on race, creed, national origin or sex." For the first time since 1940, the ERA was not specifically mentioned. Goldwater's strategy to emphasize race in order to drive a wedge into Democratic dominance in the South suggests that the lack of attention to women's rights in the platform should probably be viewed as a reflection of lack of interest rather than as a switch in party position. Civil rights consumed the national dialogue.

While addressing more paragraphs of their platform to women's rights, Democrats only diverged slightly from Republicans. As in the GOP platform, most of the attention to women's rights came in the form of general opposition to various forms of discrimination. Democrats pointed to the Equal Pay Act, Title VII, and the Kennedy Commission as evidence of their commitment to women's rights. The only exception to this emphasis on nondiscrimination was a brief, approving note of plans for child care services in forty-six states.

Interest in women's rights grew in the four years of Johnson's first full administration, although a mass women's movement had yet to emerge. NOW, founded in 1967, immediately began pressing the federal government for greater responsiveness to women's needs. One of NOW's first efforts was to lobby Johnson to add sex to his 1965 executive order prohibiting discrimination in the employment practices of the federal government and its contractors and requiring for the first time the establishment of affirmative action programs; Johnson did so in October 1967. Johnson engaged in a public campaign to end what he termed "stag government" by appointing more women to public office (Harvey 1998, 214). Both Johnson and Vice President Hubert Humphrey made public comments in support of women's changing roles and calling for greater gender equality (Spiegel 1967; Robertson 1965; *NYT* 3/1/66).

Yet just as women's rights were about to become a major issue on the national political agenda, they disappeared almost completely from the parties' platforms. If race and social welfare had consumed the attention of the parties in 1964, race and the conflict in Vietnam dominated the agenda in 1968. There is no mention of women's rights in the entire 1968 Democratic party platform. Women are noted in one paragraph of the Republican platform in which the party simply pledged "concern for the unique problems of citizens long disadvantaged in our total society by race, color, national origin, creed, or sex." The ERA, specific forms of sex discrimination, child care, and other related policy concerns are absent from both platforms.

The 1970s: Conflict and Controversy

The politics of women's rights were transformed in the four years between 1968 and 1972. In 1967, NOW adopted its first Bill of Rights, taking positions in favor of a number of issues, including the ERA (causing women from the labor movement to walk out of the organization) and legalized abortion (leading to the establishment of a more conservative spin-off organization, the Women's Equity Action League [WEAL]). While NOW was not active at either convention in 1968, the Bill of Rights was drafted as a statement to which political candidates would be asked to agree, a sign that NOW was already shifting its tactics toward the electoral arena. Scholars generally identify 1970 as the year in which women's rights emerged as a mass movement (Klein 1984). In the spring, Betty Friedan used her final address as NOW president to call for a national Women's Strike for Equality on August 26, the fiftieth anniversary of women's suffrage. Despite the fears of many feminists that a disappointing turnout would undercut the movement's momentum, tens of thousands of women (and some men) took to the streets in cities across the United States. The event was extensively covered in the press, with the result that NOW was subsequently inundated with inquiries about membership and activities, new women's rights organizations appeared across the country, and press coverage of women's rights issues exploded (Freeman 1975).

For the political parties, the most significant organizational development was the founding of the National Women's Political Caucus (NWPC) in the summer of 1971 by a group of feminist activists that included Friedan, Bella Abzug, Gloria Steinem, and Shirley Chisholm. The NWPC was created to advocate the election and appointment of women to office and the representation of women's interests by the political system, including the political parties. Membership was predominantly Democratic and independent from the beginning, but the NWPC sought to be a bipartisan organization with influence in both parties (Davis 1991; Baer and Bositis 1988; Freeman 1975).

In Congress, the parties reacted (and contributed) to the salience of feminism by passing an unprecedented amount of women's rights legislation, culminating (and cresting) with the 92nd Congress (1971–1972) in which more women's rights legislation was passed than in all previous legislative sessions combined (Freeman 1975). The momentum appeared to be on the side of the feminists; Representative Bella Abzug (D-NY) described 1972 as "a watershed year. We put sex discrimination provisions into everything. There was no opposition. Who'd be against equal rights for women? So we just kept passing women's rights legislation" (quoted in Evans 1989, 291). Support for women's rights legislation was largely bipartisan. The most noted accomplishment was the passage of the ERA by both houses in the spring of 1972, the result of an organizational effort that ranged from "the Americans for Democratic Action to the National Republican Committee" and achieved by a bipartisan vote (Freeman 1975, 216; also Costain 1992).

Regarding women's rights, the 1972 conventions were strikingly different than those of 1968. While women's rights had been literally ignored in the 1968 platforms, both parties featured specific sections devoted entirely to women's rights issues, totaling some fifty paragraphs between them, in 1972. This attention to women's rights by the parties was a function of a confluence of factors: the growing salience of women's rights and the women's movement, the organizational efforts of women's rights organizations, and the creation of a greater role for women and political amateurs, especially within the Democratic party, by changes in the rules governing the parties' delegate selection and proceedings. The McGovern-Fraser reforms specified that blacks, youths, and women be represented in each state delegation in "reasonable relationship" to their proportion in the population of the state (Sullivan et al. 1974, 17). As a result, forty percent of delegates to the 1972 Democratic convention were women, compared to just thirteen percent in 1968. While Republicans did not undertake any binding rule changes, the McGovern-Fraser reforms spilled over into the GOP's governance as party committees advised states to increase the representation of women and minorities in their delegations. Women made up almost thirty percent of Republican delegates in 1972, up from sixteen percent in 1968 (Beck 1997). Many female delegates had feminist ties. The NWPC held seminars around the country prior to the conventions to provide women with the information necessary to become delegates, and when they were successful, "bombarded" them with information about policy and procedure (Davis 1991, 188).

At the Democratic Convention in Miami, many women delegates participated in the organized Women's Caucus, led by the NWPC. The Women's Caucus had two major goals: challenge of delegations in which women were underrepresented and inclusion of a reproductive freedom plank in the platform. Their successes were limited. While the McGovern campaign featured a number of women in positions of power and had been generally favorable toward feminists, the McGovern camp came to the convention concerned that the perception of their candidate as too far left would hurt him in the November general election. McGovern's people actively sought to counter the image that the Democratic party had been, as Representative Edith Green (D-OR) put it, "taken over by the kooks" (quoted in Tolchin and Tolchin 1976, 33). The first example of this strategy was McGovern's choice of party regular Lawrence O'Brien as sole party chair, reneging on his promise to appoint a woman as an equal co-chair; McGovern named Yvonne Braithwaite Burke a vice chair instead.

Feminists' perception of betrayal by the McGovern forces was to continue throughout the convention. The Women's Caucus sought to challenge the South Carolina delegation and the Daley delegation from Illinois. McGovern told the Women's Caucus he fully supported the South Carolina challenge, but as the vote was taking place, McGovern delegates were instructed to vote against it; the vote on the crucial California challenge was to follow the South Carolina vote and McGovern forces did not want a victory on South Carolina to set the wrong precedent for California. The South Carolina challenge failed, although the Women's Caucus was successful in its challenge of the Illinois delegation the next day. McGovern's maneuvers on the South Carolina and California votes were viewed as brilliant strategic maneuvers by many pundits, but they angered and alienated feminist activists (Sullivan et al. 1974; Tolchin and Tolchin 1976; Thompson 1973).

An attempt to include a pro-choice abortion plank in the 1972 platform also failed. The proposed plank did not actually mention the word abortion, but only stated the party's support for a right to privacy and individual choice in reproductive decisions consistent with "relevant Supreme Court decisions." McGovern was personally ambivalent on abortion reform, and his campaign wanted to avoid taking a position on such a controversial issue. Similar to his reversal on the South Carolina challenge, McGovern initially told delegates to "vote your conscience," but the McGovern camp later urged their delegates to vote against the abortion plank, which was ultimately defeated (Sullivan et al. 1974; Tolchin and Tolchin 1976; Curtis 1972).

Frustrated by these failures, the Women's Caucus made one final attempt for influence at the 1972 Democratic Convention. Shirley Chisholm's campaign for the Democratic nomination had created a dilemma for feminist activists who agreed with Chisholm's positions and liked the idea of a viable female candidacy but were concerned that supporting Chisholm would sacrifice their opportunity for influence within the party. Chisholm admitted to having no chance for the nomination but hoped that she might contribute to a deadlocked convention and thus have a strong position from which to bargain with the other frontrunners. By and large, feminist activists initially stayed away from the Chisholm campaign. When it appeared that their loyalty to McGovern was not being repaid, however, the Women's Caucus seized upon the idea of a woman on the ticket, this time in the person of Sissy Farenthold, who had recently posted a surprisingly strong showing in the Texas gubernatorial primary. The push for Farenthold began with some of her young supporters but was soon latched on to by the Caucus, which showed greater unity on the Farenthold vote than they had on any of the previous disputes. McGovern's strategists were caught off guard by the initial success of the insurgent campaign but managed to pull their delegates back in line. In the end, Farenthold's vice presidential candidacy came in second only to Tom Eagleton's and was responsible for creating the infamous delay of McGovern's acceptance speech until almost three o'clock in the morning (Davis 1991; Tolchin and Tolchin 1976).

On the Republican side, Nixon's first term had not been overly encouraging to feminists within and without his party. Nixon officially supported the ERA, appointed a number of women to high-level positions within his administration and party, required affirmative action plans for hiring and promoting women from federal contractors, and made a number of public statements in support of women's rights, including the 1972 State of the Union address. However, he paid little attention to these issues until the election neared late in his first administration. Nixon vetoed the Comprehensive Child Development Act, one of the most significant child care initiatives since World War II, and consistently opposed abortion reform, limiting the liberalization of abortion rules at military hospitals and rejecting his population growth commission's recommendations that family planning services and abortion referral be made available to teenagers by the states (Melich 1996; Costain 1992).

Like their counterparts at the Democratic convention, feminists at the Republican convention in 1972 were interested in the representation of women as delegates and the adoption of specific policy planks in the platform. The major fight regarding representation was over the addition of sex to Rule 32, which claimed the party would "take positive action to achieve the broadest possible participation" of various minority groups but did not include women (Melich 1996, 25–6). The battle over this rule pitted moderate Republicans (who were also attempting to fend off other rule changes) against conservatives. The conservative wing, Melich (1996) argues, was central to what she terms the New Majoritarian strategy, proposed by Kevin Phillips in his 1969 book *The New Republican Majority* and adopted by the Nixon campaign. While Nixon was officially neutral on Rule 32, the White House actively opposed the rule change. Feminists eventually prevailed—sex was added to Rule 32 and the "positive action" language stayed in, despite attempts to weaken it—but the rules provided for no enforcement mechanism, and thus no basis for the sorts of delegation challenges available to Democratic feminists.

Yet like the Democratic document, the Republican platform contained an extensive list of women's rights planks. Despite Nixon's veto of the child care bill, Republican feminists succeeded in their hard-fought effort to add a plank in support of "federally assisted" child care, the only change in the entire Nixon campaign–dictated platform made at the convention. Republican feminists decided not to push for a minority report on abortion reform (there had been reports that Nixon strategists wanted the pro-abortion minority report to come to the floor so they could vote it down on prime time television) after their victory on child care, and the issue of reproductive freedom was absent from the 1972 Republican platform (Melich 1996; Curtis 1972). In terms of achieving actual policy change in the platform, Republican feminists were actually more successful in achieving their established goals at the 1972 conventions than were their Democratic counterparts. Delegates to the conventions, however, were more likely to express the belief that feminists were influential at the Democratic rather than at the Republican convention (Freeman 1987).

In the end, the 1972 platforms were more similar than they were different. Both platforms supported the ERA, equal pay, child care (tax deductions and federal assistance), the elimination of sex discrimination in various areas of law, and the appointment of women to the federal government. Democrats supported "guaranteeing" the proportional representation of women in the party, while Republicans merely claimed the party "welcomes and encourages" female participation. There were small, but meaningful, differences in the wording of some proposals, and each party noted a policy initiative or two vis-à-vis women's rights that the other did not, but by and large the differences were not great. While the platforms were similar, it was clear that the candidates themselves differed in their dispositions toward feminism, with McGovern being more favorable (Davis 1991). Both candidates mentioned women's rights issues in their acceptance speeches; McGovern spoke out against prejudice based on sex, while Nixon lauded the role of women in government (Sanbonmatsu 1996).

Despite the attention to women's rights in the parties' platforms, neither party's candidate gave much attention to the issue during the general election campaign. The women's rights issue that received the most attention vis-à-vis the candidates was the linking of McGovern (the "Triple A" candidate—abortion, amnesty, and acid) to abortion reform despite the success of the McGovern campaign in keeping reproductive freedom out of the platform. Bella Abzug, it appeared, had been correct to argue that McGovern might as well come out for reform because Republicans would associate him with abortion regardless (Davis 1991).

Feminist activity and political attention to women's rights grew considerably between 1968 and 1972. The ensuing four years, however, saw the rise of a backlash to the women's movement that would have considerable repercussions for the politics of women's rights. This movement has its roots in the traditionalist aspects of the conservative movement represented by Goldwater's candidacy in 1964, but is a distinct phenomenon that is in many ways antithetical to economic, or libertarian, conservatism (Brennan 1995; Klatch 1987). Social conservatism drew its support from those Nixon termed the Silent Majority, Americans disturbed and alienated by the permissive social attitudes and racial tensions of the 1960s and 1970s (Miller and Levitin 1984), and from the growing ranks of evangelical or fundamentalist Christians (Klatch 1987). Yet it was opposition to women's rights, particularly the ERA and abortion, that provided the greatest impetus to mobilization and organization of the New Right (Himmelstein 1990). As Mansbridge writes, "For many conservative Americans, the personal became political for the first time when questions of family, children, sexual behavior, and women's roles became subjects of political debate" (1986, 5).

While traditional economic conservatism emphasizes individualism, liberty, capitalism, and limited government, social conservatism is rooted in religious belief and focuses on the family as the sacred foundation of society and social order. Like traditional conservatives, social conservatives fear communism (more as a threat to religion than as a threat to capitalism, however), but immorality and spiritual decay are generally considered the most important threats to American security and stability. Social conservatives oppose women's rights because they perceive feminism as anti-family, narcissistic, degrading to homemakers, and a form of government intrusion (Evans 1989; Klatch 1987; Conover and Gray 1983). Organizationally, antifeminist groups, such as Schlafly's StopERA and Happiness of Womanhood, operated autonomously, but they were part and parcel of the social conservative movement that shared their opposition to feminism and were predecessors to many of the more well-known and broader organizations, such as the Moral Majority and Christian Coalition (Melich 1996).

The passage of ERA in 1972 and its subsequent ratification by twenty-four states was a central rallying event for organized antifeminism. In November 1972, Phyllis Schlafly devoted her newsletter, the *Phyllis Schlafly Report*, which had concentrated on the Soviet threat, to an attack on the ERA. Schlafly soon founded StopERA, the most active antifeminist organization, and dedicated herself to mobilizing and training others to join her in the cause. A long-time Republican activist (her 1964 book, *A Choice, Not an Echo*, had assisted in galvanizing Goldwater Republicans), Schlafly helped bring together fundamentalist Christians, Catholics, homemakers, and others into a powerful and well-organized opposition to feminism. While Schlafly's natural alliances were within the Republican party, she did not limit herself to that arena; indeed, initially her most powerful ally was Democratic Senator Sam Ervin (NC), who went so far as to extend her his franking privilege for anti-ERA activities (Mathews and De Hart 1990).

The second rallying event for social conservatives followed closely on the heels of the first: the Supreme Court's ruling in *Roe v. Wade* (1973) that the right to an abortion is constitutionally protected. Debate over abortion reform had largely taken place in elite circles before that time, but the *Roe* decision forced the issue onto the national agenda. Before *Roe*, the alliance of elites favoring reform could be described as nonpartisan, and included the Young Republicans (Luker 1984). There is little evidence to support the contention that the ERA had any bearing on abortion rights, but as a result of the prominence of the two issues, the fact that feminists discussed both in terms of women's rights, the linking of state ERAs and abortion rights by some feminist lawyers, and the strategy of the opposition to claim a linkage, the two soon became inextricably linked. To socially conservative Americans, the ERA and abortion symbolized everything about feminism worth opposing (Melich 1996; Davis 1991; Mansbridge 1986; Conover and Gray 1983).

The emergence of an organized opposition slowed the feminist momentum that characterized the earliest years of the 1970s and contributed to controversy over women's rights. The ERA, the "touchstone" for distinguishing between social and equality feminists in the first part of the century (Costain 1992, 115), became a litmus test to distinguish between feminists and antifeminists (Evans 1989). As controversy grew, ERA ratification slowed. Thirty states ratified by the end of 1973, but only four more would do so in 1974 and 1975, and none in 1976, while other states voted to rescind their previous ratification (Mathews and De Hart 1990; Mansbridge 1986).

Support for women's rights from the Nixon and Ford administrations was mixed. Nixon did little to implement the 1972 platform vis-à-vis women's rights, but his resignation and the subsequent ascendancy of Gerald Ford placed a far more moderate Republican in power. Ford was an ERA supporter (although that support appeared to waver at times), and his wife Betty campaigned for ratification. Under pressure from forces within his party, however, Ford came out against the *Roe* decision, although he claimed not to support a constitutional amendment prohibiting abortion, taking the position that the states have authority over abortion law (Melich 1996; Costain 1992).

As the 1976 convention season neared, the NWPC formed separate task forces for the Democratic and Republican parties. As in 1972, Republican feminists were concerned with the representation of women at the convention. While their protests resulted in the addition of a few additional female speakers, lobbying for increased representation attracted charges that feminists were seeking to "McGovernize" the party with quotas, and in the end, the rule on anti-discrimination vis-à-vis delegate selection was actually weakened. Even without any party action, the number of female delegates at the 1976 GOP convention represented a slight increase from 1972, while the percentage of Democratic women as delegates actually slipped from 1972 to 1976 (Melich 1996; Freeman 1987; Shanahan 1976; *NYT* 2/19/76).

In 1972, Republican feminists succeeded in expanding the platform to include an additional women's rights plank. Four years later, Republican feminists were on the defensive, not the offensive, and spent the majority of their time defending a plank that had not been controversial in 1972—the ERA—and attempting to block the inclusion of an anti-abortion plank. Republican feminists were in a difficult situation; Ronald Reagan came to the convention with enough delegates to mount a serious challenge to Ford's nomination, forcing feminists to balance pursuit of their demands with efforts to support Ford, who most believed was a preferred candidate vis-à-vis women's rights. Hoping to keep abortion and the ERA distinct, the Republican Women's Task Force's (RWTF—the NWPC's Republican organization) strategy for the convention was to work publicly to defend the ERA, while unofficially lobbying against the anti-abortion plank behind the scenes. Both feminists and the Ford camp were caught off guard when a platform subcommittee actually voted down the ERA, but Ford instructed his delegates on the full committee to reverse the subcommittee's recommendation; even so, the vote of the full committee was only 51-47. Anti-ERA forces threatened to force a vote of the entire convention on a minority report, but the Reagan campaign decided to concentrate their floor efforts on other issues (Melich 1996; Freeman 1987; Madden 1976a,b; Lelyveld 1976).

Feminists encountered less success with the anti-abortion plank. The same subcommittee that opposed the ERA approved support for a constitutional amendment to ban abortion, sponsored by committee member Senator Bob Dole. In the case of abortion, the full committee agreed with the subcommittee. Feminists, however, were able to gather the signatures necessary to force floor consideration of a minority report that asserted that abortion "should not be included in a political party's platform." Discussion of the minority plank on abortion took place after one a.m. on Tuesday night of the convention. After a brief debate, the convention chair refused to acknowledge the request for a roll call vote and judged the voice vote to favor those against the minority report. The anti-abortion plank stayed in the Republican platform (Melich 1996; Freeman 1987; Lydon 1976).

On the Democratic side, there were comparatively fewer public disputes at the 1976 convention. At a press conference a year earlier, Democratic feminists announced a "women's agenda," which they sought to have included in the Democratic platform, but there was little controversy over any substantive policy demands by the time of the convention. Feminists and racial minorities did clash with Carter forces over the "50–50 rule," which mandated that beginning in 1980 all delegations would be half female. Feminists were not satisfied with the negative outcome from the Platform Committee, but Carter avoided a contentious floor fight by offering a compromise in which he agreed to promote equal division at future conventions and provide for a greater role for women in the party, his campaign, and his administration (Freeman 1987; Shanahan 1975).

The 1976 platform documents suggest an emerging division between the parties on women's rights. Both parties continued to support the ERA and the elimination of sex discrimination in various areas of law, as well as expanded job training for women and the promotion of part-time and flexible work schedules that were viewed as especially beneficial to female workers. Both noted support for child care, although Democrats were more supportive of a federal role. There is no mention of pay equity in the Republican platform, but Democrats expressed their support for equal pay for *comparable* work, a step beyond the status quo, equal pay for *equal* work; comparable worth proposals seek to ameliorate the inequalities caused by the occupational sex segregation and the lack of value afforded traditionally female vocations. Finally, the Democratic platform made no mention of the abortion controversy, but Republicans, while acknowledging the diversity of opinion within the GOP, claimed to support "the efforts of those who seek enactment of a constitutional amendment to restore protection of the right to life for unborn children." Women's rights were not greatly featured in the candidates' acceptance speeches; Ford was silent on the issue and Carter limited his remarks to promising a decision-making role for women in his administration (Sanbonmatsu 1996).

From 1976 to 1980, women's rights became increasingly controversial, even as more Americans accepted many of the basic tenets of feminism both in their attitudes toward women's role and in their own lifestyle choices. In 1977, Congress sponsored a national conference in Houston in recognition of the United Nation's International Women's Year (IWY). Delegates were elected at state-level conferences in all fifty states, many of which became battlegrounds for clashes between feminists and social conservatives. While most were feminist in their attitudes, several states sent decidedly antifeminist delegations, particularly Indiana, Utah, and Mississippi. The Houston conference elicited considerable press coverage, and First Ladies Rosalynn Carter, Betty Ford, and Lady Bird Johnson all attended the event. The conference adopted a lengthy plan for action that included the ERA and, after considerable debate, reproductive freedom and lesbian rights. Claiming that the IWY was a government-funded feminist front, Schlafly staged a counter "Pro-Family Rally" in Houston during the conference (Melich 1996; Evans 1989).

Jimmy and Rosalynn Carter campaigned widely for the ERA, and the Carter administration was generally favorable to women's rights concerns. Relations between organized feminism and the Carter administration were not always smooth, however; Carter clashed publicly with Bella Abzug after naming her to head the National Advisory Committee on Women created after the IWY conference, and her eventual dismissal led more than twenty members of the Committee to resign in protest. Feminists were increasingly critical of Carter's commitment to women's rights (Melich 1996; Freeman 1987).

As the 1970s came to a close, "the mood of bipartisan consensus on ERA in the 1970s began to show stress cracks" (Costain 1992, 125). Only one state—Indiana—would ratify after 1975 (it did so in 1977), but ERA supporters were successful in achieving an extension of the ratification deadline from Congress in 1978. The vote for the deadline extension, however, lacked the bipartisanship that had characterized the original ERA vote in 1972; in both chambers, Democrats were considerably more supportive of the extension than were Republicans. On women's rights in general, the gap between the parties was widening, destroying the bipartisanship that had so briefly existed only a few years earlier.

The 1980s: The Lines Are Drawn

Both parties' conventions featured considerable debate and controversy over women's rights in 1980, but the outcomes were very different. Given Reagan's ties to Schlafly and their experience with Reagan's forces at the previous convention, many Republican feminists active in 1976 opted out of the 1980 meeting or were not delegates because they supported other candidates. While the RWTF members who did attend adopted a less public approach than in 1976, the convention's debates and decisions vis-à-vis women's rights were covered on the front pages of major newspapers and constituted the most prominent convention news, save for Reagan's choice of running mate. Reagan, who came to the convention assured of the party's nomination, began hinting early on that he might seek to drop the GOP's historic support of the ERA. ERA supporters within his party responded immediately with public pleas in defense of the amendment, but when the Platform Committee convened in July 1980, its membership, particularly as represented by the members of Congress and other notables with the greatest influence over the outcome, was overwhelmingly anti-ERA. Despite the efforts of the RWTF, opponents of the ERA simply had more supporters on the committee; the vote to reverse the party's forty-year stance was 90-9. Reagan's offer of a compromise to ERA supporters consisted of language that recognized "the legitimate efforts of those who support or oppose ratification of the Equal Rights Amendment." Mary Crisp, a former Republican National Committee (RNC) chair and current informal spokesperson for the RWTF, resigned her current post as RNC vice chair in protest. In a widely reported line, she accused her party of burying "the rights of over 100 million American women under a heap of platitudes" (Melich 1996; Raines 1980; Miller 1980; Weaver 1980a,b,c; *NYT* 7/2/80).

The same Platform Committee's decision on abortion drew less press coverage but also represented a significant step away from women's rights. The subcommittee removed all of the 1976 platform's conciliatory language regarding abortion and drafted a plank stating unequivocal support for a constitutional amendment to ban abortion, opposing the use of federal funds for abortions, and favoring the appointment of pro-life judges. Attempts at the committee level to oppose any of those proposals were obstructed by the pro-life bias in the composition of the committee and the parliamentary maneuvers of that contingent (Melich 1996).

Responding to a request from ERA supporters, Reagan agreed to meet with a hand-picked group of women (no men were allowed), including some members of the RWTF, in the midst of the convention. While participants claimed to be generally satisfied with the meeting, many expressed a sense that Reagan did not really understand their concerns or positions. Afterwards Reagan repeated his promise to appoint women to his administration and to the Supreme Court and to work to eliminate discriminatory federal laws. Feminists were unable to garner the necessary signatures for a minority report on the ERA or abortion (which would have forced a debate on the floor) and were unable to convince six state delegations to call for the suspension of the rules, which also would have allowed for floor discussion of the ERA plank. The entire platform, without the ERA and including the anti-abortion planks, passed by a voice vote (Melich 1996; Weaver 1980b).

Many feminists in attendance were supporters of George Bush; Bush had supported the ERA and other feminist issues since the earliest days of his career and had opposed the anti-abortion amendment. His wife Barbara was a long-time supporter of Planned Parenthood. Bush had called Reagan's opposition to the ERA "backward thinking," but when chosen as Reagan's running mate, he declared his now former position on the ERA to be no impediment to his active participation on the ticket (quoted in Drew 1981, 94; see also Melich 1996).

On the Democratic side, debate over women's rights was carried out in light of the nomination battle between Carter and challenger Edward Kennedy. In December 1979, the executive board of NOW, citing the failure of the Carter administration to achieve the ratification of the ERA or, in their estimation, to put enough resources and effort toward that end, announced its decision to oppose Carter's renomination. Many prominent feminists expressed their disagreement with the board's decision, and in October 1980 (following the Democratic convention), the annual NOW convention voted to retract that opposition, but did not endorse any of the three major candidates. As a result of the NOW board's decision and the skirmish over Abzug's dismissal, Carter forces at the convention operated under the assumption that all feminists were Kennedy supporters, a belief reinforced by Abzug's support for Kennedy's proposal to release delegates from their obligation to vote for their state's primary choice in the first round of voting, the success of which would make or break Kennedy's insurgent candidacy (Freeman 1987; Bennetts 1980c; Clymer 1979).

Women's rights issues were debated during the convention at separate meetings of the Women's Caucus of the Democratic National Committee (DNC) and the feminist Coalition for Women's Rights, consisting of NOW, the NWPC, and prominent feminist activists. A full fifty percent of delegates to the 1980 Democratic convention were female. Approximately twenty percent of delegates were members of NOW or the NWPC, and feminists operated a sophisticated floor operation to rival that of any other organized interest. The proposed platform already included strong feminist stands, including support for the ERA and opposition to a pro-life constitutional amendment. Feminists, led by the presidents of NOW and the NWPC, chose to push for two issues. Their central concern was Minority Report No. 10, a pledge by the party to withhold financing and campaign assistance to any candidate who failed to support the ERA. Feminists also backed Minority Report No. 11, which supported federal funding of abortions, but in order to keep the two issues—the ERA and abortion—separate, they left the lobbying on No. 11 to the National Abortion Rights Action League (NARAL), which maintained a separate organization at the convention (Jennings 1990; Freeman 1987; Bennetts 1980a; *NYT* 8/20/80).

The Carter campaign opposed both proposals, particularly that concerning the ERA, which they viewed as an inappropriate litmus test and a dangerous precedent. Kennedy took no position on the abortion proposal but favored the ERA plank. Lobbying on both sides was fierce. The decisive moment came within a few hours of the vote on the ERA by the full convention when the National Education Association (NEA), Carter loyalists who represented the largest voting bloc at the convention, threw their support behind Minority Report No. 10 (ERA). The Carter camp recognized that decision as determinative and instructed its whips to withdraw their orders to oppose. Convention chair Tip O'Neill proclaimed the voice vote to have favored the yeas, and the plank was adopted into the platform. Carter's opposition to No. 11 was less hostile, as the proposal was not considered a Kennedy plank and did not involve the party's resources. Minority Report No. 11 was voted on by a state-by-state roll call and passed by a substantial margin. These feminist victories did not go unnoticed. Germond and Whitcover found it "extraordinary" that an incumbent president would be forced to accept a platform with statements on "sensitive social questions" that he opposed (1981, 203–4). Just as the outcome of the Republican convention had been interpreted as a sign of the increasing Republican opposition to feminism, the success of women's rights activists in achieving their goals at the Democratic convention was heralded as a sign of the "growing strength of feminists within the Democratic party" and the emergence of an independent feminist power base (Bennetts 1980a; also Freeman 1987).

The Republican and Democratic platforms differed sharply. Democrats supported ERA ratification, vowed not to hold meetings in nonratified states (honoring the NOW-sponsored boycott), held that the attempts of some states to rescind their previous ratification were invalid, and promised to withhold funding from candidates who did not support the ERA. Republicans acknowledged the "legitimate efforts of those who support or oppose ratification" of the ERA and "reaffirmed" the GOP's "historic commitment to equal rights and equality for women," but did not pledge their support to ERA ratification and opposed political pressure from the White House toward that goal. For the first time, the Democratic party firmly established itself as pro-choice and expressed its opposition to the curtailment of federal funding for abortions. Republicans went even farther than they had in their 1976 platform, placing themselves solidly behind a pro-life constitutional amendment, supporting the restriction of the use of federal funds for abortions, and pledging to seek the appointment of pro-life judges. Differences were evident on less high-profile issues as well. Democrats again backed the concept of comparable worth, while Republicans only noted the need for total integration of the work force to bring about equality of pay. Democrats favored a federal role in the funding of child care; Republicans, who had suggested federal assistance for child care in 1976, left child care entirely to the private sector in 1980. Democrats opposed sex discrimination in the armed services, but Republicans specifically identified the military draft as a necessary exception to the ideal of sex equality. The Democratic platform included planks addressing women-owned businesses, affirmative action, women's health and representation in health-related professions, domestic violence, and rape. These topics were not considered in the Republican platform.

Differences were apparent in the acceptance speeches as well. Carter reiterated his support for the ERA, affirmed the right of women to choose the lifestyle they prefer, and criticized Republicans' attitudes toward women's rights, particularly their insensitivity to the problems of working women. Reagan repeated his stated goal of eliminating discrimination (without mentioning the ERA), promising to appoint a liaison to coordinate efforts to eliminate discrimination against women in all fifty states, implement current federal anti-discrimination laws, and seek new statutes if necessary (Sanbonmatsu 1996).

According to many observers, the platforms and convention proceedings represented not only an emerging distinction between the parties on specific women's rights policies but also a shift in the basic approaches of the two parties toward women's issues. The 1980 Republican party platform was taken as sign that the GOP was adopting what would be called the "family values" message of the New Right that emphasized traditional roles for women: "The [1980] platform shifted subtly but significantly away from the party's traditional championing of help for all women to singling out special treatment for homemakers and mothers and downplaying those women who worked outside the home" (Melich 1996, 135). Costain writes more generally about the shift across the period described thus far:

> Democrats had begun to adopt the traditional Republican perspective, while Republicans embraced part of the former Democratic view . . . . Yet the Republican position also differed significantly from the former Democratic one.

Republicans began to fold women's issues into the category of family issues.
... Collective values of maintaining the integrity and well-being of the family unit were promoted over presumably selfish individualistic ones for women. The Democrats, in contrast, became the party of individualism in this instance, arguing that women should be free to make all the choices available to other human beings, without legal barriers (1991, 124–5).

The 1980 conventions, platforms, and campaign rhetoric confirmed and solidified the perception of a divergence between the parties on women's rights that had been growing during the late 1970s. That image was only reinforced by the 1980 election results, in which the so-called gender gap[4] emerged. The reported difference between the estimated percentage of women and men voting for Ronald Reagan varied between four and nine percent in 1980, depending on the poll consulted. This was not the first time a gender gap had appeared; women had been consistently more likely then men to vote for Republicans in the 1950s, but had generally favored Democrats since the considerable pro-Democratic gap in 1964 (Freeman 1999; Miller 1988). In 1980, however, the leadership of NOW jumped on the statistics (which did suggest a significantly larger gap than in 1976) as evidence of the emergence of a feminist voting bloc that was expressing its dissatisfaction with Reagan's policies *vis-à-vis women's rights* by failing to support him at the same rates that men did (Mueller 1988a; Bonk 1988).

In the early 1980s, NOW and other feminist organizations were deeply concerned about the future of feminism. While still committed to the ERA fight, ratification seemed unlikely before the deadline in 1982, and Reagan's election brought into office a president who opposed most feminist positions. Women's rights activists were particularly concerned that the ERA failure would be interpreted as a death knell for feminism. Feminist leaders, especially those at NOW, heralded the 1980 poll data as proof of the relevancy of feminism and used those figures as the centerpiece of their strategy for appealing to legislators in states that had not ratified the ERA, particularly Illinois. The term "gender gap" was coined by NOW leaders in a document containing polling data created for presentation to delegates to the September 1981 DNC general meeting. By October of that same year, the expression was first used in a national newspaper (Judy Mann's *Washington Post* column), and the phenomenon began to attract intense press coverage. NOW purposefully labored to disseminate the interpretation that the gender gap in the 1980 presidential election, and also in Reagan's presidential approval ratings, was a reaction to Reagan's (and the Re-

---

[4] While definitions differ, the gender gap generally refers to gender differences in support for the winning candidate (usually for the presidency, but also other offices), although it has also been used to refer to gender differences in public opinion and partisanship, among others.

publican party's) positions on women's rights issues. Beginning in May 1982, NOW released a monthly "Gender Gap Update" to thousands of reporters in a format that lent itself to easy adoption for newspaper stories and other media. By 1983, both vacating NOW President Eleanor Smeal and former Congresswoman Bella Abzug were writing books on the gender gap, both arguing that women's rights issues played a major role in the creation of the gap. The intention was to convince politicians of the electoral consequences of opposing women's rights (Mueller 1988a; Bonk 1988; Smeal 1984; Abzug 1984).

The underlying assumption of the gender gap arguments made by feminists and the discussions carried on by pundits in the press was that the Democrats were the party more sympathetic to women's rights, and that it mattered at the ballot box. In reality, the veracity of the latter assumption (that the parties' divergent positions on women's rights issues played a role in citizens' voting decisions in such a way as to create a difference in the voting patterns of women and men) has not always been supported by the careful analyses of social scientists, many of whom have suggested that other issues and factors are more important in explaining the gender gap than feminism (see, for example, Cook and Wilcox 1991; Erie and Rein 1988; Miller 1988; Mansbridge 1985). Significantly, however, most feminist organizations were increasingly adopting the assumption that the Democratic party was the party of women's rights. Most women's rights organizations had purposefully sought to be bipartisan in dealing with Congress, presidents, and the federal bureaucracy, but after 1980 those organizations, especially NOW, found themselves working increasingly closely with Democrats while relationships with Republicans soured. Some feminist lobbyists believed this emerging alliance weakened feminists' bargaining position, but the real and perceived links between organized feminism and the Democratic party grew stronger in the early 1980s (Costain and Costain 1987; *NYT* 2/12/82).

Reagan's actions during his first administration did little to warm relations with feminists or change his administration's image as "somewhere between being apathetic about women's issues to being antiwomen," as the conservative National Federation of Republican Women complained to the president in 1983 (Clymer 1983). Several well-publicized gaffes only added to the perception of Reagan as insensitive to women's rights concerns. Addressing a conference of the International Federation of Business and Professional Women in August 1983, for example, Reagan attempted to apologize for a mix-up in which the organization was refused admittance for a scheduled White House tour by offering the following compliment: "I happen to be one who believes if it wasn't for women, us men would still be walking around in skin suits, carrying clubs." Feminists attacked Reagan's "caveman quote" as evidence of his inability to appreciate and discern the needs and experiences of American women (Costain 1992; Bonk 1988; Weisman 1983a). Later that month, Justice Department appointee Barbara Honegger resigned her post, citing the lack of real commitment to women's rights exhibited by the Reagan administration. To counter criticism of his opposition to the ERA, Reagan had promised to launch an exhaustive investigation of federal and state laws with the goal of identifying and eliminating any discriminatory provisions. Honegger termed the project a "sham" and once again focused attention on what the White House had come to call "the woman problem" (Bonk 1988; Taylor 1983).

Honegger was not the only critical voice from within the Republican party. Various Republicans—former first ladies, party leaders, and state legislators—spoke out publicly about their frustration with the Republican party's position vis-à-vis women's rights (Cummings 1983; Bennetts 1980b; *NYT* 10/13/81). At the 1983 NWPC national convention, President Kathy Wilson, a Republican, called on Reagan not to run for reelection. Claiming to represent the views of most Republican women in the NWPC, Wilson issued a fiercely worded attack on what she called Reagan's "benign bewilderment in response to the women's revolution," which was carried on the front page of the *New York Times* (Raines 1983a).

The Republican party and the Reagan administration actively sought to counter Reagan's antiwoman image. Reagan and the White House attempted to downplay the role of women's rights in explaining the gender gap in the 1980 election results and in Reagan's popularity ratings, although Reagan himself identified his "misunderstood" opposition to the ERA as part of the reason for his lower levels of support among women voters (Bonk 1988). Reagan highlighted his record of appointing women to his administration, particularly the historic naming of Sandra Day O'Connor to the Supreme Court, and his efforts to remove discriminatory laws from the books (the project criticized by Honegger), but continued to be called on to defend his record on women and women's issues (Costain 1992; see also Clines 1984; Hunter 1984; Weisman 1983b). In 1983, the Republican party hired Maureen Reagan to improve her father's image among women, and she spoke at various venues in his defense. The Reagan-Bush reelection campaign established a national Women for Reagan-Bush, charged with, as chair Sonia Landau put it, showing the voters that "Reagan is terrific on women's issues." All that was needed, Landau claimed, was "to get his record to the people" (Basler 1984; also, *NYT* 8/24/83; Clymer 1982).

In preparing for the 1984 election, Republican pollster Richard Wirthlin conducted in-depth focus groups and extensive polling of American women. Wirthlin used these data to categorize women into sixty-four different groups based largely on age, race, marital status, and employment.

These sixty-four were later reduced to eight and were arranged on a scale from most to least anti-Reagan. Those most likely to oppose Reagan were written off, while advertising, direct mail, and campaign events were designed to appeal to those who liked Reagan or who might be swayed (Mueller 1988a; Bonk 1988; Witt 1985). In many ways, the Republicans' approach to the women's vote in 1984 represented a break from the past behavior of presidential candidates of both parties; instead of emphasizing symbolic actions, such as speeches or appointments, or public policy that is directed specifically toward women (what I have called women's rights), Republicans chose to appeal to female voters as they did to male voters—by attempting to convince them that the party's policies benefited them, not because of their gender per se, but because of their income level, occupation, religion, and so on.

In policy terms, the outcome of the 1984 Republican convention was similar to that of 1980, if not more antifeminist. Women's issues were prominent in the Republican platform—the thirty paragraphs in which women's rights were mentioned represented the largest number of such paragraphs in any GOP platform during the period of this study—but the tone was in decided opposition to feminist stances. The ERA was not mentioned in the draft of the platform considered in committee prior to the convention, but Schlafly testified against it anyway. A pro-ERA motion was offered at the subcommittee hearing, but it did not receive a second. ERA supporters were more successful in the full committee; the ERA actually came up for a vote, but it was defeated 76-16. The same committee also voted down a proposal favoring the addition of sex to the equal protection clause of the Fourteenth Amendment and a statement recognizing the presence of ERA supporters within the party. Attempts to soften the party's positions in opposition to abortion and comparable worth were likewise defeated. Both NOW and the NWPC ceded the convention to the opposition and sent no delegations on what they believed would be a futile mission. While forty-eight percent of the delegates (and fifty-two percent of alternates) were women, Republican feminists were generally not among their ranks, as most opted out of convention participation (Melich 1996; Freeman 1987).

While the platform was generally hostile to feminists, the Republican party sought to counter its image as antiwoman by featuring women prominently at the convention and devoting resources to assisting female candidates. One-third of the major convention speeches were given by women. The first night of the convention was dubbed "Ladies Night" by organizers; speakers included U.S. Treasurer Katherine Ortega, Jeane Kirkpatrick, and Nancy Reagan. Maureen Reagan, who had been charged with improving her father's image with women, was considered too sympathetic to feminism and was not asked to speak. In addition to showcasing prominent women, the Republican party continued its organizational efforts to reach out to women voters, releasing reams of information regarding women, women's issues, and the GOP (Melich 1996; Freeman 1987).

Democratic strategy and positioning differed from that of the Republican party in almost every conceivable way in 1984 and the period leading up to the election. Throughout Reagan's first administration, Democrats emphasized their divergence from the GOP on women's issues. At the party's midterm convention in Philadelphia in 1982 (one week after the ERA ratification deadline expired), speeches and statements focused on women's rights. Not only did the party reaffirm its support of the ERA and abortion rights, but it also included women's rights in its statements on other issues such as economics, Social Security, and employment (Lynn 1982). Democratic presidential contenders dutifully appeared before the NWPC convention in 1983, the same convention at which NWPC president Kathy Wilson called on Reagan to step aside. Most Democratic hopefuls promised they would use the resources of the presidency to bring about ERA ratification, among other concessions, resulting in what the *New York Times* called a "bidding war . . . to see who could most energetically embrace the agenda of the [NWPC]" (Raines 1983b). When NOW announced its intention to endorse a Democratic candidate, five such candidates met with the NOW board. NOW's criteria involved the candidate's position on and priority given women's issues, his appointment of women to his staff, his willingness to consider a female running mate, and his potential for winning the election. Walter Mondale received the organization's endorsement (Freeman 1987).

Democrats were so predisposed to the feminist cause that activists had little to do at the convention itself. Prior to the convention, Representative Geraldine Ferraro (D-NY), chair of the Platform Committee, created a minor controversy when she suggested that perhaps the platform would emphasize broad principles vis-à-vis women's rights "without using capital E, capital R and capital A." Feminists immediately expressed their dissatisfaction, and within a few hours, Ferraro called most major feminist leaders to explain and issued a public statement clarifying and, in effect, changing her position. As drafted, the Democratic platform contained the ERA as well as most other feminist demands (Germond and Whitcover 1985; Perlez 1984).

Assured of getting everything they wanted in the platform, feminists turned their attention to the goal of seeing a woman named to the Democratic ticket. Polling data from the electorate as well as the delegates, and predictions for a greater, perhaps even determinative, gender gap were employed by NOW to justify what became their only demand, despite questions about the wording of poll items, the depth of support for the idea of a woman vice president, and the limited impact of running mates on presidential vote choice. Notwithstanding these potential problems, feminist leaders converged not only on the idea of a woman vice president but also on the person for the job—Ferraro. Democratic politicians soon threw their support behind both the idea and the individual; by the convention, House Speaker Tip O'Neill, New York Mayor Ed Koch, and six governors (including Mario Cuomo and Michael Dukakis) had endorsed Ferraro for the position. As a groundswell appeared to emerge, NOW toughened its stand: If Mondale did not name a woman, NOW delegates would propose one from the floor. However, some feminists within the party, including Ferraro, indicated to the Mondale campaign that they would not go along with NOW's hard line. Regardless, on July 12, Mondale named Geraldine Ferraro as his running mate, the first woman on a major party ticket in American history. With that victory, feminists had little to do at the convention, and the NWPC dismantled its floor operation. In the eyes of many observers, the events of 1984 indicated that feminists had moved from outsider to insider status within the Democratic party and were now perceived as a central Democratic party constituency (Frankovic 1988; Freeman 1987).

The 1984 platforms differed as the 1980 platforms had. Democrats continued to support the ERA, while Republicans made no mention of the amendment. The Democratic party favored comparable worth, which Republicans specifically opposed. Democrats called for "universally available day-care with federal or business funding." Republicans pointed to the expansion of child care tax credits under Reagan and pledged to "encourage private sector initiatives to expand on-site child care facilities." On abortion, Democrats expanded their commitment to the pro-choice position, opposing federal limitations on access to abortion services for poor women and the pro-life constitutional amendment. As in 1980, Republicans favored the pro-life amendment and the appointment of pro-life judges and opposed the use of federal monies for abortion services or research. In addition, the Republican platform in 1984 included a plank proposing the application of the Fourteenth Amendment's equal protection to unborn children. Democrats listed and proposed a number of programs related to women's political participation, including voter registration and party recruitment. Republicans gave little attention to those issues. There were a number of areas of agreement, reflecting changing social norms: Both parties favored the recruitment of women to government positions, improved enforcement of child support regulations, job training for women on welfare, and the general elimination of sex discrimination.

Subtle differences became more pronounced in the parties' approaches to women's rights. Most paragraphs relating to women's rights in the Democratic platform fell under the heading "Equal Justice for All," which included planks relating to minorities, workers, and the poor. While a good portion of the Republican women's rights paragraphs fell under a section called "Individual Rights," Republicans also dealt with women's rights under the heading "Family Protection." Differences in the kinds of issues raised follow this pattern. In addition to the planks just described, Democrats included women in their support for affirmative action and their opposition to the *Grove City* decision, which limited the application of sex (and other) discrimination provisions. Republicans, on the other hand, spoke out on the topic of domestic violence and supported (within constitutional limits) the control of pornography, which they argued was especially degrading to women. Democrats thus focused on rights, while Republicans gave more attention to morality (Melich 1996).

These differences were reflected in the candidates' speeches to their conventions. Mondale focused on his choice of Ferraro as his running mate and his hope that a woman would some day be president. He asserted that women should have a larger role as leaders in business and spoke out in favor of the ERA. Reagan stated his belief in sex equality but focused substantively on moral issues: the increasing rates of out-of-wedlock births and his belief in the sanctity of human life (Sanbonmatsu 1996).

Public attention to women's issues had been declining since the early 1980s, and continued to do so after the 1984 campaigns. The ERA deadline expired in 1982, three states short of the necessary thirty-eight, and women's rights activists shifted their efforts to other goals. Organized feminism became more institutionalized, shifting from movement activities, such as protest and mass action, to interest group politics and institutional reform more likely to occur out of the public view (Katzenstein 1998; Costain and Costain 1987). In addition, feminists increasingly turned to the election of women as a means to achieving public policy goals, rather than through the political parties. With feminists increasingly less focused on public displays of activism, the press either declared the supposed death of feminism, described a backlash against the women's movement, or ignored women's rights altogether in the mid-1980s (see Davis 1991, 471–4).

Mondale's choice of Ferraro as his running mate was a major victory for Democratic feminists in 1984. In the aftermath of Mondale's disastrous defeat in November, however, that goal, and the tactics used to obtain it, drew serious criticism. Almost immediately after the election Democratic strategists began to blame feminists for the failure of a determinative women's vote to materialize. Mondale staffers and Democratic party leaders accused feminists of promising something they could not and did not deliver. Feminists, on the other hand, charged the Mondale campaign with downplaying women's rights issues in the campaign and not taking advantage of what they described as an outpouring of female support available to the Democratic party following the Ferraro announcement (Dowd 1984). Conventional wisdom viewed the Ferraro nomination as contributing to Mondale's image as a candidate controlled by special interests. The emergence of a gender gap in 1980, and the interpretations and publicity that had surrounded the phenomenon, had set the stage for feminists to wield substantial power at the 1984 Democratic convention. After 1984, many concluded that a strong association with feminism had contributed to Mondale's defeat. As a result, the degree of influence publicly afforded feminists in 1988 was considerably circumscribed (Davis 1991).

As the 1988 election season neared, it was increasingly clear that the Democrats would be adopting a somewhat different approach to women's rights, at least in terms of shaping public perception of the party's positions. Feminists complained publicly that the party and the candidates seeking its nomination were ignoring women's rights issues, particularly more controversial topics such as abortion. The lesson Democrats appeared to have drawn from the 1984 election was that women voters are not a homogenous group and that emphasizing women's rights issues is not the best strategy for appealing to many women voters—an assumption that had been the foundation of the Republican approach to the women's vote in 1984, if not before. Feminists sought to counter the premise that women voters were uninterested in women's rights, arguing that the party was drawing the wrong conclusions from 1984 and would not gain by, in the words of Democratic strategist Ann Lewis, "fighting the last war" (quoted in Toner 1987b, 10; see also Toner 1987a).

In the end the 1988 Democratic platform was very similar vis-à-vis women's rights to the 1984 platform, but the process differed significantly. DNC chair Paul Kirk indicated early on that he wanted the 1988 platform to be shorter than previous platforms and to deal in broader statements and goals, avoiding the long list of specific policy proposals, which appeared designed to placate specific interests, that had characterized recent past documents. Women leaders met with Kirk before the convention and pointed out that leaving out specific references to women's rights issues such as the ERA or abortion would attract more attention than leaving them in. The initial draft of the platform still made only vague references to equal rights and freedom of choice. The Platform Committee that considered the document, however, included many women's rights supporters, including members of the Dukakis and Jackson camps who were the most influential voices. The platform approved by the committee and by the delegates in convention in Atlanta included specific references to the ERA and abortion rights, as well as other women's rights concerns. Unlike recent platforms, women's rights issues were not given a unique section but were addressed throughout the document. As Kirk had desired, the 1988 Democratic platform is by far the shortest document in this period; thus the number of actual mentions of women's rights issues is comparatively circumscribed (Sanbonmatsu 1996; Davis 1991; Freeman 1988).

The relationship between feminist organizations and the Democratic party differed in 1988 as well. In 1984, NOW representatives had virtual approval power over all women's rights language in the platform. No such authority was granted to any group or person in 1988. Nonetheless, the platform represented little real policy change vis-à-vis women's rights from 1980 or 1984. Unlike past years, feminists were less interested in women's representation to the convention, despite the fact that the percentage of female delegates had declined since 1984. This decrease was largely attributed to the greater number of seats reserved for superdelegates (public and party officials not chosen by the caucus and primary processes) in 1988, and NOW president Molly Yard called for a reduction in the number of those seats prior to the convention. Largely as a result of pressure from Jesse Jackson, the rules adopted by the DNC in 1988 did specify a smaller number of superdelegates for future conventions. For the most part, however, that battle was not a priority for feminists. Instead, women's rights activists focused on the underrepresentation of women in elective office and party leadership, pushing for and receiving a platform plank calling for "full and equal access of women and minorities to elective office and party endorsement." Unlike 1984, NOW and other feminist organizations declined to endorse any presidential candidate, and none of the major candidates addressed the Women's Caucus at the convention, as they had in 1984. At the same time, women did play a larger and more influential role in the Dukakis campaign than they had in Mondale's, even if feminist organizations themselves were less publicly courted (Freeman 1988).

While feminists were less visible at the Democratic convention than they had been four years earlier, they were slightly more so at the Republican convention. Yet, for the GOP as well, while the process differed, in the end, the platform mirrored that of 1984. Bush's campaign had brought moderates and some feminists back into active participation in the Republican party, after being shut out by the Reagan campaigns. The ERA had ceased to be a salient issue, and feminist efforts at the 1988 GOP convention largely focused on abortion. While a proposed change in the abortion plank was quickly put down at the Platform Committee hearings in 1984, representatives from both NOW and NARAL were permitted to present proposals regarding abortion to the Subcommittee on Family and Community in 1988, although neither expected to achieve any real change as a result of their presentations. Long-time Republican activist Tanya Melich was cut off by the chair when she proposed the committee eliminate all abortion language from the platform so as to recognize the diversity of views within the Republican party and substitute the abortion plank with a statement in a support of family planning services for unwanted pregnancies. Motions, most proposing to substitute the 1976 language (in which the party favored "a continuance of public dialogue on abortion") for the 1984 language, were at least put to a vote in the subcommittee (unlike 1984), but they were quickly defeated. The full Platform Committee voted on a statement opposing U.S. funding of any organization involved in abortion; an attempt to delete that sentence (and another critical of the World Bank) was tabled by a vote of 36-30. The other abortion-related vote came when Marjorie Bell Chambers (who had chaired the National Advisory Committee on Women after Carter fired Bella Abzug) proposed removing the last four words of the sentence, "the unborn child has a fundamental individual right to life *which cannot be infringed*" (italics added). Chambers argued that the language placed the life of the fetus above that of the mother, the most extreme pro-life position. After extended debate (itself an achievement), the motion was defeated 55- 32. While the motion only countered the most extreme pro-life stance, the relative success of the somewhat pro-choice vote, compared to 1984, was viewed as a sign of moderate strength at the convention. An attempt to gather the twenty-seven signatures necessary for a minority report on Chambers's motion, however, quickly fizzled when Chambers herself refused to sign. A final proposal to include support for the ERA was quickly voted down, as it had been in the subcommittee (Melich 1996; Freeman 1989).

Feminists and moderates were ultimately unsuccessful with the two issues—ERA and abortion—that defined women's rights in the 1970s, but the Republican party did address extensive attention to a women's rights issue that was gaining significant attention in the 1980s—child care. The GOP dedicated an unprecedented sixteen paragraphs (two percent of the platform, by one estimation) to the issue of child care. The Republican approach to child care was still greatly distinguished from that of the Democrats (and that preferred by most organized feminist groups); the Democratic-sponsored child care bill currently before Congress was denounced for limiting parental choice and religious participation, and the approved federal role was generally limited to tax credits for lower income families. Yet the platform claimed to favor public policy that acknowledged the wide variety of family circumstances; identified parental, rather than only maternal, care as the most preferred form; and encouraged employers to offer flexible and part-time work opportunities to accommodate the diversity of family needs. There was no debate at the Platform Committee over what was generally considered "a step . . . in the feminist direction" (Melich 1996, 220; see also Freeman 1989).

Feminist influence was also felt on the issue of recruitment, support, and funding for women candidates, resulting in a statement that was remarkably similar to the Democratic plank on the same issue. Few participants at the GOP convention realized that the plank was linked to a feminist organization specifically, but it had indeed been first suggested by the Women's Campaign Fund (WCF, a political action committee that supports women candidates). The WCF sent the proposed text to Representative Nancy Johnson (R-CT), a member of the Republican Platform Committee. Johnson, who had received assistance from the WCF, favored the plank but wanted to expend her energies on other issues, so she passed it on to fellow Committee member Nancy Thompson, who had the led the RWTF at the 1980 convention. Thompson made the proposal to the full Committee, which was itself half female. Even the most conservative members were supportive; it was Angela Buchanan, wife of arch-conservative Pat Buchanan, who objected to a proposal to add the word "qualified" in front of "women candidates," asserting that if it was not necessary to single out only qualified male candidates, then it was not necessary to do so for women. The Committee did change "funding" to "campaign support" and "parity" to "seeking an equal role," but the proposed plank survived mostly intact and was adopted by an overwhelming voice vote (Melich 1996; Freeman 1989).

Despite these achievements, feminists were hardly visible players at the GOP convention in 1988. Most moderates put their support for George Bush ahead of their commitment to feminist goals. As feminism became increasingly linked to the Democratic party, Republicans came to view women's rights organizations as extensions of the opposition. The RWTF, which had organized feminist efforts at conventions prior to 1984, had become unable to function effectively within the Republican party because of its ties to the NWPC, despite the avowed bipartisanship of that organization. While the group attempted to remobilize, it was not present as an organized force at the 1988 GOP convention. Efforts toward feminist goals were pursued by an informal and very loose network of like-minded individuals. Such was the lack of communication that on more than one occasion, feminist participants were surprised when an unknown individual made a feminist proposal from the floor of committee meetings or by who joined in voting for the feminist position (Melich 1996; Freeman 1989).

Despite the few subtle shifts in a more feminist direction, organized women's groups were vocal in their criticism of the Republican platform. NOW coordinated marches at the Republican conventions in 1976 and 1980, but not 1984. In 1988, they were back, although the size of the march was relatively small. The presidents of NARAL and Planned Parenthood held a press conference to condemn the Republican platform as antiwoman. The NWPC sponsored a meeting at the convention that featured well-known Republicans claiming that feminism should have a place in the GOP. These organizations had a more limited role at the Democratic convention in 1988 than they had had in 1984, but that party still heard and responded to organized feminism. Such was not the case with the Republican party, which had "ceded sovereignty over social issues to conservatives" (Freeman 1989, 46).

The 1988 platforms differed on many of the major women's issues as they had since 1980. Democrats favored the ERA and abortion rights, regardless of ability to pay. Republicans were silent on the ERA and favored a constitutional amendment outlawing abortion, restriction of funds for abortion services or research, application of the Fourteenth Amendment's equal protection clause to unborn children, and the appointment of pro-life judges. Democrats did not mention comparable worth in their 1988 platform, but Republicans stated their opposition. On child care, Democrats pledged assistance to lower- and middle-income families, assistance to the states for the creation and maintenance of a "child care infrastructure," and the development of minimum standards for the health and safety of child care facilities. Republicans, as I have noted, dedicated a large portion of their document to child care. Policy proposals were wide ranging, including repealing the Social Security earning limitation to allow grandparents to care for children and changing the tax code to promote in-home child care. Solutions, however, were largely intended to be state and private funded; the platform pledged to "encourage" states to promote child care programs for teenage mothers who stay in school and to "encourage" business and government child care programs. The form of that encouragement was not specified. Republicans were silent on several additional issues that Democrats supported: affirmative action, domestic violence programs, and an issue new to the platforms, family leave.

Dukakis's attention to women's rights in his acceptance speech focused on child care, declaring that families should not be forced to choose between their jobs and their children, and criticized the Republicans for their failure to understand the difficulty some families have in finding affordable, adequate child care services. Bush lauded the role of women in creating and filling the new jobs created by the Reagan-Bush administration, claimed economic empowerment was necessary for gender equality, and made note of the BPW. He emphasized abortion as well, proclaiming his belief in the sanctity of human life and urging a shift from abortion to adoption (Sanbonmatsu 1996).

Neither candidate gave much attention to women's rights during the general campaign. Republicans continued their strategy of courting women voters by emphasizing economic issues, particularly child care but also more general issues of economic stability and security. Bush also concentrated on crime and violence, partly in an attempt to appeal to women's concerns and fears. In addition to the women's rights references noted earlier, Bush used his acceptance speech to pledge to be the "education president" and describe his vision of a "kinder, gentler nation," while campaign advertisements emphasized his role as a family man. Such images were intended to appeal particularly to women. Bush did stumble over abortion in the first debate; when asked if he thought women who had abortions should go to prison, Bush was unable to articulate the sorts of penalties he thought should be established if abortion was illegal, as sought by his party's platform. In general, Republicans worked to keep the issue of abortion out of the campaign; the Reagan Justice Department went so far as to withhold their brief asking the Supreme Court to overturn *Roe* until after the election (Melich 1996; Mueller 1991; Drew 1989; Baker 1988).

Dukakis's campaign did not highlight his or his party's positions on women's rights, despite the strong feminist stands taken in the Democratic party platform. Instead the campaign attempted to portray Dukakis as strong on crime and foreign affairs in an effort to counter Republican attacks on those issues and to coax white male voters back to the Democratic fold. Dukakis sought to avoid the special interest label that had plagued Mondale by distancing himself from groups such as organized labor and feminists. Only in the last weeks of the campaign did Dukakis speak to the economic issues that many believed were highly salient for women voters. On women's rights, however, he remained largely silent. He did effectively criticize Bush's lack of a response to the abortion question in the first debate, but voters were more likely to remember his stiff answer to a question in the second debate about his stance on the death penalty if his wife Kitty was raped and murdered (Sanbonmatsu 1996; Mueller 1991; Baker 1988).

The 1990s: Party Polarization over Women's Rights

In the late 1980s, the debate over women's rights included both new and old issues. Abortion, which along with the ERA had been the major women's rights issue in the 1970s, had not, like the ERA, gone away but was as salient and polarizing as ever, if not more so. With varying levels of success, pro-life forces sought to limit access to abortion services through state and federal rules and regulations, restrictions which the courts were increasingly willing to let stand. This trend culminated in *Webster v. Reproductive Health Services* (1989) in which the Supreme Court held many of Missouri's restrictive abortion rules constitutional and, in doing so, allowed states to greatly circumscribe abortion rights. At the same time, the tactics of pro-life groups and individuals were growing more radical and attracting more attention. Operation Rescue, founded by Randall Terry in 1987, garnered extensive press coverage with its targeting of cities in an attempt to close down all abortion clinics and services. Around the country, violence against clinics swelled. On the other side, pro-choice groups lobbied for passage of the federal Freedom of Choice Act, which limited the ability of states to restrict access to abortion services, and provided greater protection of clinic access (Melich 1996).

The Republican party had been officially pro-life since 1980 (and had leaned in that direction in 1976) and had never taken a pro-choice stance in its history. Yet the abortion issue remained controversial within the party. In 1989, a group of pro-choice Republicans created the National Republican Coalition for Choice (NRCC), with Mary Crisp (who had resigned her RNC post over the party's reversal on the ERA in 1980) as its head. That same year, President Bush vetoed four abortion-related bills; eight of the twelve Republican women in the House joined in the vote to override the veto of a bill allowing federal funds for abortions for rape and incest victims. As the abortion controversy heated up, Republican party leaders emphasized the "big tent" concept—all views are welcome in the GOP—while refusing to consider a change in the party's position. Bush strategist Lee Atwater went so far as to encourage the creation of a second pro-choice Republican organization, Republicans for Choice. The NRCC generally viewed Republicans for Choice as an attempt by Republican conservatives to keep tabs on pro-choice supporters within the party and to siphon off support from the NRCC. Before the 1992 conventions, five state Republican parties (all from the east coast—New York, Maine, Vermont, New Hampshire, and Massachusetts) adopted pro-choice planks (Melich 1996; Freeman 1993).

New women's rights issues gained attention as well. The accusations made by attorney Anita Hill at the confirmation hearings of Bush's appointee to the Supreme Court, Clarence Thomas, focused public attention on the issue of sexual harassment. Public awareness of sexual harassment had been growing since the 1970s. In 1980 the EEOC declared sexual harassment to be unlawful employment discrimination under Title VII, a decision Congress codified into law in 1985. Sexual harassment claims, however, were few and discussion of the issue limited until the 1991 Thomas-Hill hearings. As one indicator of the impact of the hearings, the EEOC reported receiving more than 10,000 sexual harassment complaints in 1992, a seventy percent increase over the previous year (McGlen and O'Connor 1998).

The Thomas-Hill hearings also drew attention to the severe underrepresentation of women in the Senate specifically and elected office generally. A number of women attributed their decision to seek elective office in 1992 in part to being angered by the sight of Anita Hill telling her story to an all-male Senate Judiciary Committee. Women's rights activists were increasingly seeking the election of women as a means to achieving their public policy goals. The traditional feminist organizations, such as NOW and the NWPC, shifted resources and effort toward that goal, while new organizations emerged that single-mindedly sought the election of women. The first such women's political action committee (PAC), the Women's Campaign Fund (WCF), was formed in 1974; by the 1991–1992 election cycle, almost fifty women's PACs were registered with the Federal Election Commission. The most successful of these, by far, was EMILY's List.[5] Founded in 1985, EMILY's List supports pro-choice, female Democratic candidates with campaign funds, training, and other support. In 1986, EMILY's List raised $350,000 for two Senate candidacies; by 1992, it could claim to have contributed or funneled (using its innovative bundling techniques) $6.2 million to its candidates and was one of the largest PACs in operation. In 1992, pro-choice Republicans created WISH List,[6] modeled after EMILY's List, to support pro-choice female Republican candidates. Taking advantage of the unusually large number of open seats, an anti-incumbent mood, the attention devoted to female candidacies, and an emerging fund-raising network, an unprecedented number of women ran for political office in 1992, earning it the moniker the Year of the Woman. While some observers noted that a more appropriate term would be the Year of the Liberal, Democratic Woman, both parties devoted significant resources to the recruitment and election of women. The attention and enthusiasm generated by the Year of the Woman created significant interest in women's issues at both parties' 1992 conventions (Biersack and Herrnson 1994; Nelson 1994; Wilcox 1994).

Finally, the family values debate was front and center in American political discourse. While family values includes some issues not directly related to women's rights—parental control, prayer in schools and church-state relations, sexuality and violence in the entertainment industry, for example—it does share a number of concerns, such as child care, women's role in the family and workplace, abortion, and so on. Social conservatives laid claim to the family label and accused feminists of being anti-family because of their advocacy of nontraditional roles for women, sexual freedom, and reproductive choice (Klatch 1987). By the early 1990s, family values was the touchstone for a broad cultural debate in American politics, a debate that had repercussions for public policy and party positioning on women's rights. In May 1992, Vice President Dan Quayle made his famous comment criticizing TV character Murphy Brown for having a child out of wedlock. The remark was front-page news and generated extended debate. Quayle later spoke out against the "cultural elite," who he described as lacking respect for tradition, morals, or standards. The phrase quickly became another buzzword in the battle over cultural values (Melich 1996).

In 1992 party divergence on women's rights was sharp, public, and omnipresent. Jo Freeman writes, "The 1992 conventions . . . saw the culmination of trends that ha[d] been developing for 20 years. The two major

[5] EMILY's List is an acronym for Early Money Is Like Yeast (it makes the dough rise), highlighting the organization's focus on helping pro-choice female Democratic candidates raise money, particularly in the important early stages of the campaign.

[6] WISH List is an acronym for Women in the Senate and House.

political parties ha[d] now completely polarized around feminism and the reaction to it. Each party's position ha[d] become institutionalized to the point where it is not seriously questioned within the national party and where the differences are clearly evident to the voting public. . . . [The two parties we]re presenting two different and conflicting visions of how Americans should engage in everyday life" (1993, 21). The bipartisanship that had appeared both present and possible on the issue of women's rights in the late 1960s and early 1970s had disappeared. Each party adopted an opposing position on the major women's rights issues. Yet while there was little real potential for change vis-à-vis women's rights within the party organizations themselves or at the conventions, these positions were not without controversy, particularly those of the Republican party. As has been the case since 1972, dissident voices continued to be present within both organizations. After 1980, however, dissidents were unable to mount any real challenge to the adopted positions of either party. This pattern continued in 1992.

Women's rights were not the subject of much debate at the Democratic Platform Committee meetings the previous May or at the convention itself. The Platform Committee was made up of an equal division of Clinton campaign and DNC Chair Ron Brown appointees. Bill Clinton had emphasized health care issues in his campaign, and the platform, as drafted and approved, contained an extensive list of policy pledges related to women's health. The ERA, pay equity, and other traditional women's issues had a less featured place in the document, although they maintained what was now an accepted place in the platform. The platform did not contain a specific section on women; women's rights were included under the "Choice" and "Strengthening Families" headings and were incorporated into discussions of labor, civil rights, health care, and so on. Pennsylvania Governor Robert P. Casey did request an opportunity to speak to the Platform Committee in opposition to its abortion plank, but Chair Ann Richards turned down his petition. No other deviations from the party's positions were noted (Freeman 1993).

Feminists were officially organized by the Women's Caucus. The Caucus held daily meetings, and Clinton addressed the group during the convention. Since the platform already covered most feminist demands, there was little of the complicated floor organization and maneuverings that had occupied feminists at past conventions; indeed, the lack of organization was so pronounced the feminists were often working at cross-purposes with receptions and marches coinciding on the schedule. NOW, however, boycotted the conventions because, according to President Patricia Ireland, "parties are irrelevant." Regardless, the image presented to the public was one of unified support for women's rights. Nearly every speaker proclaimed her support for the pro-choice position and was greeted with loud applause. Six pro-choice Republican women appeared before the convention to endorse Clinton. Clinton himself mentioned abortion four times in his acceptance speech. In addition, he touched on women's health, child support enforcement, women's role in and out of the home, and child care (Sanbonmatsu 1996; Freeman 1993).

The image projected to the American people by the 1992 Republican convention differed strikingly. Conservative commentator Pat Buchanan's insurgent campaign for the Republican nomination forced Bush and the Republican party to be particularly responsive to social conservatives. After 1988, Evangelist Pat Robertson used the list of supporters from his unsuccessful campaign for the Republican nomination to form the foundation of a new religious right organization, the Christian Coalition. By 1992, the Christian Coalition commanded an extensive grassroots operation of 550 chapters in all fifty states and 250,000 members. The Christian Coalition specialized in what executive director Ralph Reed described as "stealth tactics" by which it quietly labored to place its members in positions of power in state and local Republican organizations; at the 1992 convention it claimed to control more than a dozen state delegations, three hundred delegates, and twenty members of the Platform Committee. Phyllis Schlafly's Republican National Coalition for Life, the organizational successor of StopERA, was also active at the convention (Freeman 1993).

Representatives for both Republican pro-choice organizations, the National Republican Coalition for Choice and Republicans for Choice, were allowed to speak at platform hearings in Salt Lake City prior to the convention, as were Phyllis Schlafly and the head of Concerned Women for America on the pro-life side. After the debate attracted headlines, pro-choice Republican leaders announced their intention to lead a caravan of supporters to the convention, but that effort quickly fell apart. At the subcommittee and full committee meetings of the Platform Committee before the convention, a number of individuals spoke against the document's anti-abortion language adopted verbatim from the 1988 platform, but they were generally shouted down. Attempts to substitute less stridently pro-life language were defeated 17-3 in subcommittee and 84-16 by the full committee. A proposal to exclude victims of rape or incest was defeated by voice vote. Both pro-choice organizations promised to force a debate on the floor but were unable to garner the necessary six state delegations (Melich 1996; Freeman 1993).

The tone of the convention itself was widely perceived as intolerant and extremely conservative, an attitude that extended to women's rights. In his speech to the assembly, Pat Robertson accused Bill Clinton of wanting "to destroy the family," while Marilyn Quayle denounced liberals for being "disappointed because most women do not wish to be liberated from their true natures as women" (quoted in Melich 1996, 273). Republicans were especially critical of Hillary Clinton as the quintessential liberated woman, failing in her duty to her family and advocating antifamily public policies, although direct attacks were toned down after that strategy appeared to backfire with sympathy for Mrs. Clinton. The most noted speech was delivered by Patrick Buchanan. The Bush camp was only concerned that Buchanan issue a ringing endorsement of their candidate, which he did, and thus he was allowed carte blanche over the content of the speech. Buchanan issued a call to arms, claiming, "There is a religious war going on in our country for the soul of America." He included women's rights in his litany, claiming that "radical feminism [is] the agenda Clinton & Clinton would impose on America—abortion on demand . . . women in combat . . . . It is not the kind of change we can tolerate in a nation that we still call God's country" (quoted in Freeman 1993, 27). Bush's acceptance speech was mild by comparison, but it still included a number of nods to social conservatives vis-à-vis women's rights, citing his belief in "families that stick together, fathers who stick around" (reminiscent of Quayle's Murphy Brown attack) and in "the worth of each human being, born or unborn" (Sanbonmatsu 1996).

The platforms themselves continued the pattern of polarization evident since 1980. Democrats stated their now largely symbolic support for the ERA. The Democratic party pledged to ensure quality and affordable child care, while Republicans continued to favor private solutions to child care needs. On abortion, Democrats affirmed their pro-choice stance and backed national legislation to protect reproductive freedom. The Republican abortion plank remained untouched from 1988. Both parties made note of the need for greater attention and research on women's health concerns, particularly breast cancer, but while Democrats supported family planning programs, including greater access to contraception, Republicans pointedly opposed the provision of contraceptive or abortion information in schools. Republicans were not alone in their use of "family" language; Democrats promised a "family preservation" program to combat domestic violence. They also pledged tougher penalties for rapists. For their part, Republicans spoke out against pornography (including the sale of sexually explicit materials on military bases), military combat roles for women, and sexual harassment in Congress and the military.

In the period following the 1992 Republican convention, press accounts focused on the perception of the event as intolerant and extremist, particularly in relation to women's rights. Some commentators noted the discrepancy between Marilyn Quayle, a lawyer who gave up her profession and was particularly critical of feminism in her address, and Barbara Bush, who never pursued a career outside the home but whose convention speech was noted for being comparatively tolerant and progressive. The image of the GOP as antiwoman, perceived by many since Reagan's nomination in

1980, was only reinforced by the convention's tone; said one woman interviewed by the *New York Times*, "I don't think the Republicans are really for women" (Stanley 1992; Tabor and Applebome 1992).

Not all women or men criticized the family values agenda promoted at the GOP convention, and many citizens and activists shared Pat Buchanan and Marilyn Quayle's distrust and disdain of feminism. The 1992 conventions simply made clear just how polarized the two parties had become on women's rights.

Summary

This analysis suggests a considerable transformation of the politics of women's rights across this forty-year period. In the 1950s and 1960s, the few positions the parties took on women's rights issues attracted little internal debate or controversy. Republicans were generally perceived as more supportive, but the parties' platforms reveal few major differences. The issue of women's rights was almost entirely absent from the political agenda. Beginning in the late 1960s, this situation changed dramatically as women's rights issues leapt to the forefront of political debate and the parties' agendas. Women's rights were the subject of considerable controversy at both parties' conventions throughout the 1970s. While both parties were generally favorable to women's rights in 1972, their positions increasingly diverged, culminating with the events of 1980. After 1980, women's rights continue to occupy relatively large portions of the parties' platforms, but one view dominated each party, and real dissension from each party's positions at the conventions was almost nonexistent. Democrats maintained a strong pro–women's rights position. Republicans, on the other hand, favored some women's rights issues, but opposed many others, including the ERA, abortion rights, and federal funding for child care. While the salience of women's rights declined somewhat with the institutionalization of organized feminism, debates over family values and culture wars continued to shape political discourse.

One indicator of the evolution of the politics of women's rights is a comparison of the attention paid by both parties to women's rights issues before and after 1970. While their positions are often in opposition, both parties have recognized that women's rights deserve a place on their political agendas. Generally, but not always, the paternalistic attitudes evidenced by most politicians regarding women's rights in the 1950s has been replaced by a more progressive perspective. For example, both parties acknowledge that women are likely to have careers outside of the home and that some form of child care other than a parent is a necessity for many American families. Both Democrats and Republicans publicly encourage the participation of women in their parties, and unlike the earlier period, this position is likely to be backed up with party resources furthering that goal, although discrimination and barriers do still exist. The basic anti-discrimination laws that were enacted in the 1960s and early 1970s have unanimous support; in nearly every platform since 1972, both parties vow to vigorously enforce existing anti-discrimination statutes.

This narrative points to the enormity of change in women's rights politics. In the 1950s and early 1960s, there was little or no controversy or even discussion of women's rights. The small amount of elite activity centered around the Women's Bureau of the Department of Labor, but for most Americans, elites and the public alike, women's rights did not exist as a political issue. By 1972, however, women's rights had moved to the forefront of political debate as Americans discovered the previously ignored, denied, or unseen concerns of women. The parties' positions were reevaluated in light of the changing context, a context that involved new cleavages, meanings, and symbols. Each party experienced fierce fighting within its ranks regarding its stances on women's rights issues throughout the 1970s. These clashes eventually resulted in the development of new, different, and greatly polarized positions for both parties. By 1984, intraparty conflict on women's rights had largely been quelled. A few dissenting opinions were expressed at each convention, but those voices were quickly drowned out. While the agenda changes, there are no significant shifts in the parties' positions on women's rights after 1980.

PARTY PLATFORMS

This chapter has provided a detailed overview of the evolution of the parties' positions on women's rights over a forty-year time period, with attention given to the changing context in which those positions were established. In this section, I provide an additional investigation of the parties' platforms across this period, examining the level of attention and the priority given to women's rights. The unit of analysis is the party platform paragraph. For the most part, platforms during this period consist of short, concise paragraphs that are well focused on an idea or policy; thus the paragraph provides a convenient and substantively appropriate unit for analysis (see Carmines and Stimson 1989). A paragraph is coded as involving women's rights when it contains any mention of women's rights issues, however large or small. To qualify as a women's rights paragraph, the policy discussed must clearly relate to women. As a result, paragraphs that concern, for example, general anti-discrimination statutes but do not specifically mention sex are not included. Clearly, feminists have been interested in the enforcement and expansion of general equality and affir-

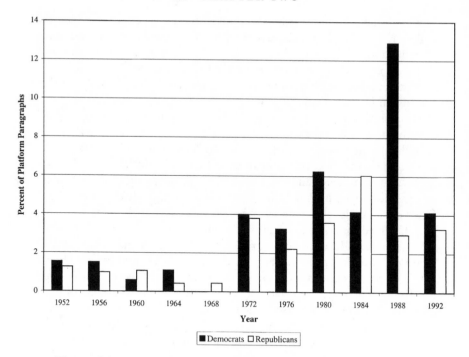

Figure 2.1. Percent Women's Rights Paragraphs, Democratic and Republican Party Platforms, 1952–1992.

mative action programs. This conservative coding scheme is intended to focus the measurement on women specifically and not on differences between the parties in their approaches to and emphasis on discrimination more generally.

Figure 2.1 shows the total number of paragraphs concerning women's rights issues in each party's platforms from 1952 to 1992, controlling for the number of paragraphs in each platform. This control is prudent as the platforms vary from more than 840 paragraphs each (Democrats in 1980, Republicans in 1988) to less than 100 paragraphs in the 1988 (31 paragraphs) and 1992 (97 paragraphs) Democratic platforms. As expected, neither party apportions much of its platform to women's rights concerns prior to 1972. During that period, Democrats devote more of their platform to women's rights than do Republicans in three out of five years. Differences are not great, and the parties are not sharply distinguished by this crude measure. As I have indicated, the substance of the parties' platforms vis-à-vis women's rights did not vary greatly during this period; distinctions between the parties on women's rights were more subtle. In 1972, the par-

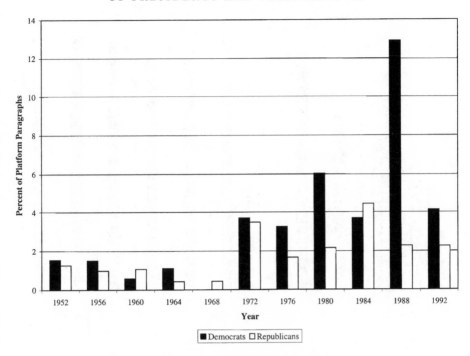

Figure 2.2. Percent Pro–Women's Rights Paragraphs, Democratic and Republican Party Platforms, 1952–1992.

ties give substantially equal amounts of their platform to women's rights, which in both cases represents a significant increase from past years. After 1972, however, Democrats consistently dedicate more of their platform to women's rights than do Republicans, with the exception of 1984. The 1988 data are somewhat exaggerated; the 1988 Democratic platform contained only thirty-one paragraphs, but each paragraph was quite long and covered an extensive list of topics and pledges. Seeking to deemphasize special interests that year, Democrats incorporated women's rights into various sections of the document rather than a single section. As a result, women's rights issues can be found in a comparatively large percentage of paragraphs. In general, post-1972 differences are still fairly moderate.

Figure 2.1 shows the level of attention to women's rights but does not indicate the direction of that attention. In Figure 2.2, the paragraphs included are limited to those considered favorable to women's rights. Paragraphs were only coded as anti–women's rights if they contained statements clearly in opposition to women's rights. Examples include expressed opposition to abortion rights, the concept of comparable worth, or federal

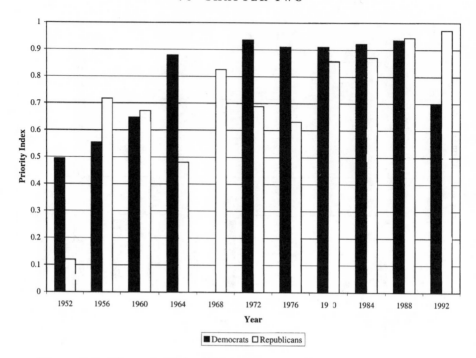

Figure 2.3. Women's Rights Priority Index, Democratic and Republican Party Platforms, 1952–1992.

financing of child care services. Statements that might be open to interpretation or that use language that might be considered misleading were given the benefit of the doubt and allowed as pro–women's rights. For example, a paragraph that acknowledges the many work situations of American women while suggesting a preference for traditional roles is permitted as pro–women's rights.

From 1952 through 1968, there is no difference between the data in Figures 2.1 and 2.2. In 1972, there is a very slight decrease in the percents for both parties, but the similarity between the two parties remains. Post-1972, looking only at pro–women's rights paragraphs increases the divergence between the two parties: The level of attention afforded women's rights by the Democrats does not change greatly, but the Republican percentage declines, and thus the divergence is exacerbated, and the 1984 discrepancy is lessened. Again, the pattern that emerges is one of increasing attention over time. Democrats and Republicans dedicate similar portions of their documents to women's rights through 1972. After 1972, however, Democrats almost uniformly devote more attention to women's rights, a difference that is exacerbated when one looks at pro–women's rights paragraphs only.

Finally, we can obtain a sense of the importance of the issue to each party. I adopt Carmines and Stimson's (1989) priority index, which is created by taking 1.0 minus the number of paragraphs preceding the first mention of the issue divided by the total number of paragraphs in the platform. The higher the score, the greater the priority given the issue by the party. Figure 2.3 shows the results of this analysis for women's rights (in every case, the first mention of women's rights by both parties is favorable). Before 1972, neither party consistently gives more priority to women's rights than does the other. (There is no priority index for Democrats in 1968 because the Democratic platform contained no references to women's rights that year.) Beginning in 1972, Democrats always give more priority to women's rights than do Republicans, by this measure. The two exceptions to this rule are 1988 and 1992, where small platform size means that the comparatively high placement of women's rights in the Democratic platforms is undercut by this measurement strategy. Differences, it should be emphasized, are often not great, suggesting that women's rights was considered an important issue by both parties across the latter time period.

CONCLUSION

The detailed overview of the positions adopted by the political parties and their presidents and presidential candidates over the forty-year period from 1952 to 1992 provided in this narrative suggests that the parties' positions on women's rights have been characterized by significant change. In the 1950s and early 1960s, neither party afforded a great amount of attention to women's rights, but while their platforms were not greatly differentiated, Republicans were generally more favorable to the few women's rights issues discussed, such as the ERA. In the late 1960s and early 1970s, this equilibrium was disturbed as women's rights issues came to the fore of public discourse. Beginning in 1972, both parties devoted an unprecedented portion of their platforms to pledges and statements related to women's rights. Throughout the 1970s, women's rights were hotly debated at both parties' conventions as activists and party elites clashed over positioning. By 1980, the parties had shifted from a generally favorable consensus regarding women's rights to a situation of increasing polarization. Democrats, despite their earlier opposition to such issues as the ERA, largely sided with feminists, supporting a myriad of policy initiatives intended to facilitate greater equality and opportunity for women. Republicans, on the other hand, developed positions in opposition to women's rights on issues such as the ERA, abortion, comparable worth, child care funding, and so on. After 1980, the level of dissension within both parties declined as one view came to dominate each party.

When previous authors have noted the phenomenon of changing and polarizing party positions on women's rights, they have generally been referring to the change in the party's positions as represented by the platforms and presidential actions and statements. The evidence reviewed here confirms their impressions. In the next chapter, I turn to the positions of party elites in Congress.

CHAPTER THREE

Women's Rights in the House and Senate

THUS FAR, my discussion of the transformation and polarization of the parties on women's rights has focused on the political parties as represented by their national organizations, presidents, and presidential candidates. Examination of the parties as organizations and executives has indeed suggested a change in relative positioning vis-à-vis women's rights. Before the late 1960s, Republicans were perceived as more supportive of most women's rights issues, particularly the ERA, but differences in terms of platforms were not particularly great. The parties were quite similar on women's rights in the late 1960s and early 1970s, but as the decade of the 1970s wore on, each party adopted increasingly divergent positions. After 1980, the two parties stood on opposing sides, with the Democrats embracing, and the Republicans eschewing, feminism. The goal of this chapter is to determine if and to what extent this transformation has characterized the parties in Congress as well.

Previous scholarship in this area has focused almost exclusively on party organizations and executives, with the parties in Congress receiving only cursory attention (cf. Costain 1991; Freeman 1987). Information culled from various sources, however, suggests a similar pattern to that described in chapter 2: greater Republican support before the 1970s, general bipartisanship in the early 1970s, and greater Democratic support thereafter. For example, in her study of the women's movement, Costain (1992) finds Republican membership positively associated with ERA sponsorship from 1963 to 1971. Accounts of Congressional activity on women's rights in the early 1970s emphasize bipartisanship (Orfield 1975; Freeman 1975). Research on female legislators has examined whether women in elected office are more supportive of women's rights than are their male counterparts, often including party as a control. These studies generally find Democratic party membership correlated with support for women's rights since the early 1970s (cf. Burrell 1994). As this brief discussion suggests, previous work has not tracked the partisanship of women's rights support in Congress consistently from the early 1950s to the early 1990s. Students of Congressional realignment examining all or part of this period have given little or no attention to women's rights (cf. Rohde 1991; Sinclair 1982).

This analysis thus represents a unique attempt to systematically track the phenomenon of changes in the relative party positions on women's rights among members of the House and Senate over the forty years from 1952 to 1992. The central data of this chapter are the cosponsorships of all women's rights bills offered in the House and Senate during this time period. Beginning with the 82nd (1953–1954) and ending with the 102nd (1991–1992) Congress, I do indeed find substantial evidence of a transformation similar to that observed between the parties as national organizations, presidents, and presidential candidates. In the 1950s and early 1960s, Republicans in both chambers were more likely to be supporters of women's rights than were Democrats. Beginning in the late 1960s and early 1970s, this situation reverses (dramatically in the House, less so in the Senate), and Democrats become the party in Congress more likely to support women's rights. The parties grow increasingly polarized across the 1980s and into the early 1990s.

In this chapter, I begin by identifying challenges to measuring relative party position on women's rights in Congress across this time period. I propose bill cosponsorships as a primary indicator, and the advantages and disadvantages of this measurement strategy, particularly as compared to the more commonly used measure of Congressional activity and preferences, roll call votes, are discussed. Next, I describe the process of identifying and coding women's rights bills introduced into the House and Senate across this time period. After reviewing the resultant data, the findings regarding party activity on women's rights are presented and discussed. Finally, I supplement the analysis of bill cosponsorships with a brief examination of available roll calls.

MEASURING SUPPORT FOR WOMEN'S RIGHTS IN CONGRESS

The 535 members of Congress produce quantifiable outputs that are particularly appropriate for systematic research into party realignment. Party organizations produce platforms every four years; presidents and presidential candidates can be counted on to give nomination acceptance speeches with the same regularity and State of the Union addresses annually. For the period of this study, however, there have been only twenty-two platforms and nomination speeches. Forty State of the Unions have been presented to Congress, but by only eight different presidents. In contrast, during this forty-year span there have been thousands of Representatives and hundreds of Senators who have been variously involved in the process of creating the parties' images and positions vis-à-vis women's rights.

Yet measuring support for women's rights in Congress is a difficult task. The vast majority of research on Congressional behavior focuses on roll call votes. Roll call votes have the advantage of being public, consequential, and, not incidentally, readily available in machine-readable form. Unfortunately, the scarcity of votes related to women's rights in the first half of the period under study generally discommends roll call behavior as a measure of support for women's rights by members of Congress; before 1969, there are fewer than a handful of women's rights votes on the floor of either chamber. Even during the height of legislative activity on women's rights in the early 1970s, women's rights proposals were often lumped together with other issues in omnibus legislation. Moreover, the women's rights votes available in the second half of the period are skewed toward the topic of abortion. My intention is to provide a sense of relative party positioning in Congress on women's rights broadly; while evolving party polarization on abortion rights has been demonstrated (Adams 1997), a determination of the degree to which party polarization characterizes women's rights generally, including but also above and beyond abortion, merits investigation as well. By offering a means to observe the behavior of the parties' delegations on a broad spectrum of women's rights issues, cosponsorship provides a more comprehensive view of women's rights politics. In the final section of this chapter, I analyze available roll call votes to supplement the cosponsorship results and offer further evidence of this transformation.

Bill Cosponsorship as a Measure of Support for Women's Rights

I use cosponsorship[1] of women's rights bills as an individual-level indicator of support for women's rights that is then aggregated to the parties' delegations in Congress for a measure of party support. Bill cosponsorship has a tradition of usage among students of gender politics. Klein describes the introduction of a bill relating to women's issues as an "expression of sympathy and interest" (1984, 11) for women's rights and uses the level of bill introduction as a measure of women's access to political decision makers. Costain (1988) similarly views bill introduction as a signal of sympathy, interest, and awareness and tracks change in the agenda for women's rights through the content of women's bills introduced into Congress.

Yet as a less common strategy for measuring members' policy positions, this approach warrants justification and explication. While cosponsorships differ from floor votes in important ways, many of these differences actually bolster the case for using cosponsorship as a measure of preferences. First, a floor vote involves a decision between yea or nay. The decision to

---

[1] Technically, these data include both bill introduction (the act, usually individual, of initiating legislation) and cosponsorship (adding one's name as a cosponsor to a bill already introduced). For the most part, I do not distinguish between the acts of introduction and cosponsorship in this analysis. By cosponsorship I mean to reference both acts of attaching one's name to proposed legislation.

cosponsor, on the other hand, may be better conceived as a choice between yea and don't care, not interested, or no opinion. Said another way, roll call voting suggests a sharp distinction between favoring and not favoring legislation. Bill cosponsorship, alternatively, indicates support for the policy, but not cosponsoring does not necessarily denote opposition. Instead, failing to cosponsor might suggest disinterest or that the member does not consider the issue relevant to her constituents or supporters. Because no roll is actually called, members may fail to cosponsor legislation they favor simply because their scarce resources (e.g., time, effort) are directed elsewhere. Yet many fighting for a cause have contended that those who do not act on behalf of an interest or cause are necessarily in opposition (see King 1963). Moreover, as Schiller suggests regarding bill introduction in the Senate, "unlike roll-call voting, where senators face a predetermined set of alternatives they had no part in shaping, bill sponsorship is under the control of the individual legislator" (1995, 186–7). On a roll call vote, members are forced to make a choice between the public policy proposed and the status quo, regardless of their intensity of preference. Members are not required to cosponsor any piece of legislation, and thus the degree of choice associated with cosponsorship activity is greater than with roll calls (members, of course, may choose to abstain from voting, but significant absence can provide fodder for potential challengers). Thus as an action over which members have substantial discretion, cosponsorship of a bill may be more indicative of member preferences and policy interests than a roll call yea or nay.

Second, a floor vote is a more public act than bill cosponsorship, and, as a result, potential constituent response may be a greater concern with floor votes as compared to bill cosponsorship. On the other hand, Mayhew (1974) lists bill cosponsorship as an electorally motivated position-taking activity, and cosponsorship is sometimes used by challengers to link members to unpopular policies (Schiller 1995). In the one study employing an explicit measure of constituent characteristics, Regens (1989) finds constituency to be a predictor of cosponsorship of environmental legislation. More generally, policy preferences are consistently shown to be important determinants of cosponsorship of specific bills (Wolbrecht and Martin n.d.; Kessler and Krehbiel 1996; Krehbiel 1995; Regens 1989). Thus, even if cosponsorship behavior is not only or primarily directed at constituents (see Kessler and Krehbiel 1996), there is reason to believe that it is an activity that reflects members' positions on given issues.

Third, roll call voting is a more consequential act than bill cosponsorship in terms of policy outcomes. The vast majority of bills proposed do not make it out of committee, much less become law. For example, Wilson and Young (1997) report that in the 99th Congress (1985–1986) only eighteen percent of the almost 3,000 bills introduced into the Senate and fourteen percent of the more than 5,000 bills introduced into the House reached the floor. In both chambers, about nine percent of all bills introduced were passed. As a result, members may be willing to sign on to bills they do not expect to pass as a way to take a position or appease an interest without actually achieving a policy outcome. Krehbiel (1995), for example, examined the behavior of cosponsors to a certain bill on subsequent attempts to move that bill out of committee via a discharge petition and found that approximately thirty of the more than 219 members who had cosponsored refused to follow through by signing the petition. On the other hand, cosponsorship is not entirely divorced from policy outcomes. Commentators often note the number of cosponsors to a bill as an indication of potential for a successful legislative outcome. Research suggests that cosponsorship may impact success in the early stages of the legislative process (Wilson and Young 1997). Moreover, Krehbiel argues that "cosponsorship behavior is not significantly different from other more explicitly outcome-based forms of legislative behavior, such as roll call voting" (1995, 910). In short, members cosponsor legislation with expected policy consequences that they prefer to the status quo. Consistent with this view, the decision to cosponsor a bill appears to be related to the same sorts of factors that influence roll call behavior, including policy preferences, relevant constituency characteristics, and ideology (Krehbiel 1995; Regens 1989).

In addition, the weak connection between bill cosponsorship and policy outcome, compared with that for roll call voting, makes the activity in some ways more comparable to the party platforms discussed in chapter 2. Both can be conceived of as representing positions with which an individual or party wishes to be identified (Schiller 1995), even if in neither case does the member or party necessarily follow through by devoting energy or resources to making the bill or pledge a reality. Like party pledges, bill introduction and cosponsorship are often responses to pressures from organized interests. Again, such a reality does not negate the usefulness of the bill cosponsorship data but simply indicates that like platform pledges, bill cosponsorship might provide insight into the types of interests and policies with which a member, and a party, chooses to be associated.

Fourth, one might expect Democrats, who tend to favor government activism, to be more likely to cosponsor legislation than are Republicans. In that case, conclusions about the differing cosponsorship behavior of each parties' members on any specific set of issues would be suspect. Research on bill cosponsorship, however, suggests that partisanship is not a significant determinant of level of cosponsorship activity (Kessler and Krehbiel 1996; Schiller 1995). Campbell (1982) found a party effect for cosponsorship in the House, but it was weak and in the opposite direction expected—that is, Republicans were more likely to cosponsor.

Fifth, the content of bills introduced changes from session to session, reflecting the shifting political agenda. As a result, over time comparison of members' cosponsorship behavior on a particular type of bill might be considered inappropriate. Yet roll call voting or interest group ratings based on roll call behavior over a period of time are subject to the same vagaries of the Congressional agenda. Furthermore, for my purposes change in the content of the bills being introduced from Congress to Congress is not problematic in that bill cosponsorship behavior is meant to measure support of (or opposition to) women's rights at a specific point in time. In the 1950s, supportive behavior vis-à-vis women's rights might mean cosponsoring the Equal Pay Act, while in the 1980s, it might include cosponsorship of the Domestic Violence Prevention Act. Both elites and citizens evaluate a member's stance based on her position on the relevant women's rights issues of the time. This measure is one way in which to record that position at a particular moment in history.

Two additional distinctions between roll call votes and bill cosponsorships deserve note: Unlike bill cosponsorships, roll call votes have a history of application in the social sciences and are readily available in machine-readable form. It should be emphasized that neither tradition nor ease of use should necessarily recommend one measure over another. Students of Congress continually note the need for measures of Congressional preferences in addition to roll call voting because, as so often employed, these indicators suffer from the weakness of circular reasoning: They are vote-based measures used to predict voting behavior (Krehbiel 1995). While bill cosponsorships do not solve all of the problems associated with the analysis of roll call votes, they do provide a means for expanding the ways in which Congressional preferences are observed.

Finally, bill cosponsorships possess certain characteristics particularly useful for this research: They can be observed over time and they are partisan. Women's rights bill cosponsorships occur in both the House and the Senate in every Congress from 1953 to 1992. In addition, like a roll call vote, bill cosponsorship is an individual-level activity that can be assigned to an individual, partisan member. As such, bill cosponsorship is distinguished from other Congressional activity concerning women's rights that can be observed over time, such as committee hearings, but are not as clearly attributed to partisans or parties. Bill cosponsorships thus serve two crucial purposes: They attach women's rights positions to partisan individuals, and thus by inference, parties, and they do so over time.

Identifying and Coding Women's Rights Bill Cosponsorships

Women's rights bills were identified by consulting each year's *Congressional Record Index* (1953–1992) under the following index headings:

women, discrimination, equal/equality, female, gender, rights, and sex. In the end, the vast majority of bills coded were listed under women (including the "see also" subheadings), with few found under the other headings. The abstract or title of each referenced bill is used to determine if it is related to women's rights. Following from the definition of women's rights in chapter 1, the decision rule is that the bill must concern women *directly* and *only*. The coding rule is conservative; bills that group women together with ethnic, religious, racial, or other minority populations are not included, nor are bills that include provisions related to women rights with other non-women's rights–related provisions.

A few comments regarding this decision rule are appropriate. Various programs and policies that disproportionally impact women's lives but for which women are not the direct or only intended beneficiary or focus are not included. Under this rule, for example, bills pertaining to the Women, Infants, and Children (WIC) program are precluded. While such legislation is certainly relevant to many women's lives, cosponsorship of such bills is probably more suggestive of a member's views toward another policy area (such as, in this example, public responsibility for children as well as general attitudes toward social welfare) than of a position on women's rights.

Second, these rules obviously exclude a great deal of legislation, some of it of major importance, where women's concerns are part of broad legislative initiatives. For example, the Civil Rights Act of 1964 as introduced would not be included under this coding strategy, although Title VII of that act represents one of the most important legal achievements for women's rights in the twentieth century. The purpose of this coding, however, is not to identify legislation that has had significant policy consequences for women. Instead, the intent is to use identified bills to determine support for women's rights by individual members of Congress. Further, while this coding scheme may eliminate bills that eventually became laws of significance for women, it does include many of the women's rights–related bills that were eventually incorporated into those laws. Indeed, using bill cosponsorship instead of roll call votes allows me to disaggregate the final pieces of legislation into the myriad of smaller bills that are often incorporated into the final legislation and to identify better the various supporters of specific aspects of such laws.

Bills determined to be related to women's rights are then coded as pro-women's rights or anti–women's rights. As suggested by the definition in chapter 1, pro–women's rights bills are those that have greater equality and opportunity for women as their goal, either by legislating such equality of treatment and practice or by addressing the unique needs of women. Anti–women's rights bills, on the other hand, are those that seek to restrict or deny women's rights, equality, or opportunity.[2] It should be emphasized that the coding of bills, both for inclusion as relevant to women's rights and in coding of directional category, relies solely on the brief title or abstract in the *Congressional Record Index* (1953–1992); I did not consult the full text of the proposed legislation. Clearly, relying on such limited information poses potential problems. The names and abstracts attached to bills are often vague and broad, possibly suggesting an impact and role for bills beyond their actual scope or emphasizing certain policy aspects of the proposal while failing to mention others. Bill titles may be designed to convey particular interpretations of the consequences of the legislation that do not reflect their full or specific intent.

Despite these realities, bill coding decisions were, by and large, straightforward, partly because the coding required was simple: Bills either had to be pro–women's rights or anti–women's rights. Perhaps because members seek to aid the ease of decision making on the myriad of bills they are called to evaluate, bill titles/abstracts tend to be quite direct and are rather easily categorized. I include a number of examples in Table 3.1. to illustrate this point. A small number of bills could not be categorized as pro–women's rights or anti–women's rights and are excluded from all analysis.

Finally, I aggregate bills by Congress rather than by year or by session. Bill cosponsorship activity is not randomly distributed across each Congress but tends to be clustered, usually in the first year. Cosponsorship data from the second year are considerably thinner than those from the first, and thus are potentially unrepresentative. This is particularly troublesome in the earlier period when fewer women's rights bills were introduced.

The Data

Almost 2,300 bills were identified during the 83rd (1953–1954) to the 102nd (1991–1992) Congresses. Figures 3.1 and 3.2 present the number of pro–women's rights and anti–women's rights bills introduced into the House and Senate, respectively, by Congress (note that the scale varies greatly by chamber). For the most part, I focus my attention and the following analysis on the far more numerous pro–women's rights bills and cosponsorships.

Figure 3.1 suggests a surprising pattern of pro–women's rights bill in-

[2] Honorific bills, those which demand no real substantive activity on the part of the federal government and/or have no real effect or meaning, are excluded from analysis. Examples of honorific bills include the declaration of days, weeks, or months and expressions of the "sense of Congress." The action of cosponsoring any piece of legislation can be more symbolic than consequential, but in the case of such purely honorific bills, the action is wholly symbolic in both behavior and outcome. I have chosen to focus my analysis on bills that would have an impact on women's rights and opportunities if implemented.

TABLE 3.1
Coding of Women's Rights Bills

Index Subheading[a]	Title/Abstract	Category
Sex, prohibit discrimination on account of	To prohibit discrimination on account of sex in the payment of wages by certain employers engaged in commerce or in the production of goods for commerce, and to provide for the restitution of wages lost by employes by reason of any such discrimination	Pro–women's rights
National Center for Prevention and Control of Rape, establish	To amend the Community Mental Health Centers Act to authorize a program for rape prevention and control	Pro–women's rights
Small business owned by women, development of program	A bill to amend the Small Business Act to establish programs and initiate efforts to assist the development of small business concerns owned and controlled by women, and for other purposes	Pro–women's rights
Abortion, availability of services under federally funded programs	A bill to amend various provisions of law to ensure that services related to abortion are made available to the same extent as are all other pregnancy-related services under federally funded programs	Pro–women's rights
Musical programs, prohibit sex discrimination in	To amend section 901(a) (relating to the prohibition of sex discrimination) of the Educational Amendments of 1972 to exempt from the prohibition of such section musical programs or activities designed for parents and students	Anti–women's rights
Abortion, deny tax deduction of medical expenses	A bill to amend the Internal Revenue Code of 1986 to deny the deduction of medical expenses incurred for certain abortions	Anti–women's rights

[a]All examples were found under the major heading "women" in the *Congressional Record Index* (1953–1992).

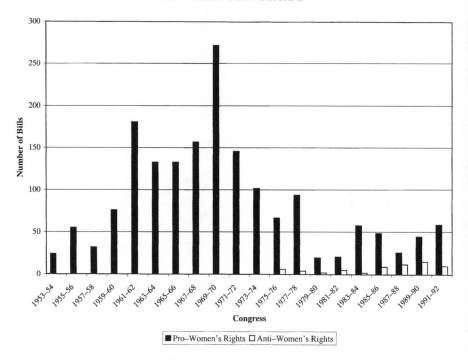

Figure 3.1. Number of Women's Rights Bills Introduced, by Category, House, 1953–1992.

troduction: The number of pro–women's rights bills introduced into the House actually declines from the early 1970s onward. However, the number of bills provides an inaccurate picture of women's rights activity in both chambers because it does not reflect the number of cosponsors to each bill. Specifically, the bill count does not indicate if such bills attracted the cosponsorship of a few members or involved more extensive participation. Moreover, the two chambers were characterized by different cosponsorship practices across this period. Multiple sponsorship of bills has been the norm in the Senate since the late 1930s. The Senate graph (Figure 3.2) thus adequately reflects the growth of women's rights bills, although it masks any variation in the number of cosponsors to those bills. In the House, on the other hand, multiple cosponsorship was explicitly banned until 1967 when the House passed a resolution allowing up to 25 members to join a bill; unlimited cosponsorship was adopted in 1978 (Wilson and Young 1997). The unexpected findings in Figure 3.1 can thus be explained in large part by the fact that after 1967, members who wished to sponsor women's rights legislation could join together on the same bill in-

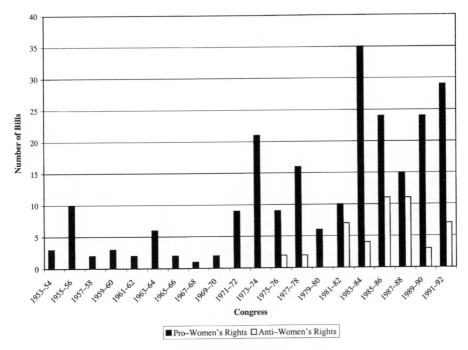

Figure 3.2. Number of Women's Rights Bills Introduced, by Category, Senate, 1953–1992.

stead of introducing multiple versions of the same legislation, as was the practice in the earlier period.

The number of bill cosponsorships thus provides a more accurate picture of the extent of Congressional activity on women's rights. More than 21,400 cosponsorships were coded during this time period. Figures 3.3 and 3.4 present the number of pro–women's rights and anti–women's rights cosponsorships for each chamber by Congress (again, note the difference in scaling). In both chambers, the number of bill cosponsorships grows slightly in the early 1970s, with greater increases in the mid-1980s and after. Compared to the later part of the series, the relatively small increases in cosponsorship in the early 1970s are actually somewhat surprising, given the large amount of women's rights legislation being passed by both chambers during the period. The House graph suggests a pattern of generally steady growth, with some falloff in the late 1970s and early 1980s. The Senate figure is more erratic, but it likewise reflects a falloff in the period around 1980 and a substantial increase in pro–women's rights cosponsorship activity in the 1990s.

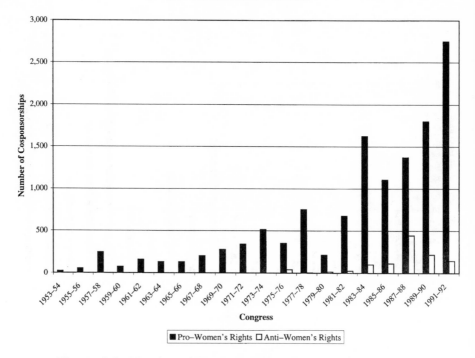

Figure 3.3. Number of Women's Rights Bill Cosponsorships, by Category, House, 1953–1992.

In addition to the *level* of women's rights activity, it is also possible to gauge the *extent* of women's rights activity by examining the number of members in any Congress who cosponsor any pro–women's rights or anti–women's rights bills. While the count of cosponsorships provides a sense of how much women's rights activity is occurring, it does not provide information about the extent to which members are participating; it is entirely possible, for example, that the more than 2,700 pro–women's rights cosponsorships during the 102nd House (1991–1992) were the work of just a handful of dedicated members. Figures 3.5 and 3.6 show the number of members cosponsoring any pro–women's rights and anti–women's rights legislation in the House and Senate, respectively (note that the scale of the graphs reflects the total membership of each body; i.e., the limit for possible participation). In both chambers there is evidence of greater numbers of members engaging in women's rights cosponsorship activity in the 1970s than in the 1950s or 1960s, with even broader participation in the 1980s and 1990s. Both series are characterized by outliers, and again,

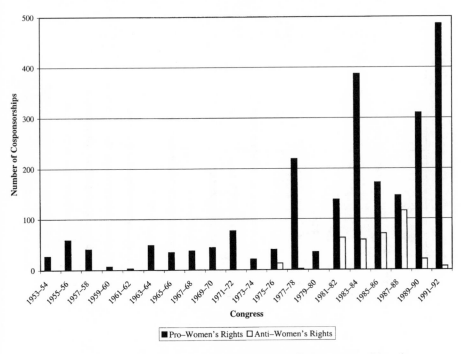

Figure 3.4. Number of Women's Rights Bill Cosponsorships, by Category, Senate, 1953–1992.

the pattern in the Senate is more erratic than in the House.[3] Even in the earlier periods, it is interesting to note that women's rights cosponsorship activity extended to considerable portions of both chambers in some years. The rate of increase in extent of participation is not nearly as steep as that for cosponsorship activity, suggesting increasingly greater levels of activity for those who do cosponsor across this period rather than an increase in the portion of members engaging in such behavior.

[3] The large increase in number of members cosponsoring any pro–women's rights legislation in the House during the 1957–1958 Congress can be explained in part by an unusual effort on behalf of the ERA in which supporters obtained the permission of members to petition the Speaker to add their names *en masse* to the list of ERA cosponsors. This activity was unusual during the early period, and probably more suggestive of the level of support among pro-ERA activists in and outside of the House than of the members who agreed to allow their name to be added.

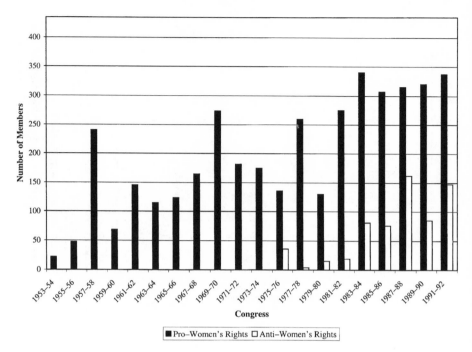

Figure 3.5. Total Number of Representatives Cosponsoring Any Women's Rights Bills, by Category, 1953–1992.

THE TRANSFORMATION OF PARTISAN SUPPORT FOR WOMEN'S RIGHTS IN CONGRESS

In this section I address the central goal of this chapter: determining if and to what extent the transformation and polarization over women's rights observed among the parties as organizations, presidents, and presidential candidates characterizes the parties in Congress as well. I employ bill cosponsorship activity as a measure of support for women's rights. This activity is specific to individual members. Each member, however, claims a partisan label and represents her party, individually and collectively. By aggregating individual member's policy positions, we can attain a sense of a general party position or tendency.

I focus on cosponsorship of pro–women's rights bills as a measure of each party's relative position on women's rights. As the descriptive graphs have shown, pro–women's rights bills have been introduced in both chambers in every Congress across the period of study, while anti–women's rights bills do not occur until the mid-1970s. Furthermore, in every Con-

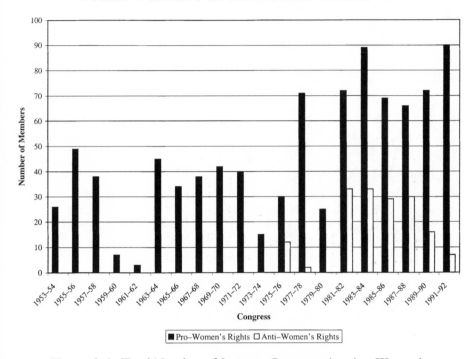

Figure 3.6. Total Number of Senators Cosponsoring Any Women's Rights Bills, by Category, 1953–1992.

gress pro–women's rights cosponsorships are far more numerous and thus provide a richer source of information. This analysis is supplemented with a brief examination of anti–women's rights bill cosponsorships at the close of this section.

Position: Bill Cosponsorship by Party

To measure each party's support for women's rights, I focus on the portion of the parties' delegation displaying supportive behavior and compare the levels of such support by each party. To do so, I take the percentage of Republicans cosponsoring *any* pro–women's rights legislation and subtract it from the percentage of Democrats doing so. Thus, a negative observation indicates Republicans are more likely than Democrats to cosponsor any pro–women's rights legislation, and a positive observation shows Democrats are more likely to do so. The resulting series, presented in Figures 3.7 and 3.8, represent the interparty difference on cosponsorship of any

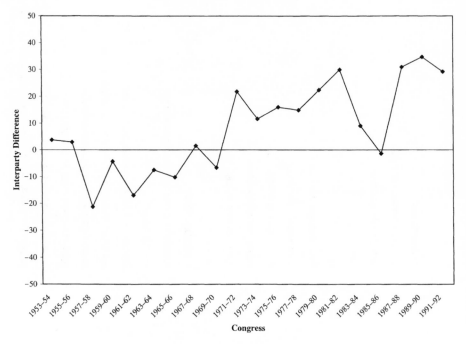

Figure 3.7. Interparty Difference in Cosponsorship of Any
Pro–Women's Rights Bills, House, 1953–1992.

pro–women's rights legislation. Table 3.2 reports this analysis, along with
tests of significance for each difference.

Turning first to the House, Republicans were generally more likely to
cosponsor pro–women's rights legislation before 1971, a difference that is
statistically significant in three Congresses. There are three exceptions to
the pattern of greater Republican support, but none are statistically significant. The 1953–1954 and 1955–1956 findings somewhat confound attempts to identify a strong trend, but greater support from Republicans
appears strongest in the late 1950s and early 1960s. In the late 1960s, interparty differences waned. In short, Republicans were generally more
likely to be cosponsors of pro–women's rights legislation before 1971–
1972, with a few exceptions, and differences appear to be diminishing as
the 1970s neared.

The situation in the House reversed dramatically during the 92nd Congress (1971–1972), as Democrats became significantly and consistently
more likely to be cosponsors of pro–women's rights legislation than Republicans. The one exception to that pattern is 1985–1986, during which

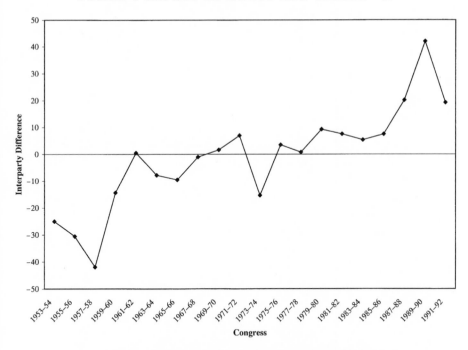

Figure 3.8. Interparty Difference in Cosponsorship of Any
Pro–Women's Rights Bills, Senate, 1953–1992.

there was no statistically significant difference between the parties' rates
of cosponsorship. I can only speculate as to the causes of 1985–1986 and,
to a lesser extent, 1983–1984, outliers in the post-1970 period. Closer
examination of the data (see Table 3.2) shows that in 1983–1984, Democratic rates of cosponsorship remained stable from the previous Congress,
while Republicans greatly increased their level of cosponsorship behavior.
In 1985–1986, Republicans continued to cosponsor at relatively high
rates, while Democratic cosponsorship fell off. In the next Congress, and
those following, Democratic rates of cosponsorship rebounded to their
highest levels of the series. Republicans, on the other hand, fell back to
rates in the 50s, above where they had been in the early 1980s, but below
their 1983–1984 and 1985–1986 levels, which represent the high points
of Republican cosponsorship for the entire period. As discussed in chapter 2, the period around the 1984 election was characterized by considerable salience and controversy vis-à-vis women's rights and the parties.
Republicans in Congress may have perceived themselves to be suffering
from association with a Republican president widely viewed as at best in-

TABLE 3.2

Percentage of Democrats and Republicans Cosponsoring Any Pro–Women's Rights Bills, House and Senate, 1953–1992

Congress	House			Senate		
	Democrats	Republicans	Difference	Democrats	Republicans	Difference
1953–1954	6.9 (218)[a]	3.2 (221)	3.7	10.7 (56)	35.7 (56)	−25.0***
1955–1956	12.3 (235)	9.4 (202)	2.9	32.7 (55)	63.3 (49)	−30.6***
1957–1958	44.8 (239)	66.0 (203)	−21.2***	16.1 (56)	58.0 (50)	−41.9***
1959–1960	14.1 (284)	18.5 (157)	−4.4	1.4 (70)	15.8 (38)	−14.4**
1961–1962	25.9 (274)	42.9 (175)	−17.0***	2.9 (68)	2.4 (41)	0.5
1963–1964	23.0 (261)	30.4 (181)	−7.4	39.4 (71)	47.2 (36)	−7.8
1965–1966	24.8 (298)	35.0 (143)	−10.2*	28.8 (73)	38.2 (34)	−9.4
1967–1968	38.3 (251)	36.7 (188)	1.6	35.8 (67)	36.8 (38)	−1.0
1969–1970	58.4 (250)	65.0 (197)	−6.6	40.3 (62)	38.6 (44)	1.7

Year						
1971–1972	50.4 (258)	28.6 (182)	21.8***	40.3 (62)	33.3 (45)	7.0
1973–1974	44.8 (248)	33.2 (193)	11.6*	7.9 (63)	23.3 (43)	−15.4*
1975–1976	36.2 (296)	20.1 (144)	16.1***	29.9 (67)	26.3 (38)	3.6
1977–1978	63.9 (296)	49.0 (145)	14.9**	69.2 (65)	68.4 (38)	0.8
1979–1980	37.6 (282)	15.2 (158)	22.4***	28.8 (59)	19.5 (41)	9.3
1981–1982	75.1 (195)	45.1 (195)	30.0***	76.1 (46)	68.5 (54)	7.6
1983–1984	80.9 (272)	71.9 (167)	9.0*	91.1 (45)	85.7 (56)	5.4
1985–1986	69.4 (258)	70.7 (181)	−1.3	72.3 (47)	64.8 (54)	7.5
1987–1988	84.0 (263)	53.1 (177)	30.9***	74.6 (55)	54.4 (46)	20.2*
1989–1990	86.1 (266)	51.4 (177)	34.7***	90.9 (55)	48.9 (45)	42.0***
1991–1992	87.5 (272)	58.3 (168)	29.2***	96.6 (58)	77.3 (44)	19.3**

[a]N in parentheses.

* $p \leq 0.05$, ** $p \leq 0.01$, *** $p \leq 0.001$. Significance indicated by Z-test for the difference in rates between two sets of binomial data described in the Appendix. Membership totals may exceed 435 (House) or 100 (Senate) because of turnover during the session.

sensitive and at worst antagonistic to women's rights and sought to counter that image by adding their name to pro–women's rights legislation. Following the 1984 election, conventional wisdom, and many Democratic elites, blamed Mondale's image as beholden to special interests, especially feminists, for the party's devastating defeat. An effort to distance themselves from feminism might explain the dropoff in Democratic cosponsorship in 1985–1986. These explanations, however, are purely speculative and post hoc.

Those outliers notwithstanding, Figure 3.7 and Table 3.2 show that the period after 1970 represents a significant change in the parties' relative positions vis-à-vis women's rights in the House, as reflected by their cosponsorship behavior. Before that Congress, Republicans were generally more likely to cosponsor, but after, Democrats were consistently (with one exception) more likely to cosponsor, and the differences were usually larger than any in the preceding period.

A similar, but distinct, pattern characterizes the Senate (see Figure 3.8 and Table 3.2). From 1953 through 1960, Republicans in the Senate were significantly more likely than their Democratic colleagues to cosponsor pro–women's rights bills. From 1961 through 1986, however, there are no statistically significant differences between the two parties' rates of cosponsorship, although the pattern is generally one of increasing Democratic cosponsorship vis-à-vis their Republican colleagues. The one exception is 1973–1974, when Republicans were significantly more likely than Democrats to cosponsor pro–women's rights legislation. Yet, with that one exception, Democrats cosponsored at higher rates than Republicans after 1968. It is not until 1987 that Democrats were significantly more active as cosponsors, a pattern that continued into the 1990s.

Differences between the parties' respective rates of cosponsorship thus generally confirm a realignment of the parties' positions on women's rights across this period. These findings are particularly striking because the bar for support is so low: A member need only add her name to *one* bill to be considered a women's rights supporter. Moreover, there is considerable variation in the policies included here; a member who cosponsors a bill to fund breast cancer research or retirement equity for women under Social Security receives the same credit as a member who cosponsors controversial legislation to fund abortion services or allow women in military combat. This measurement approach only emphasizes the divergence between the parties: The diversity of bills and the focus on cosponsorship of *any* pro–women's rights bills make it relatively easy (theoretically) to be considered a women's rights supporter, and still, Republicans were more likely to be supporters before 1970 (often statistically more likely), and Democrats are more likely after, consistently significantly in the House, and eventually significantly in the Senate.

Intensity: Rate of Bill Cosponsorship

The analysis thus far has focused on the rate at which each party's members cosponsor *any* pro–women's rights legislation as an indicator of a member's, and by aggregation, each party's, position. As I have noted, this approach does not reflect intensity or strength of position; a member who puts her name on one pro–women's rights bill receives the same credit as a member who cosponsors twenty such bills in the same session.[4] Comparing the average number of cosponsorships per each party's members provides an alternative gauge of the parties' relative positions that takes into account possible differences in level of cosponsorship activity. The interparty difference scores (pro–women's rights cosponsorships per Democrat minus per Republican) are displayed in Figures 3.9 and 3.10.

In both the House and Senate, the comparatively fewer bills introduced and cosponsorships offered in the 1950s and 1960s (see Figures 3.3 and 3.4) mean that intraparty differences during the first period are easily dwarfed by the potential for differences in the later sessions, when literally thousands (in the House; hundreds in the Senate) of cosponsorships were offered. In the House, differences between the average number of bills cosponsored by each parties' delegation are statistically significant in three Congresses prior to 1970 (1957–1958, 1961–1962, and 1965–1966), with Republicans cosponsoring more bills on average. Interparty differences are always statistically significant after 1970, with Democrats consistently cosponsoring more pro–women's rights bills on average. In the Senate, interparty differences are statistically significant from 1953 to 1960, with Republican averages exceeding those of Democrats. While the Senate pattern is again more erratic, Democrats cosponsored a significantly greater number of bills, on average, than Republicans in 1977–1978, 1985–1986, 1989–1990, and 1991–1992. More generally, by providing a window into differences in the levels of activity by each party, this approach highlights the growing polarization of the parties over time. In the House, while Republicans cosponsored slightly more pro–women's rights bills on average before 1971, the pattern after 1971 is one of comparably greater Democratic cosponsorships on average, with greatly increasing differences in the late 1980s and 1990s. As with the other graphs, the pattern in the Senate is less straightforward, but in some ways mimics the pattern revealed in Figure 3.8: Republicans are responsible for a greater number of cosponsorships on average in the 1950s followed by a period in which each party var-

---

[4] In these data, the greatest number of cosponsorships in any one Congress are attributed to Representative Nancy Pelosi (D-CA), who cosponsored thirty-seven pro–women's rights bills in 1991–1992. Representatives Patricia Schroeder (D-CO) and Jolene Unsoeld (D-WA) are her nearest competition with thirty-three each that same Congress.

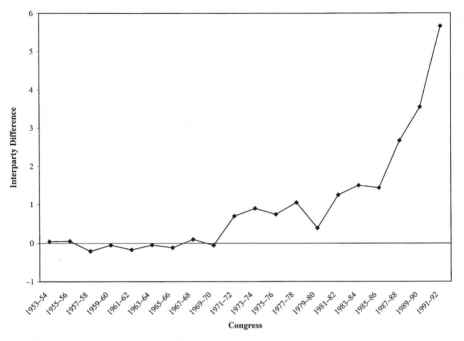

Figure 3.9. Interparty Difference in Average Number of Pro–Women's
Rights Cosponsorships, House, 1953–1992.

iously cosponsors more bills on average lasting until the mid-1980s, with
relative increases in Democratic activity in the mid-1970s. Similar to the
pattern in the House, however, Senate Democrats cosponsor many more
pro–women's rights bills on average beginning in the mid-1980s, and the
difference grows across the end of the series.

Women's Rights Realignment in Congress

In response to the central question of this chapter—if and to what extent
the transformation and polarization of party positions on women's rights
characterized the parties in Congress—the answers appear to be yes and
substantially. These data reveal a pattern similar to what was observed for
party organizations and presidential candidates, but with their own unique
trajectories. In chapter 2, the historical narrative suggested that while the
parties were not greatly distinguished by their relative positions on women's
rights before the 1970s, Republicans were slightly more supportive. Consensus grew across the 1960s and by the early 1970s, the two parties

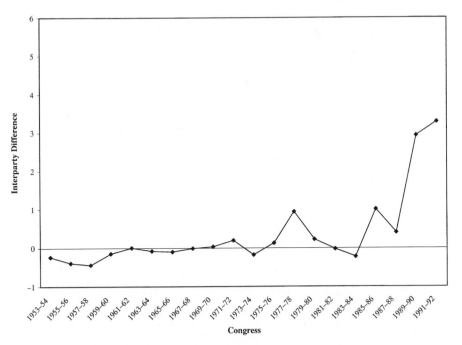

Figure 3.10. Interparty Difference in Average Number of
Pro–Women's Rights Cosponsorships, Senate, 1953–1992.

adopted similar stands vis-à-vis women's rights. Analysis of the Congressional data supports the elite insight of stronger Republican support, especially in the 1950s, and provides further evidence that the two parties behaved with increased similarity across the 1960s. In the Senate, and to a lesser extent in the House, Republicans were more likely to cosponsor any women's rights legislation in the 1950s and early 1960s, but differences narrowed or disappeared across the latter decade.

For the party organizations and presidential candidates, the 1970s were a decade of upheaval and dissension regarding women's rights; both parties' conventions witnessed public debates over the parties' platform planks, while presidents and presidential candidates of both parties both supported and opposed feminist initiatives. The House series reflects little of this ambivalence. Beginning dramatically in the 92nd Congress (1971–1972), Democrats became the party more likely to cosponsor any pro–women's rights legislation, a state of affairs that remains the status quo (with one exception) for the duration of the series. The Senate series, however, is perhaps more similar to the pattern suggested by the party organization and presidents narrative; throughout the 1970s and into the 1980s, Democrats are slightly more likely to cosponsor, but the difference is not statistically significant.

After the 1980 convention, the two parties' relative positions on women's rights as suggested by their organizations and presidents reached a new equilibrium, with Democrats generally more supportive and Republicans largely in opposition. This finding is repeated in the House and later in the Senate as well. In both chambers, Democrats were consistently more likely to have cosponsored any pro–women's rights bills than were Republicans after 1980. Comparison of the number of cosponsorships per each party's members further confirms increasing polarization across the late 1980s and early 1990s.

Coda: Cosponsorship of Opposition

The data presented thus far have focused on pro–women's rights cosponsorship, as such activity can be observed consistently across this time pe-

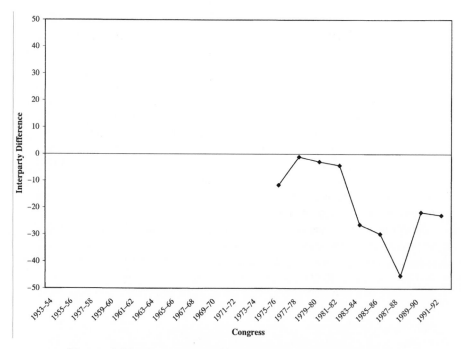

Figure 3.11. Interparty Difference in Cosponsorship of Any Anti–Women's Rights Bills, House, 1953–1992.

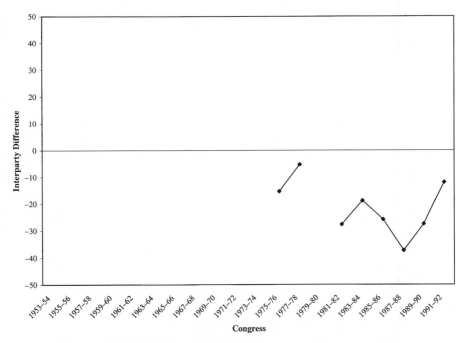

Figure 3.12. Interparty Difference in Cosponsorship of Any
Anti–Women's Rights Bills, Senate, 1953–1992.

riod and provides a useful indicator of support for women's rights. Yet, as
suggested earlier, *not* cosponsoring does not necessarily reflect opposition.
The examination of the parties as organizations and presidents in chapter
2 showed not only that Democrats were more supportive of women's
rights but also that Republicans adopted policy positions in opposition to
women's rights beginning in the late 1970s. Did such behavior characterize the parties in Congress as well? While not occurring during the entire
time period, it is possible to track anti–women's rights bill cosponsorship
after 1975, thus providing additional insight into the extent to which the
behavior of the parties in Congress follows the pattern observed among
the parties' organizations and presidents.

Figures 3.11 and 3.12 show the interparty difference scores (Democrats
minus Republicans) between the percentage of each party's membership
cosponsoring *any* anti–women's rights legislation in those Congresses in
which such bills were introduced. In both chambers in all Congresses, Republicans were more likely to cosponsor anti–women's rights legislation
than were Democrats. Generally, the difference between the two parties
grew across the 1980s but narrowed in the 1990s. Table 3.3 presents these

TABLE 3.3

Percentage of Democrats and Republicans Cosponsoring Any Anti–Women's Rights Bills, House and Senate, 1953–1992

Congress	House			Senate		
	Democrats	Republicans	Difference	Democrats	Republicans	Difference
1975–1976	4.4 (296)[a]	16.0 (144)	−11.6***	6.4 (63)	21.6 (37)	−15.2*
1977–1978	0.3 (296)	1.4 (145)	−1.1	0.0 (65)	5.3 (38)	−5.3
1979–1980	2.1 (281)	5.1 (158)	−3.0			
1981–1982	2.4 (249)	6.7 (195)	−4.3**	17.8 (45)	45.5 (55)	−27.7**
1983–1984	8.5 (272)	34.7 (167)	−26.2**	22.2 (45)	41.1 (56)	−18.9*
1985–1986	5.0 (258)	34.8 (181)	−29.8***	14.9 (47)	40.7 (54)	−25.8**
1987–1988	18.6 (263)	63.8 (177)	−45.2***	12.7 (55)	50.0 (46)	−37.3***
1989–1990	10.5 (266)	32.2 (177)	−21.7***	3.6 (55)	31.1 (45)	−27.5***
1991–1992	9.2 (272)	32.0 (169)	−22.8***	1.7 (58)	13.6 (44)	−11.9*

[a] N in parentheses.

* $p \le 0.05$, ** $p \le 0.01$, *** $p \le 0.001$. Significance indicated by Z-test for the difference in rates between two sets of binomial data described in the Appendix. Membership totals may exceed 435 (House) or 100 (Senate) because of turnover during the session.

same data with tests of the significance of interparty differences. In the House, differences are almost always statistically significant, with only two exceptions in the late 1970s. The results are even stronger in the Senate, where differences are statistically significant in every Congress except 1977–1978, when traditional levels of statistical significance are only narrowly missed.

In short, these data show that since the mid-1970s, Republicans have been more likely to support anti–women's rights initiatives than have Democrats. As was the case with pro–women's rights cosponsorships, these findings suggest that the pattern in Congress vis-à-vis women's rights and the parties is similar to that observed for the parties' organization and presidents in chapter 2.

ROLL CALL DATA

As I have argued, bill cosponsorships provide an appropriate and useful indicator of the issue positions of members of Congress and, by extension, the Congressional parties. In the case of women's rights, these data are particularly advantageous because the general absence of women's rights from the active political agenda in the first half of the time period means that traditional gauges of members' policy positions—roll call votes—are either unavailable or inconsistent for a full half of the series. However, given the centrality of roll call analysis to the study of Congressional behavior and the more direct connection between roll call votes and policy outcomes as compared to cosponsorship behavior, the analysis of women's rights cosponsorships is supplemented with an examination of available roll calls. In this section, I employ two approaches to examining roll calls related to women's rights: the classification provided by Poole and Rosenthal (1997) across the entire period and the interest group ratings produced by the NWPC since 1977.

One of the difficulties with roll calls is that each vote can involve multiple issue areas, making it difficult to disentangle the various policy preferences the vote reflects. One solution is to rely on the judgment of an interested party, such as an interest group, to identify those votes it deems relevant. Groups may consider a wide variety of roll calls important to their interests, thus creating a measure based on a diverse collection of votes. A second solution is to consider only those votes where the issue in question is clearly the primary, if not only, consideration. As in the case of cosponsorship, such an approach may miss legislation, possibly of considerable import, related to women's rights. The advantage, on the other hand, is that the votes examined can be considered relatively clear signs of one's position on women's rights. The NWPC ratings are an example of the former, and are subject to the identified considerations, while the Poole and Rosenthal (1997) roll calls represent the second approach, with all the associated benefits and drawbacks.

Roll Calls

Poole and Rosenthal (1997) classify all roll calls through the 100th Congress (1987–1988) into 99 substantive issue categories. I consider all votes categorized as either "women's equality" and "abortion/care of deformed newborns" as potential women's rights roll calls. The description of each roll call in the *Congressional Quarterly Almanac* was consulted to determine if the vote did indeed involve the issue of women's rights as defined by this research and the meaning of each yea and nay in terms of support for women's rights. Votes on rules, compromise proposals, and procedural tactics (unless clearly favoring one side or the other) are not included (see Adams 1997). Some seventy women's rights roll calls were identified in both the House and the Senate across this forty-year period. For each session where such votes occurred, a party score was computed as the number of pro–women's rights votes cast by each party's members divided by the total number of women's rights votes cast by the party's members (Adams 1997; Carmines and Stimson 1989). An interparty difference score was calculated (Republican score minus Democratic score); as with cosponsorship, a negative value indicates a relatively higher rate of pro–women's rights voting by Republicans, and a positive value indicates a comparatively higher rate of pro–women's rights voting by Democrats. The results are presented in Figures 3.13 and 3.14.

The House data, in particular, underscore the problems endemic to using roll calls to examine party positions on women's rights when the available data in the early period are thin and possibly unrepresentative. In both Congresses with women's rights roll calls before 1970, the interparty differences are based on a single vote. The first, during the 85th Congress (1957–1958), concerns the cutting of funds from the Women's Bureau of the Department of Labor. In the analysis of this one vote, Democrats emerge as relatively more supportive of women's rights, even though this is a period in which other measures have suggested Republicans were comparatively more supportive. A case can be made for attributing this unexpected finding to Democratic support for organized labor; that is, the vote may be more indicative of different party positions on labor than on women's rights. Without additional votes, it is impossible to evaluate the generalizability of this finding. Likewise, the second vote, during the 87th Congress (1961–1962), concerns the creation of an Assistant Secretary of Labor to address the concerns of women in the labor market. While not

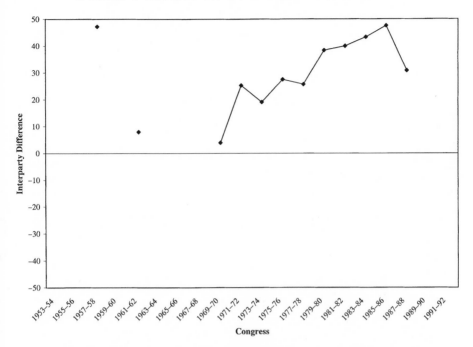

Figure 3.13. Interparty Difference in Women's Rights Roll Calls, House, 1953–1988.

resulting in such a dramatic Democratic advantage, this vote might also be influenced by the pro-labor tendencies of the Democratic party during this period. During the 92nd Congress (1971–1972), the number of relevant roll calls increases dramatically, and the rest of the series strongly confirms the cosponsorship findings: Democrats become increasingly more supportive of women's rights as compared to Republicans across the period.

A similar pattern emerges in the Senate. The two votes during the 83rd Congress (1953–1954) involve the ERA, and the Republican party is characteristically (for the period) more supportive. The one vote during the 88th Congress (1963–1964), however, concerns the addition of sex discrimination to the 1964 Civil Rights Act; the amendment in question was offered by Senator Strom Thurmond, then a Democrat from South Carolina, as one of numerous attempts on the part of Southern Democrats to sink the bill (Davis 1991), perhaps explaining the relatively and, for the period, uncharacteristically strong Democratic support for the pro–women's rights measure. Yet as with the House, when the number of relevant votes increases in the early 1970s, the picture painted by the cosponsorship data

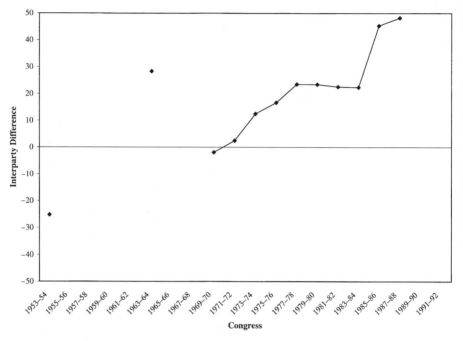

Figure 3.14. Interparty Difference in Women's Rights Roll Calls, Senate, 1953–1988.

is confirmed: Across the 1970s and into the 1980s, Senate Democrats became increasingly supportive of women's rights as compared to their Republican colleagues, with polarization increasing in the late 1980s.

The issue of abortion dominates these data; in both the House and Senate, approximately half of all women's rights roll calls concern abortion. In contrast, only six and four percent of all pro–women's rights cosponsorships in the House and Senate, respectively, relate to abortion (anti–women's rights cosponsorships, on the other hand, are also dominated by abortion). An important goal of this research is to determine the extent and nature of party realignment on women's rights generally, as opposed to the more narrow issue of abortion alone (see Adams 1997). Unfortunately, purging the roll call data of all abortion-related votes further reduces the available data considerably; indeed, in a number of Congresses, analysis is no longer possible because every women's rights vote concerns abortion. The interparty differences for the available women's rights roll calls are presented in Figures 3.15 and 3.16. Through 1972, the series are identical to those in

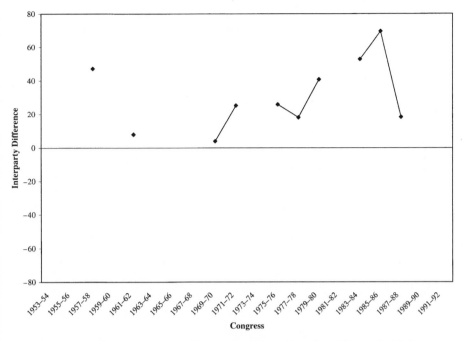

Figure 3.15. Interparty Difference in Non-Abortion Women's Rights
Roll Calls, House, 1953–1988.

Figures 3.13 and 3.14 (note the change in scale), but with the advent of
abortion on the national agenda in the early 1970s, the roll call analysis for
the rest of the period is clearly affected. In general, where observations are
available, the non-abortion roll call series affirm the growing polarization
of the parties across the second half of the series. In the House, focusing
on non-abortion women's rights roll calls suggests even greater polarization; interparty differences never exceed fifty points with the abortion roll
calls included, but without abortion votes, differences reach almost seventy
points during the 99th (1985–1986) Congress. In the Senate, all women's
rights roll calls after 1980 involve abortion, but the available data from the
1970s generally follow the pattern of increasing polarization. These results
thus confirm the findings of the cosponsorship analysis: The realignment
of the parties' relative positions on women's rights, while surely affected
by the abortion debate (see chapter 5), is not limited to that specific issue
but has characterized women's rights more generally.

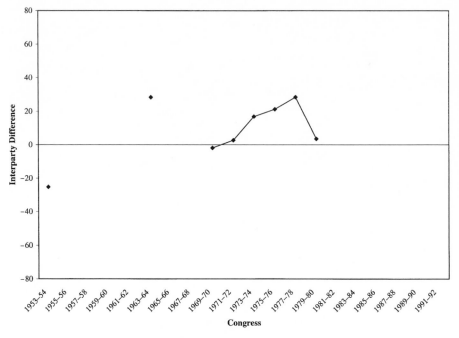

Figure 3.16. Interparty Difference in Non-Abortion Women's Rights Roll Calls, Senate, 1953–1988.

National Women's Political Caucus Scores

Scholars have long relied on the judgment of organized interests to identify those roll call votes particularly relevant to an issue area. From 1977 (1979 for the Senate) to 1990 the NWPC rated members of Congress on the basis of their votes on a selection of roll calls. In addition, in 1972, the Virginia state NWPC published comparable ratings of members for the 92nd (1971–1972) Congress (Shanahan 1972).[5] The major shortcoming of the NWPC ratings is that they were not produced prior to 1971 (the year in which the NWPC was founded), and only consistently after 1976. Thus, unlike cosponsorships, the NWPC ratings cannot provide insight into the process of party realignment during the late 1960s and early 1970s. The NWPC ratings can, however, render further evidence of the process of party polarization over women's rights across the 1970s, 1980s, and early 1990s.

[5] Copies of *The Woman Activist*, the newsletter of the Virginia National Women's Political Caucus, from 1972 were provided by the staff of the Schlesinger Library on the History of American Women at Radcliffe College.

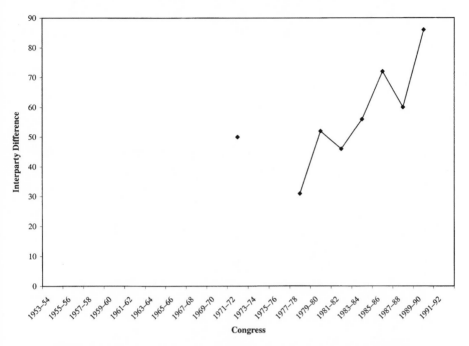

Figure 3.17. Interparty Difference in Median National Women's
Political Caucus Scores, House, 1971–1990.

The roll calls selected by the NWPC differ from those generated by Poole
and Rosenthal's (1997) classification; while the two Poole and Rosenthal
categories analyzed earlier focus narrowly on the specific topics of "women's
equality" and "abortion/care of deformed newborns," the NWPC takes a
broader view of what constitutes a feminist vote. Thus, for example, the
NWPC's ratings for the 96th Congress include not only votes on pregnancy
discrimination, abortion, domestic violence, and the ERA deadline extension, but also roll calls covering full employment, food stamps, welfare reform, and the establishment of a Department of Education. As a result, the
NWPC scores and Poole and Rosenthal categories result in two different
measures, the former with a wider sweep than the latter. It should also be
noted that the NWPC selection criteria differ somewhat from the more narrow definition of women's rights employed in this work. Together, however, the Poole and Rosenthal and NWPC roll calls provide a somewhat bal-
anced complement to the cosponsorship analysis.

For each Congress, each member is rated on the basis of her vote on a
number of NWPC-selected roll call votes. The median NWPC score for

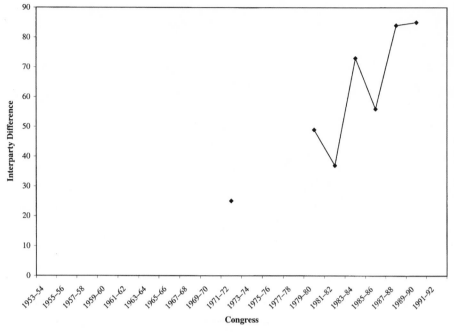

Figure 3.18. Interparty Difference in Median National Women's
Political Caucus Scores, Senate, 1971–1990.

each party's members is employed as an indicator of the party's support for
women's rights. The difference between the two parties' median scores is
then calculated as a measure of interparty difference on women's rights
(median Democratic NWPC score minus median Republican NWPC score),
so a negative score indicates greater Republican support and a positive
score indicates relatively greater Democratic support. The results for the
House and Senate are presented in Figures 3.17 and 3.18.

The Democratic median NWPC score exceeds that of the Republican
contingent in both the House and the Senate in every year for which
NWPC ratings are available. Consistent with the cosponsorship analysis
and the analysis of the Poole and Rosenthal (1997) roll calls, the difference
between the parties grows across the 1980s and 1990s; by the 100th Congress (1989–1990), the Democratic and Republican medians are separated
by almost 90 points in both chambers. Differences between Republicans
and Democrats are sharper in the early 1970s in the House than they are
in the Senate (the interparty difference in the House during the 92nd Con-

gress is twice that in the Senate), but eventually become quite comparable. In short, this second investigation of roll call voting further confirms the results of the cosponsorship analysis, insofar as the limited NWPC scores are able: The Democrats are somewhat more supportive of women's rights, as measured by NWPC-selected roll calls, beginning in the early 1970s, and the difference between the parties grows steadily across the 1980s and into the 1990s.

CONCLUSION

In this chapter, I employed women's rights bill cosponsorships to determine if the transformation and polarization of the parties' positions vis-à-vis women's rights witnessed among the parties' organizations and presidents have characterized the parties in Congress as well. Various comparisons of the parties' actions regarding pro–women's rights cosponsorships, as well as supplementary analysis of anti–women's rights cosponsorships and available roll calls, suggest that this has indeed been the case. Before 1970, Republicans were almost always more likely to cosponsor pro–women's rights bills than were Democrats, although the distance between the two parties narrowed across the 1960s. In the House, this period was followed by a dramatic shift in 1971–1972, as Democrats became far more likely to cosponsor pro–women's rights bills than were Republicans, a pattern maintained, with one exception, throughout the duration of the series. In the Senate, while Democrats were slightly more likely to cosponsor women's rights legislation in the 1970s, differences between the two parties are not statistically significant until the late 1980s. By the late 1980s and into the 1990s, the divergence of the parties over women's rights in both chambers is clearly reflected in the parties' cosponsorship behavior. This general pattern is largely confirmed by supplementary analysis of anti–women's rights cosponsorships and available roll call votes.

This and the preceding chapter have established that a transformation of the relative positions of the Democratic and Republican parties on women's rights has taken place across the forty year period from 1952 to 1992. Employing both qualitative and quantitative sources, I have shown how the parties moved from a situation in which Republicans were slightly more favorable to a period of general consensus to a reemergence of division in which Democrats were far more favorable. The central goal of this work is to provide an explanation for that outcome. It is to that task that I turn in chapter 4.

CHAPTER FOUR

Explaining Party Issue Realignment

THE PREVIOUS two chapters discussed the realignment of the Democratic and Republican parties' relative positions on women's rights from 1952 to 1992. This transformation has characterized the parties in their various elite institutional forms—as formal organizations, presidents and presidential candidates, and Congressional delegations. How can we explain the positions adopted by the parties? Why have the parties' relative positions changed across the period? In this chapter, I develop a general explanation of party issue adoption and change and briefly relate that model to the case of women's rights. The application of the model to women's rights from the early 1950s to the early 1990s is detailed in chapters 5 and 6.

PREVIOUS WORK

The role of parties in the representation of policy interests is crucial to the legitimacy of a democratic system. If elections are the central mechanism for transferring the people's preferences to public policy in a representative democracy and if parties structure the choices available to citizens in those elections, then the policy positions espoused by the parties reveal a great deal about the functioning of our republic as a truly representative political system (Burns 1997). As a result, various lines of inquiry have been concerned, directly and indirectly, with the connection between political parties and public policies. In particular, I draw from previous work on spatial models, critical realignment, issue evolution, Congressional behavior, and agenda setting. The insights and findings of these works provide the foundation for the model I develop to explain why parties adopt issue positions and under what circumstances parties might shift those positions, particularly in opposition to each other.

Spatial Models

Why do parties establish certain policy positions? Perhaps more importantly, why do parties develop positions in opposition to each other? An important tradition in democratic theory suggests that the answer to the latter question is that they should not. The classic spatial, or economic, model associated with the work of Anthony Downs (1957) predicts that in a two-party system where the distribution of mass preferences is single-peaked across a single-issue dimension, vote-maximizing parties will move toward the median voter. Said another way, the two parties are expected to locate their policy positions as close as possible to the center of the distribution of mass preference in an attempt to attract a majority of voters. The result is parties that are not greatly distinguished from each other in terms of their policy platforms.

The Downsian prediction of two parties grouped at the center rings true for some observers of American politics. Activists with strong ideological inclinations have often accused their own parties of being too centrist. In the 1950s and 1960s, for example, conservatives Barry Goldwater and Phyllis Schlafly contended that the GOP was dominated by "Me-Toos" who differed little from the Democrats. In contrast to Downs's logic, however, Schlafly, Goldwater, and supporters argued that a centrist strategy so alienated those on the right end of the spectrum that they abstained from voting, leading to a poor showing by Republican presidential candidates (Converse, Clausen, and Miller 1965; Schlafly 1964). Others have observed that candidates' campaigns are often ambiguous on many salient issues, emphasizing broad and even meaningless themes on which there is public consensus. In keeping with Downs, these authors suggest that ambiguity (even when candidates or parties actually hold divergent positions) is a rational strategy for candidates seeking an electoral majority (Carmines and Gopoian 1981; Page 1978; Shepsle 1972a). Finally, the degree of disagreement within the American political system generally pales in comparison to the political systems of other advanced industrial societies. Few people or parties, for example, advocate government control of the means of production or the elimination of democratic processes, yet socialist and, to a lesser extent, fascist parties are active in other countries. Political debate and partisan competition in the United States largely takes place in a context of extensive consensus on many major issues, with the result that the spectrum of both public opinion and party position-taking is relatively circumscribed (Beck 1997; Hibbs 1977).

Yet within that narrow spectrum, the two American parties have in fact adopted differing positions on a wide range of issues throughout their histories. Many of these differences reflect broad, even ideological, predilections that differentiate the parties. Democrats tend to be more liberal, Republicans more conservative (Bruce, Clark, and Kessel 1991; Erickson, Wright, and McIver 1989; Kessel 1988). Since the New Deal, Democrats have generally preferred an active federal government. Republicans, on the other hand, have favored a more limited federal role (Page 1978). Differences in specific policy positions, consistent with those distinctions, can be

found in the platforms forged by the parties in convention every four years
(Monroe 1983; Pomper and Lederman 1980). The issue distance between
the parties' platforms and presidential candidates varies by election (the
1964 and 1972 elections are often noted as the most divergent in recent
history) but in each, differences are apparent and largely consistent with
basic party divisions (Page 1978). Members of Congress likewise vary in
the extent to which they reflect their parties' issue cleavages, but partisanship has been consistently related to the structure of Congressional decision making throughout American history (Poole and Rosenthal 1991; see
also Grofman, Griffin, and Glaser 1990; Brady and Lynn 1973; Fiorina
1974; Clausen 1973), with party polarization increasing in recent years
(Rohde 1991).

The failure of the pure spatial model to account for the existence of divergent platforms is in part attributed to the structure of the American electoral process, where candidates first compete for nomination within their
own party and then in a general election (Wittman 1990; Monroe 1983;
Coleman 1972; Aranson and Ordeshook 1972). Office-seeking candidates
must appeal to the subset of voters who participate in the party nomination process as a necessary precondition to competing for the office itself.
Activists in the nomination process appear to differ systematically from activists in the opposing party in the distribution of their policy preferences,
although the extent of this divergence varies over time (Carmines and Stimson 1989; Kessel 1988; Miller et al. 1986; Nexon 1971; McClosky, Hoffman, and O'Hara 1960). In addition to their direct role in choosing nom-
inees, parties and candidates rely on activists for various forms of support,
ranging from sheer manpower to technical expertise to financial contributions. Having adopted certain positions in pursuit of the nomination, candidates are constrained from shifting entirely to the population median
during the general election campaign. Models that extend the spatial model
to include the nomination process and the dependence of candidates and
parties on activists generate predictions closer to observed reality; that is,
parties are predicted to articulate divergent policy positions (Aldrich 1983;
Monroe 1983). Some forms of activism may be especially valued; if there
is a systematic difference in the interests of those contributing to the parties and their candidates (as indeed appears to be the case), parties might
be particularly encouraged to diverge in the policies they advocate
(Schlesinger 1984; Page 1978).

Others have noted that party elites may derive utility not only from votes
and seats but also from the platform itself. Such an assumption is consistent with studies that suggest that while electoral success is a primary mo-
tivation, politicians do have personal policy preferences that they value and,
within electoral constraints, pursue (Page 1978; Mayhew 1974; Fenno
1973). As Wittman writes, "It would be strange if the voters were inter-

ested in policy and not the members of the political party, especially so because government policy is a public good shared by all" (1990, 66). Models that allow parties to consider the trade-off "between the utility of such a platform and the expected utility once the likelihood of winning is considered" show that under such conditions, platforms do not converge on the median but are distinct (Jackson 1996, 3; see also Morton 1993; Wittman 1990, 1983, 1977, 1973; Alesina 1988; but see Kollman, Miller, and Page 1992; Calvert 1985).

Other refinements of the classic Downsian spatial model have been offered. Parties' long-term interest in protecting the parties' reputation and credibility may contribute to the emergence and persistence of diverse policy positions (Wittman 1990; Alesina 1988; Bernhardt and Ingberman 1985; Shepsle 1972b). The threat of third-party entry (Palfrey 1984) and relaxed information assumptions (Morton 1993; but see Kollman, Miller, and Page 1992; Calvert 1985) also lead to divergent political parties.

The classic spatial model predicts that parties will converge on the mass preference median, with party platforms and positions not greatly distinguished from each other. Extensions within the spatial framework have recognized that the institutional structure of the American electoral system forces candidates and parties to consider first the distribution of preference among their activists, delegates, contributors, and primary and caucus participants, and that doing so can lead to divergent party platforms. Vote-maximizing parties, then, should develop distinct platforms on issues when the distribution of preferences over those issues varies systematically between each party's supporters. Here, interparty differences in the issue preferences of party activists and contributors are especially important because of the desire of parties to attract such individuals' energy, effort, and dollars. At the same time, if party elites derive utility not only from winning but also from the platform, policy positions are further predicted to diverge. Assuming that party elites do value the platform itself, we should likewise expect the platforms to be distinct when party elites differ systematically in their preferences on the issue within the constraints of electoral competition.

Critical Realignment

The classic theory of party change in political science—critical realignment—was first proposed by V. O. Key (1955, 1959) more than forty years ago. The stated goal is to theorize about and describe electoral alignments—in Key's words, to build "a more general theory of elections" (1955, 3). Realignment theories seek to explain changes in patterns of mass partisanship and voting behavior. Attempts to build from and elaborate on

Key's seminal work, both theoretically and empirically, have been so numerous and diverse (see Bass 1991 for a short discussion and extensive bibliography) that some have suggested that to speak of realignment as a coherent, or useful, theory is not possible (Carmines and Stimson 1989; see also Shafer 1991). Some basic and relevant contours of the original argument, however, remain identifiable. Broadly speaking, critical realignment theory assumes that American electoral history can be divided into eras or systems in which one party or the other dominates in terms of both office-holding and mass identification. Each party era is characterized by various factors, the most important of which is its defining alignments. While these alignments (economic, ethnic, regional, and so on) define the party system during that era, new issues and conflicts eventually arise to challenge the saliency of the dominant cleavage. As the established partisan order becomes increasingly unable to mediate conflict brought on by broad societal change of various potential sorts, political strain results. When the tension reaches a breaking point (for some, these points come at regular intervals, adding a notion of periodicity [Burnham 1970]), an election occurs that ushers in a new party system with a new defining alignment and, in some cases, a new majority party. This critical election is characterized by unusually high levels of voter interest and involvement and the disruption of traditional voting patterns (Key 1955; Burnham 1970).

Critical realignments are fundamentally issue-based. In realignment narratives, mass party support and identification are formed and shaped by the alignment of issue positions the parties represent. In a very real sense, parties reflect the dominant issue cleavage in the electorate. If issues emerge that cut across the existing party alignment, they can result in a transformation of party loyalties and the creation of a new party system, with party loyalties based on the new cleavage instead of the old (Sundquist 1973).

Yet while party positioning on new issues is central to the critical realignment narrative, realignment theory is less clear about why parties choose the sides they do vis-à-vis new issue cleavages. Burnham (1970), for example, generally assumes that the party in power will end up on the losing side of new issues. Institutionalized and tied to the status quo, the previously dominant party is unable to adequately manage the emerging issue cleavage, allowing the minority party to use the new issues to gain electoral advantage. For Sundquist (1973), the degree of cross-cutting created by the new issues is crucial; if the dissenters are a relatively small minority within a party, the scale of realignment will be likewise minor, with little shift in either party's position. For realignment theory generally, the emphasis is not on changes in position or on why the parties would develop opposing positions where once they were characterized by a degree of agreement. Instead, realignment theory sees one dominant issue cleavage replaced by another. Parties' previous positions are relatively unimportant because it is the cleavage over a new set of issues that matters for the alignment of voters.

A second, related, point pertains to the nature of the issues to which realignment theory has been applied and, more fundamentally, from which it has been derived. Realignments are generally assumed to come about as the result of "national crises and major, widespread tension within society" (Clubb, Flanigan, and Zingale 1980, 30). The scale of realigning issues is often grand and the nature of the emergent cleavage opaque: major events like wars and depressions and vast socioeconomic restructuring on the scale of the Industrial Revolution. The new issues are not sharply defined or constrained, but represent broad themes that pit equally broad demographic groups, sectors of the economy, and interests against each other. Because of this focus on the dramatic and diffuse, realignment theory is not particularly concerned with the myriad of smaller position changes the parties experience. Despite extensive investigation, no election since 1932 has been determined to clearly resemble the critical realignment model (see, e.g., Shafer 1991; Carmines and Stimson 1989; Converse, Clausen, and Miller 1965; Converse et al. 1961). While major cleavages are of course important and interesting, parties have often changed their positions on issues of smaller scope than the sort of major economic cleavage that defined the New Deal realignment. These issues deserve investigation and explanation as well (Ladd 1991; Carmines and Stimson 1989).

It is incorrect, however, to suggest that realignment theory offers no insights into the process of party position-taking of this sort. First, realignment theory points to the importance of issue saliency. Parties can avoid taking positions on issues that divide their coalition as long as the issue fails to capture public attention. As realignment theory suggests, various factors, both external and internal to the world of politics, can move a crosscutting issue onto the political agenda, forcing parties to take positions and destabilizing existing alignments. Party coalitions organized around one set of aligning issues will not necessarily be in agreement on a different set of issues, thus contributing to realignment when the new set becomes salient. Second, critical realignment highlights the role of underlying social change in disrupting existing party issue alignments. As the real circumstances of citizens' lives are transformed, the distribution of preference in the electorate, as well as among elites, may be affected, with important consequences for party position-taking. Finally, realignment theory points to the consequences of elite positioning on issues. In the realignment narrative, parties live and die (in terms of dominance) by their ability to articulate positions on salient issues. While traditional realignment theory emphasizes major realignments, the reality is that parties are continually shifting their issues stances, and citizens (some—like new entrants into the political system—more than others) are continually adjusting their voting choices and partisanship in response (cf. Franklin and Jackson 1987; Carmines and Stimson 1989).

Issue Evolution

An explicit attempt to construct a theory that addresses the shortcomings of the critical realignment model (see Shafer 1991 and Carmines and Stimson 1989 for a more thorough critique) is provided by Carmines and Stimson (1989). Carmines and Stimson are purposefully countering critical realignment theory, and like critical realignment, the crux of their argument concerns the impact of party elite realignment and the distribution of mass preferences and identification. Specifically, the authors are interested in developing a general theory of "how issue alignments and realignments are driven by mass response to the behavior of participants in national political institutions" (1986, 915). To a considerable extent, they take the change or polarization in elite party position as a starting point for their investigation into the process of mass response. As a result, their attention to the causes of elite change is limited. They do, however, provide some insights that are useful in this task.

Most issues that make it onto the political agenda, Carmines and Stimson (1989) argue, are easily incorporated into the existing party system; that is, each party clearly favors one side or the other in keeping with its basic perspective. Occasionally, however, issues arise that cut across party lines and do not map easily onto existing party alignments. Under certain circumstances, the result is the transformation of the parties' positions on an issue or the polarization of elite party positions on a previously nonpartisan issue. Significantly, Carmines and Stimson assert that party elites move first (although they are driven in large part by electoral concerns), and mass realignment on the issue follows (some recent realignment theorists also emphasize elite initiation [cf. MacDonald and Rabinowitz 1987]).

Why would parties change their positions or develop opposing positions where previously there had been consensus? Carmines and Stimson identify four possible sources of issue competition that can lead to what they call issue evolution, a change in the parties' positioning on an issue that is eventually consequential for the alignment of mass preferences and partisanship. The first, strategic politicians, presumes that party elites use issues to maximize votes. Politicians, they argue, have an incentive to deemphasize controversial or divisive issues that work against that goal, while emphasizing and politicizing those issues that advantage their party. For majority party elites, this means highlighting those issues that characterize the current alignment and treating new issues as extensions of that framework. For minority party elites, however, the incentive is to use new issues to drive a wedge in the existing alignment, and pry voters away from the majority party. The second, external disruptions, acknowledges that events outside the political sphere constantly impinge on that world, raising new issues and disrupting the existing partisan balance. Local variation is Carmines and Stimson's third source of issue competition. The authors argue that over time, issues that once fit existing partisan alignments can change as the result of a new context, changing conditions, or specialization. As a result, the issue in question may no longer fit the present alignment of party issue positions and thus may lead to a change in the parties' positions. Finally, internal contradictions refers to the sorts of conflict endemic to any coalition. Certain issues can divide a party alignment formed largely on the basis of other issues, so that when those divisive issues become salient, the existing equilibrium is threatened, and change is possible.

Carmines and Stimson highlight four main points. First, elites use issues strategically to attract voters and better their party's position. As I have noted, this is an assumption shared by most party theorists. Second, the political world does not exist in a vacuum. Events outside of politics can affect party alignments. They do so in large part because of Carmines and Stimson's third insight: Issues change. For a variety of reasons, the real and perceived meaning of issues evolve over time, and this evolution can be consequential for the response of strategic party elites. Finally, party coalitions are inherently unstable. Diverse interests united under a party banner because of their shared interest on one set of issues can find themselves at odds over new issues, thus destabilizing the coalition. As party coalitions evolve, so too can the parties' positions on various issues.

Congressional Behavior

Overwhelmingly, the literature on U.S. legislative behavior finds that legislators are highly consistent in their policy positions, as reflected by their roll call activity, over time (Poole and Rosenthal 1997, 1991; Sinclair 1982; Asher and Weisberg 1978). Change in Congressional policy outputs, these authors assert, derives almost exclusively from the replacement of existing members with new individuals, not the conversion of those already in office to new policy positions or voting behaviors. If members are consistent then turnover is a crucial mechanism for bringing about a change in the aggregate policy choices of Congress generally or a subset of Congress—such as parties—specifically. Rohde, for example, argues that membership replacement is the "main driving force" (1991, 162) behind increasing party polarization in the House since the early 1970s. In their analysis of racial issue evolution in Congress, Carmines and Stimson "postulate membership replacement as the principal agent of interparty change over time"

(1989, 63). Specifically, the declining size of the Southern contingent of the Democratic party, and concomitant rise of the Northern contingent, constitutes their central explanation for the transformation of the parties' positions on race. Thus, as the distribution of a party's Congressional delegation shifts in a systematic way, a change in the observed behavior of that party on a particular set of issues may result.

Yet research also emphasizes the importance of context and policy definition in explaining change in Congressional policy outputs and party positions. When conversion, a change in the behavior of a member or members, is observed, scholars repeatedly point to a shift in the perception or the meaning of the issue as the cause. Asher and Weisberg, for example, identify "change in the policy debate surrounding an issue" as the main cause of conversion, arguing that "in short, policy redefinition may result in vote change" (1978, 392). Similarly, Poole and Rosenthal assert that while the dimensionality of voting in Congress may be stable, "how specific issues map onto the dimensions may change over time" (1991, 232).

If a changing policy definition creates a shift in members' behavior in a systematically partisan manner, the result can be a change in the partisan alignment in Congress around an issue. For example, Burns and Taylor contend that their study of the evolution of the Republican party's position on income tax policy illustrates "the importance of ideas in party position change" (1996, 18). Changing conceptions of an issue are particularly consequential when linked to the parties' constituencies and electoral strategy. Thus, Burns and Taylor argue, "[Supply-side ideas] made political sense given the signals Republicans were receiving about public discontent on federal tax policy and what supply-side economics could do to the Democratic agenda and for traditional Republican constituents" (Ibid, 17). While Carmines and Stimson (1989) assert the centrality of replacement as a mechanism for issue evolution, their sources of issue evolution (discussed earlier) suggest a role for issue redefinition in shaping the partisan consequences of replacement as well.

Similarly, change in the substantive content of the issue agenda can influence the debate and meaning attached to an issue and thus alter the partisan alignment. Sinclair, for example, argues that replacement contributed to the Republican party's shift away from civil rights, but "the underlying cause of the declining support since the mid 1960s seems to be a change in the type of civil rights issues coming to the fore" (1982, 128; but see Carmines and Stimson 1989). Like issue redefinition, agenda change is important when it affects party elites' evaluation of the relationship between the issue and valued constituencies; Sinclair asserts that racial agenda change was consequential because new policies such as open housing, school busing, and equal employment opportunity "all directly affected the Republican middle-class and business constituency" (1982, 128).

Finally, research on Congressional behavior highlights the importance of the constituencies to whom members owe their positions. While the composition of members' electoral coalitions may be stable over time (e.g., business interests and the Republican party), various developments may contribute to an adjustment of members' electoral calculus vis-à-vis a particular issue and those constituents over time, with consequences for members' positioning on salient issues (Burns and Taylor 1996; Sinclair 1982). Alternatively, changes in the composition of members' constituent bases may impact policy choices. Rohde (1991), for example, attributes the increase in party issue polarization in the 1980's House to, among other factors, the reenfranchisement of Southern blacks and consequent impact on the Democratic party in the South.

Agenda Setting and Issue Redefinition

The agenda-setting literature does not specifically focus on parties, much less the question of how parties develop issue positions and when they might be expected to shift those positions vis-à-vis each other. However, this literature does address relevant questions concerning why some issues receive political (party) attention while others do not and how ascribed meaning and definition affects cleavages and alliances over an issue. In doing so, this work offers important insight into when we might expect parties to shift or polarize on an issue.

For my purposes, two areas of inquiry in this field are of particular interest: how issues come to occupy the agenda of political decision makers and how issues are defined, and redefined, by context and the purposeful actions of interested actors. The former has been a major focus of agenda-setting theorists. Kingdon defines the agenda as "the lists of subjects or problems to which governmental officials, and people outside of government closely associated with those officials, are paying some serious attention at any given time" (1984, 3). Given scarce resources, the agenda is necessarily limited at any one time, thus creating competition for access and attention. For those interested in policy making, how issues get on the agenda is of central concern since agenda access, and the definition of alternatives, is crucial to the determination of policy outcomes. For those concerned with the representation of interests, agenda access is an important indicator of the responsiveness of government officials to that interest and, thus, of the relative power of that interest in the political sphere.

Descriptions of policy-making systems emphasize the characteristics of limited involvement, specialization, reciprocal relationships, and stability. These relationships have been variously termed iron triangles, subsystem politics, issue networks, subgovernments, policy whirlpools, and so on (cf.

Heclo 1978; Ripley and Franklin 1976; Redford 1969; Freeman 1965; Cater 1964). While each term suggests somewhat different conceptions of the policy-making process—of considerable interest to students of those processes—they generally share the characteristics I have identified. Similarly, Baumgartner and Jones (1993) describe an issue as in a state of equilibrium when it is characterized by stability in the policy itself, the terms of the debate, and the extent of participation. Decision making over the issue is limited to clearly defined institutions, and participants agree on the scope and nature of the issue. From time to time, these relationships can be disrupted and the system forced out of equilibrium. According to the authors, equilibrium disruption is usually the result of previously uninvolved actors in or outside of government entering the debate. When equilibrium disruption occurs, the issue is drawn onto the agenda of presidents, Congress, and parties. While an issue in equilibrium is characterized by stability of involvement and alignments, when disturbed, the alignment of interests and actors around the issue is likewise disrupted. In periods of instability, a realignment of actors, including, or even especially, party elites, around that issue becomes more likely (Baumgartner and Jones 1993, 21).

To understand why the realignment of interests, and thus parties, over an issue is probable during periods when issues are brought out of equilibrium directs us to the second area of inquiry in the agenda-setting literature that is relevant for this work: issue redefinition. When issue equilibrium is disturbed, Baumgartner and Jones argue, the reason is "typically a new understanding of the nature of the policies involved" (1993, 8). Any specific policy can be interpreted as embodying various conflicts and interests. Cobb and Elder (1983, 44) use the example of fluoridation policy: Initially, proposals to add fluoridation to public water supplies were debated in terms of public health, but opponents of the policy attempted to redefine the issue as one of individual rights and menacing government intrusion. This redefinition changed the contours of the debate, attracting those not initially interested in fluoridation and transforming the way in which individual actors approached the policy proposal. Definition and redefinition of policy issues are crucial because the way an issue is characterized affects where the cleavage lines over the issue develop and significantly, how they might be changed (cf. Riker 1986). A policy seen as involving questions of regulation of the economy might divide elites one way, while an issue of individual rights might generate a different division.

There are a number of means by which issue redefinition can occur. The most common sources of new meaning are those who are disadvantaged by the present interpretation. Disadvantaged interests seek to cast the debate in new terms as a means of attracting supporters and improving their strategic position. This is one of Schattschneider's (1960) central insights: Those on the losing side have an incentive to expand the scope of the dispute, thereby widening the sphere of actors involved to attract potential supporters. By purposively broadening the debate to mobilize those likely to side with the current losers, the disadvantaged interest can attain a better strategic position.

An important way that issues are defined and redefined involves the use of symbolism (Edelman 1964). The creation of public policies involves a fair amount of complexity and calls for substantial expertise. Yet most issues can be characterized in fairly simple and symbolic terms. For both elites and the public, these images are meaningful methods of conceptualizing policy debates (Baumgartner and Jones 1993). Those on either side of an issue invest significant effort in the creation and maintenance of symbols as a useful medium for casting the debate in a way that will attract support (Cobb and Elder 1982). While a symbol has an empirical component, its dominant function is evaluative. Different symbols evoke different reactions from different groups. Attaching certain symbols to an issue might lead certain elites to one position, while other symbols might result in the opposite response. Thus, symbols are an important aspect of the way in which issue definition determines the lines of cleavage, including partisan cleavage, over an issue.

The realignment of interests, including parties, over an issue following issue equilibrium disruption is thus likely because of the redefinition and new meaning that often accompany such a disruption. The expansion of the scope of actors involved in the issue, the definition of or frame associated with the issue, and the symbols and images used to shape that definition play an important role in determining the alliances that will form around a particular issue. Because of the importance of issue definition to the alignment of interests, the changing debate over and perceived meaning of an issue are important to understanding the evolution of the parties' position on the policy.

EXPLAINING ELITE PARTY CHANGE ON WOMEN'S RIGHTS

I assume that in pursuit of electoral success party elites adopt positions on issues that they believe will attract and expand the coalition that constitutes the party's base of support. The parties' relative positions are thus determined by three factors: the issue, the party coalitions, and the party elites. Party elites take those positions they believe will maximize their ability to attract votes. Because of the institutional structure of elections (i.e., the nomination process), party elites must care about maximizing some votes more than others, thus constraining future position-taking, at least in the short run. Thus in adopting issue positions, party elites must be particularly responsive to the party's coalition of interests; that is, its activists, contributors, and identifiers. The way in which issues are defined and re-defined are consequential for the cleavages that form around them and, as a result, for the calculations of elites regarding the link between issue position and the party coalition. Finally, elites themselves may vary in their beliefs about the relationship between the issue and electoral success, as well as in their personal issue preferences.

Change in any of the three factors can bring about a shift in the parties' positions. If the issue definition changes, party elites may update their calculus as to how that issue contributes to their ability to attract support (from the party coalition in particular) and may shift their policy position. If one or both of the parties' coalitions evolves in a systematic manner, this too can lead to a changed calculus for elites regarding how an issue position will satisfy and expand the coalition and thus serve to achieve electoral goals. As replacement puts new individuals into elite positions, newcomers may reflect a revised understanding of what issue positions benefit the party strategically or may bring with them systematically different personal issue preferences.

The impact of these three factors is most likely to register on the parties' relative positions during periods of issue equilibrium disruption. Issues in equilibrium are characterized by limited and stable participation, under-standing, and alliances (Baumgartner and Jones 1993). The disruption of equilibrium moves an issue onto the political agenda, increasing the issue's salience and, thus, electoral relevance. As a result, party elites have reason to examine and possibly reevaluate their issue positions. If relevant changes in the meaning of the issue, the parties' coalitions, or the composition of the elites themselves have occurred, the outcome may be a shift in one or both of the parties' positions vis-à-vis the issue.

In the following sections, I detail my argument regarding each of the three factors—issues, coalitions, and elites—and the process of issue equilibrium disruption. In addition, I provide a glimpse into the application of the model to the specific case of women's rights. The evidence in support of those propositions is evaluated in chapters 5 and 6.

Issues

Party elites use issues to attract and maintain support, particularly from the party coalition. The positions party elites take on issues should thus shift when the relationships those elites perceive between the issue and their party's coalition are altered. Changes in the meaning and definition of an issue are likely causes of changed perceptions of the link between issue and electoral support. Moreover, issue redefinition is closely related to issue equilibrium disruption as the former is a common cause of the latter

(Baumgartner and Jones 1993). While I focus specifically on issue equilibrium disruption in a later section, many of the processes and factors that contribute to redefinition are related to issue disruption as well.

To explain party position change, it is thus important to identify the mechanisms by which issues are moved out of equilibrium and the understanding and meaning of the issue shifts in ways that are meaningful for elites' electoral considerations. I identify three such potential mechanisms. The first is *strategic elites*. Politicians use issues to secure electoral goals. In doing so, strategic politicians may attempt to shape issue definition in a way that advantages themselves and their party. Scholars have long emphasized the importance of competition in motivating elites to focus attention on one set of issues rather than another or to frame a debate in such a way as to advantage their side (Carmines and Stimson 1989; Schattschneider 1960). In addition, strategic elites often act to better their own position within the party or the political sphere generally and, in doing so, may act to change the meaning given an issue or mobilize constituencies on one side of the issue or the other, thus changing the party's calculus of the relationship between that issue and its coalition.

The role of strategic elites can be proactive, reactive, or both. Elites may seek out and publicize issues that are out of the public eye in an attempt to better their own or their party's position. In that case, they are placing the issue on the agenda and creating the opportunity for a change in the issue cleavage. If an issue comes to public attention in another manner, strategic elites may react by attempting to shape debate in such a way as to benefit themselves and, in doing so, contribute to a meaningful redefinition of the issue.

The second mechanism is a *new context*. As the real and perceived circumstances surrounding an issue change, the understanding and meaning of the issue can change as well, shifting the cleavage over the issue as a result. A new context can arise from broad demographic change, such as rising or falling economic conditions, migration or immigration, changing employment patterns, and so on. As a consequence, old issue-related concerns may lose saliency and new concerns may arise, or the distribution of interest in society may be rearranged. Change in context can be the result of developments that transform the legal landscape in which the issue is understood or discussed. Other developments not directly related to the issue may introduce new or revised symbols or language that influence the debate. A new context may take the form of a change in the issue definition and meaning of other issues in a way that affects the issue in question. Dramatic events can bring an issue to the fore of the political agenda as well as shape the context in which issues are debated and understood. By directing attention to an issue, such disruptions disturb the existing equilibrium—little public attention, stable alliances, limited participants—and influence the public debate that ensues (Carmines and Stimson 1989; Kingdon 1984).

Changes in the context of issue debate can call into question the assumptions and paradigms by which the issue had been considered. Previously inactive constituencies may be politicized and, as a result, bring about a modification in the calculus of party elites as to the relationship between the issue and the party coalition. As I have suggested, contextual changes may be secular and long-term or sudden and dramatic. In either case, the environment in which both elites and the public approach and understand an issue is transformed, with the potential for meaningful issue redefinition.

Finally, and often as a result of the first two, *agenda change* can play an important role in contributing to issue change that is consequential for party alignments. Agenda change occurs when new issue-related concerns are raised or new proposals to old problems are introduced (Sinclair 1982). Broad issue categories or domains, such as women's rights, civil rights, or urban affairs, encompass different specific policies and concerns at different times (Heinz et al. 1993). While broadly related, different policies may be of varying concern to different interests. The sources of agenda change are myriad. Many issue-related concerns may exist and be voiced in the political system, but there is a limit to the number that elites can give real attention to at any one time (Kingdon 1984). If one is resolved, entrepreneurs and interested actors may see the opportunity for another to be considered. Attention to one problem may sensitize elites to another issue-related problem (Sinclair 1982). Events or agenda change in other issue areas may provide the impetus for the expansion or transformation of the agenda.

Agenda change can be conceived of as the empirical component of issue redefinition. Strategic elites and new contexts can frame an issue in a new manner, even if the actual policy content remains the same. That is, issue definition can change without a change in the actual policy or policies being debated; the fluoridation case cited earlier is one example. However, when the issue agenda—the actual policies being considered under a general issue heading—is transformed, redefinition becomes more likely, if not probable.

While all mechanisms for issue redefinition affect the terms with which individuals and groups evaluate issues, agenda change can mean a very real and concrete shift in the effect of that issue. When civil rights, for example, was expanded to include employment practices in the North (not only political practices in the South), it involved many who had no reason to actively oppose civil rights previously, but who now felt their own interests being affected by affirmative action claims (Sinclair 1982). This example suggests that as an agenda expands and/or changes, the constellation of interested actors around the issue can be expected to expand and/or change as well. As various interests feel the impact in different ways, the parties' responses to that issue can likewise be expected to shift as a result of what Sinclair calls a change in "constituency signals" (1982, 172).

It should be noted that agenda change is one cause of issue evolution that Carmines and Stimson (1989) explicitly disregard in the case of race. While acknowledging that the specific content of racial legislation changed across their time period of study, they point to the consistency of individual members' actions over time as evidence that there has been no change in the basic segregation/desegregation dimension. Specifically, they take issue with the conventional wisdom that civil rights policy changed after the mid-1960s from an emphasis on legal rights and equality to "far less tractable social and economic issues" (1989, 87). They admit that the rhetoric shifted but argue that the consistency of individual members' responses to civil rights policy shows that the core dimension remained unchanged. In part, Carmines and Stimson are able to make this argument because, as they point out, much of the new civil rights agenda was nonlegal and thus not the topic of legislative action. Moreover, many of the newer components of the race agenda were policies, such as welfare and law and order issues, that Carmines and Stimson exclude from their study. This is relevant to women's rights as well; for example, welfare policies are of great interest to feminist activists, especially since the 1980s, but are generally not included in the definition of women's rights employed in this research. Yet as I show, agenda change has been reflected in the legislative and political action on women's rights to a significant extent and has been important to explaining changing party alliances.

Strategic elites, new context, and agenda change are thus all potential mechanisms for issue redefinition. To differing degrees, each has been important in the evolution of women's rights, with consequences for partisan alignment. Prior to the mid-1960s, the limited debate over women's rights was largely defined as one of protection versus equality. The equality position was consistent with the Republican penchant for individualism and free markets. The ERA, in particular, was understood by many as a means of easing employment regulations. For Republicans, the equality position benefited two important constituencies: employers, who favored deregulation, and, to a lesser extent (in terms of perceived importance to the party), pro-equality businesswomen who were the backbone of the Republican grassroots. The protectionist status quo, on the other hand, was compatible with the New Deal tradition of the Democratic party—an active government looking out for the powerless and oppressed. Perhaps more importantly, the protectionist position satisfied important members of the Democratic coalition: organized labor and (again to a lesser extent) working-class women in the reform and Progressive traditions. In general, policy making (to the extent any took place) vis-à-vis women's rights was conducted in a system similar to the equilibrium described by Baumgartner and Jones (1993): limited participation and stability of institutions and actors, cleavages, and issue meaning.

Beginning in the mid-1960s, the issue of women's rights began to evolve and change, largely in response to what might most accurately be described as a revolution. While a few activists (in and out of government) and groups pressed for women's rights during the 1950s and early 1960s, most citizens, both elites and the public, simply did not conceptualize women's rights as an issue relevant to political debate or policy making. Betty Friedan famously identified "the problem that has no name" in 1963's *The Feminine Mystique*; while she was describing the concerns of a particular group of women (white, educated, middle-class), her characterization applies to the interests and concerns of all women insofar as they were invisible and unacknowledged by most Americans. The situation changed dramatically with the general discovery of women's rights issues in the late 1960s. The result was a disruption of the equilibrium that had characterized the small women's rights debate, with significant consequences for the alignment of the parties around the issue.

What brought about this transformation in the issue of women's rights? A new context was one cause. Important long-term secular trends in women's experience—the influx of women into the labor market, rising female educational attainment, increasing divorce rates, to name just a few— exposed women to inequalities and contributed to the development of a female group consciousness (Klein 1984). The protection versus equality dimension became far less salient as the courts and EEOC increasingly struck down legislation that differentiated on the basis of sex (Mansbridge 1986). As a result, most traditional opposition to women's rights dissipated, opening the door for an unprecedented degree of activity on women's rights in the early 1970s. This in turn contributed to the possibility of agenda change: As Congress acted on equality concerns by legislating prohibitions against sex discrimination in a number of areas, space was cleared for other women's rights concerns to gain a place on the agenda (Mueller 1988b; Costain 1988). At the same time, women's rights became increasingly linked to civil rights in the construction of law, in the symbols and language employed, and in the goals pursued. This linkage was particularly meaningful because a new partisan division over civil rights had already emerged (Carmines and Stimson 1989).

Other changes in the context even more directly affected the women's rights debate. Foremost among these was the emergence of the second wave of the women's movement in the late 1960s. The women's movement politicized the changing interests of women; that is, feminists argued that politics was the appropriate venue for addressing the various problems women faced (Smeal 1984). Feminists greatly expanded the women's rights agenda, voicing issues and concerns that had not previously been subject to political debate. In a real way, feminists were prototypical Schattschneider "losers"—a group whose interests were not being served employing symbols and actions to expand the scope of conflict by drawing attention, and thus supporters, to their cause. The symbols employed by the women's movement defined women's rights in terms of equality and rights, instead of regulation or protection, thus casting the issue in a new light and contributing to its redefinition. Finally, feminists claimed to represent an important and powerful constituency—the fifty-one percent of the voting population that is female—and thus injected a new consideration into elites' calculus of the perceived relationship between position on women's rights and electoral success.

Responses to organized feminism further transformed the context of the women's rights debate. In particular, the rise of social conservatism generally, and antifeminism specifically, contributed another set of meanings and symbols to the debate over women's rights. The opposition cast women's rights as an attack on traditional gender roles and family structure, which many consider ordained by God (Klatch 1987). The ability of the opposition to mobilize voters and activists shaped the electoral strategies of party elites vis-à-vis women's rights. Opposition to feminism was particularly motivated by the Supreme Court's establishment of abortion rights in 1973. More generally, *Roe v. Wade* moved abortion from a very limited discussion involving specialists and elites to the center of public controversy (McGlen and O'Connor 1998). Abortion quickly became linked to the feminist agenda (Mathews and De Hart 1990) with important consequences for how both elites and mass evaluate women's rights in general.

Strategic elites were important in shaping the parties' responses to women's rights across this time period as well. Perhaps the best known is Phyllis Schlafly. Schlafly's leadership against feminism helped establish her, at least for a period in the 1970s and early 1980s, as a major player in the Republican party as well as a household name (Davis 1991). In some cases almost single-handedly, Schlafly's successful efforts to attract supporters to the antifeminist cause redefined women's rights in ways that struck a cord for many Americans and, therefore, was meaningful for the strategic calculations of party elites.

Other elites used opposition to or support for women's rights to better their own political position in ways that had partisan consequences. The manner in which politicians pursued women's votes was particularly important. John Kennedy, for example, sought to attract women's votes following his narrow election in 1960 by establishing the President's Commission on the Status of Women. While his goal was to demonstrate his advocacy for women's interests and divert attention away from the ERA, the Kennedy Commission's effectiveness in publicizing and providing evidence of women's unequal status helped make women's rights part of the public discourse, not to mention leading to the formation of NOW (Costain 1992; Freeman 1975). In general, Kennedy and other presidents of both parties in the 1950s and early 1960s employed symbolic actions like speeches, appointments, and commissions as their sole strategy for winning over women voters. Presidents and their advisors, however, have pursued increasingly sophisticated and issue-based campaigns directed at women since the late 1960s (Harvey 1998). As the issue definition changed, the strategies presidents and other elites pursued shifted in response, with each party coming to adopt dissimilar strategies.

Finally, and as a result of many of the changes described here, there have been important shifts in the content of the women's rights agenda. In the 1950s and early 1960s, most items on the agenda concerned equality issues, such as the ERA, equal pay, and employment discrimination, with limited discussion of issues such as Social Security reform and child care. By and large, these policies did not involve significant federal outlays or involvement. Indeed, in the case of the ERA, the proposed policy was expected to entail a rolling back of federal regulation in the workplace.

Beginning in the late 1960s and early 1970s, the women's rights agenda substantially expanded and diversified. New policies under the women's rights rubric included abortion, affirmative action, education, family leave, and violence against women, while old policies, such as child care, received unprecedented attention. This agenda expansion was significant for several reasons. Unlike the policies that dominated the 1950s and early 1960s, many of these policies involved direct federal action or budget outlays. Furthermore, many of these proposals sought to address the interests of women in nontraditional roles, particularly in the extent to which these policy proposals treated women's work force participation as not secondary or temporary, but as a permanent interest. Abortion particularly challenged traditional conceptions of women's principal role as mother. Affirmative action policies were viewed as substantial government interference in the economy. Finally, the new policies being addressed touched on the interests of individuals and groups who had not previously been involved in the debate. Homemakers, for example, felt their position threatened by many of the new agenda items. Employers were dissatisfied with the government intrusion into their business practices. Professional women generally favored the role of government in assisting their progress in the workplace. The changing and emerging participation of various groups and individuals in the women's rights debate was significant for the parties' response.

The causes of agenda expansion were several. The women's movement raised and politicized many issues that had previously not been considered appropriate for politics (Smeal 1984). As old issues were resolved, newly sensitized elites were open to the possibility of additional women's rights policies being added to the agenda. The legislating of prohibitions against discrimination for everything from the Little League to higher education in the early 1970s (Mueller 1988b) meant that women's rights activists and entrepreneurial elites could shift their attention to other concerns (Costain 1988). Finally, the impetus for agenda expansion came from the changing social and economic position of women themselves. With the massive influx of women into the work force, for example, new problems were encountered (Klein 1984). Public policy offered one possible, if only partial, solution to problems such as child care, sexual harassment, and workplace safety.

Party Coalitions

Systematic shifts in a party's coalition might also contribute to a change in the positions adopted by party elites. I have defined the political parties in this work as the various individual elites—presidents and presidential candidates, members of Congress, and party leaders—that constitute the national-level party. The parties' coalitions are a separate and more amorphous entity. By party coalition, I mean those interests that commonly comprise each party's base of support. Coalition members can be identified through the organized interests (e.g., labor unions within the Democratic party) and the less organized interests (e.g., business and upper-class interests within the GOP)[1] active within the party and the sources of the parties' electoral and other support (blacks and the Democratic party, for instance). These coalitions are subject to practical political considerations; while corporate interests are identified with the Republican party, for example, such interests have supported Democratic candidates, particularly when those candidates hold positions in the majority (Sorauf 1992). Coalitions can and do change over time, with interests once clearly identified with one party becoming associated with the other. Yet observers and scholars have long been able to identify certain interests with each party, despite their amorphous and shifting nature (Kessel 1988; Monroe 1983). Indeed, one of the central components of realignment theory is the division of American history into eras characterized by the specific alignment

---

[1] Business and the upper classes are certainly not unorganized; if anything, they are the best organized interest in American politics (Schlozman and Tierney 1986; Schlozman 1984; Schattschneider 1960). I am simply referring to the fact that there is no "Rich People's Protection Association" active within the Republican party, but rather a clear presence of various groups and individuals with an interest in the protection and creation of wealth and free enterprise (see Hibbs 1977).

of interests with the two parties (Key 1955, 1959; Beck 1997). Perhaps the most widely recognized party coalition, the Democrats' New Deal coalition, was comprised of urban, Southern, Catholic, Jewish, labor, black, and white ethnic minority interests. This coalition was evident not only in the party's successful voting coalition but also in the organized interests active at Democratic conventions and in Democratic administrations, the ties of Democrats elected to various offices, and the conception of ordinary citizens and activists as to what interests the Democratic party represented. It is this sort of phenomenon I mean to evoke when I refer to the parties' coalitions of interests.

Party elites attempt to adopt those issue positions that will maximize their ability to garner and retain support from the party coalition, as well as expand it (within limits) so as to better the party's electoral success vis-à-vis the other. Those who do not espouse positions favored by the party's coalition are unlikely to rise to elite status and are unlikely to hold onto leadership positions very long if they do. In particular, the structure of American elections forces most potential party representatives to appeal directly to the party coalition via the nomination process as a necessary prerequisite to party elite status. Subnational differences are apparent as the composition of the parties' coalitions varies by state and locality, but national party coalitions still retain distinct and divergent identities.

The relationship between elites and the party coalition is reciprocal. Elite party positioning on an issue can be influenced by a change in the nature of the party's coalition, and it can also affect the shape of the coalition as well. Change in the distribution of a party's coalition can occur as a result of long-term secular change, changing population patterns, the emergence of new interests and the decline of old, or in reaction to changing party positions. As the latter suggests, when party elites articulate new positions, some current coalition members may be repelled from party activity and identity, while others either once identified with the other party or not distinguished by party might be attracted. As the coalition's composition shifts, elites may update their beliefs about the attractiveness of other issue positions to the changing coalition, and an alteration of the party's position on other issues becomes possible. This cyclical process, it should be emphasized, occurs over the long term. Partisanship at the individual level is highly stable over a lifetime, and conversion to a new party is relatively rare. New or newly mobilized entrants into the party system are the most likely mechanisms for party coalition change (Carmines and Stimson 1989; Salisbury and MacKuen 1981; Andersen 1979).

I am predominantly concerned with one half of the cycle: the impact of party coalition change on issue position. The major shifts in the composition of the two parties' coalitions during the period examined here include the declining size of the conservative wing of the Democratic party and the liberal/moderate wing of the GOP, both of which contributed to increased homogeneity within the parties (Rohde 1991; Kessel 1988). Party positions on women's rights have been affected by these changes. In particular, the growing power of conservatives within the Republican party has been identified as an important factor in that party's retreat on women's rights in the 1970s (Costain 1991; Hartmann 1989; Freeman 1988). As I have emphasized, it is a specific form of conservatism, social and religious conservatism, that has been so influential in shaping the GOP's position vis-à-vis women's issues (Melich 1996). What Brennan (1995) calls the traditionalists have been a part of the conservative movement in the GOP since the early 1960s, but they have become especially influential since the 1970s, as witnessed by the role played by such evangelical interest organizations as the Moral Majority and the Christian Coalition in Republican party politics. While social conservatism existed prior to the reemergence of the women's movement, opposition to feminism (particularly the ERA and abortion rights) was a major factor in mobilizing the New Right, especially within the Republican party (Himmelstein 1990; Baer and Bositis 1988). The emergence of a politically potent social conservative force contributed to the redefinition of women's rights and created a new constituency for Republicans to consider when adopting positions vis-à-vis that issue.

Other long term changes in the party's coalitions have been important as well. The decline of the Solid South, the identification of blacks and civil rights with the Democratic party, and the movement of white ethnics, especially men, away from that party, have all had consequences for women's rights. These three developments are clearly related; the decline of the Southern wing of the Democratic party and the replacement of those individuals with moderate Northern Democrats, for example, was determinative in bringing about the transformation of elite party positions on civil rights (Carmines and Stimson 1989). For women's rights, this regional shift is important as well; to the extent that Southerners represent a distinctive set of policy preferences and attitudes—specifically social conservatism and traditionalism—the declining importance of white Southerners to the Democratic coalition has been meaningful for the calculus of party elites vis-à-vis women's rights. The establishment of the Democratic party as the party of civil rights in the 1960s (as Carmines and Stimson show) was also significant. As the issue of women's rights became linked with that of race, opposition to the former became increasingly incompatible with the party's position on the latter. Likewise, Republicans were forced to reevaluate their position regarding women's rights as it increasingly became seen as part of a larger effort to use government to eradicate forms of discrimination. Republicans had come to oppose that policy regarding race, and thus extended that opposition to gender.

Party Elite Membership and Preferences

For both factors described thus far—issue redefinition and coalition change—the underlying assumption has been one of vote-seeking and office-seeking elites. Issue redefinition matters because it can lead elites to reevaluate the utility of their position in appealing to and expanding the party coalition. Change in the party's coalition may shift the distribution of preference over the issue within the party, leading strategic elites to adjust their position in response. Previous research, however, suggests that individual elites are generally consistent in their behavior vis-à-vis issues over time (cf. Poole and Rosenthal 1991). Thus, the most likely mechanism for a transformed response from elites in response to issue redefinition or coalition change is the replacement of longer-term elites with newcomers who are more likely to reflect the evolving understanding of the issue or party coalition. Elite replacement processes—changes in the actual individuals holding positions of party leadership—are thus potentially important means for the effects of issue redefinition and party coalition change to impact party position-taking.

These factors—changing issue definition, coalition composition, and elite membership replacement—are not unrelated. One can expect that a failure to respond in an appropriate and timely manner to a new or increasingly important party interest or to a shift in the understanding of an issue will spur replacement. Such replacement might occur via a challenger using a member's apparent insensitivity to the new issue definition and/or party coalition as a successful strategy to unseat her, in the case of elected party elites, or in the case of other party leaders, a loss of favor as new ideas and interests gain power in the party.

At the same time, change in behavior, often referred to as conversion, is possible; in cases of issue redefinition it may even be likely. As the literature on Congressional behavior suggests, while elites are generally consistent in their behavior vis-à-vis public policy, behavioral changes do occur, particularly when policy redefinition takes place (Poole and Rosenthal 1991; Asher and Weisberg 1978; Sinclair 1982). Again, such conversion is probably more likely for newer elites who are less constrained by prior beliefs, assumptions, and cues regarding the issue. At the same time, one does not maintain elite status over a long period of time without having to adjust and readjust on some issues in order to keep hold of a position. Given the revolutionary changes in the issue of women's rights over this period, this may be a case where conversion—changed behavior on the part of elites—has functioned as a mechanism for party change.

In addition, while I view party elites as primarily vote-seeking and office-seeking, elite behavior may be motivated by other considerations as well (Page 1978; Mayhew 1974; Fenno 1973). Women's rights is a case where we might expect to find elites with strong personal preferences, as the issue involves fundamental, and often highly personal, beliefs about appropriate gender roles and relationships. There are more than a few examples of elites basing their position-taking vis-à-vis women's rights not on electoral considerations, but on their personal beliefs or preferences. Such issue ideologues have been important to the development of the parties' positions on women's rights. When a party's position is in flux and public opinion is likewise diffuse or ambivalent, elites may stake out positions that influence their party's relative position on the issue by giving cues as to appropriate party response to members who do not have strong opinions and by attracting others with similar preferences to the party. Many women in Congress, for example, believed strongly in women's rights and were responsible for instigating much of the successful women's rights legislation of the early 1970s. Many, but not all, were Democrats, and they played an important role in moving their party in a new direction.

In sum, then, general elite replacement processes represent the most likely mechanism for the realignment of party positions on any issues, including women's rights. Yet given that the forty years under examination here include some of the greatest changes in the reality, assumptions, and beliefs relating to women's roles and experiences, the possibility of conversion on the part of long-term elites certainly exists. Finally, given the degree to which the women's rights debate touches on personal views regarding sex roles, this is a case where individual preferences, in addition to strategic electoral considerations, may be more likely to enter into elite position-taking decisions.

Equilibrium Disruption

It is when an issue moves out of the sort of equilibrium described by Baumgartner and Jones (1993) that we are most likely to observe the effects on party positioning of the three factors identified. Whereas there had been low or even no salience, a stable and limited set of participants, and agreement as to the scope and nature of the issue, the extent of participation expands, the definition of and symbols associated with the issue are transformed, and the public's awareness of the issue grows. During such a disruption, previous cleavages and understandings are disturbed, and new alliances and definitions may emerge. In this time of instability, it can be difficult for elites to determine the issue position that best suits their electoral goals. Elites may use their personal preferences as a guide, adopt ambivalent positions that allow future adjustment, or shun the issue altogether, although the latter is difficult as the issue has become so salient. As time passes and the new meanings and alliances become apparent, elites have more information with which to update their beliefs, and positions become more established as a new equilibrium is constructed.

Equilibrium disruption is a central component of this model, as it is under such conditions that change in elite membership, issue definition, and coalition composition are highlighted and consequential. When issue equilibrium is disturbed, any tension between the old issue position and the new or evolving issue, coalition, or elite composition is emphasized. As I have asserted, because of the instability inherent in such a disruption, the initial response by parties may be mixed. As conditions stabilize, so do the parties' positions, with the potential outcome of new and revised positions.

This appears to be what occurred in the case of women's rights. When the issue of women's rights was discovered by elites and the public in the late 1960s and early 1970s, elites rushed to capitalize on the issue but had little information on which to base their beliefs about the strategically wise position to take. Public opinion on women's rights underwent rapid change but provided few clear guidelines as to the location of lines of cleavage around the issue. Citizens appeared to favor the concept of equality for the sexes in theory, but responses were ambivalent and contradictory when it came to specific changes in gender roles and sex-related public policy (Mansbridge 1986). Previous organized opposition to women's rights was crumbling, while new opponents had yet to materialize (Freeman 1975). In this context, a spurt of women's rights legislation was accomplished in a largely bipartisan manner. Elites acted on their perceptions of their constituent's preferences, but also on their own preferences and beliefs. As the decade wore on, however, lines of cleavage over women's rights emerged. Opposition was articulated and mobilized. At the same time, the women's rights agenda shifted from what had become generally (although not entirely) noncontroversial equality and nondiscrimination measures to other types of policies that dealt more clearly with the consequences and realities of gender equality, often challenging traditional notions of appropriate roles and behaviors. In this new context, the parties diverged and polarized, eventually establishing a new equilibrium.

CONCLUSION

The model developed here is premised on the assumption that parties are primarily vote-seeking, interested in using issues as electoral tools rather than in the issues per se. Three factors are expected to contribute to a change in the issue positions adopted by parties: the issue itself, the composition of one or both of the parties' coalitions, and the parties' elites. Changes in one or a combination of these factors are most likely to lead to party issue position change in times of issue equilibrium disruption—

when the issue moves from a situation in which participation, debate, and public attention are limited and stable to the broader political agenda with the associated greater participation, widened and transformed debate, and heightened salience. These factors are related in that changes in the issue, party composition, or party elites can lead to issue equilibrium disruption. When such disruption does occur, it focuses mass and elite attention on the issue, and the resultant salience encourages party elites to consider, and possibly reevaluate, the link between the issue and the party's electoral constituencies.

The argument presented here relies on *change*—of issues, party coalitions, and the composition of party elites. In reality, dramatic changes are rare. The composition of party coalitions and the elites that lead the parties is generally stable and consistent over time. Partisanship is itself highly stable, and individual party elites are overwhelmingly consistent in the policy positions they adopt (Poole and Rosenthal 1991; Sinclair 1982; Asher and Weisberg 1978). Finally, most issues are characterized by stability and constancy most of the time (Baumgartner and Jones 1993; Carmines and Stimson 1989).

Women's rights, however, clearly represents a case of dramatic issue change. For myriad reasons, frames of reference regarding women's issues were transformed during this forty-year period. The women's rights revolution cut a wide swath, affecting virtually every area of social, economic, and political life in the United States. So fundamental was this transformation that to compare women's rights politics in the 1950s to those in the 1980s borders on comparing the proverbial apples and oranges. Moreover, the emergence of women's rights in the late 1960s and early 1970s represented not simply a new or returning issue on the political agenda but, moreover, a challenge to the very political institutions themselves.

Understanding the transformation and polarization of the parties on women's rights thus tells us not only something about how parties position themselves on salient issues but also about the ability of parties to successfully react to, and even absorb, vast social transformations. In 1952, there were two major parties, Democratic and Republican. Forty years later, the same two parties still structure electoral choice. In the period between, a virtual sexual revolution occurred. That the parties, weakened as so many claim they are, could and did translate such foundational demands into electoral choice stands as a testament to the enduring power of parties to mediate conflict.

How did the parties adapt to the dramatic shifts in the politics of women's rights? Why did they adopt the positions they did, and why did they polarize around the issue? Having developed an explanatory framework, I now turn to the task of applying this model to the specific puzzle of women's rights realignment.

CHAPTER FIVE

Equilibrium Disruption and Issue Redefinition

CHAPTERS 2 and 3 detailed the evolution of the parties' relative positions on women's rights from the early 1950s to the early 1990s. While there is some variation in the behavior of each party in their various elite-level incarnations—organizations, presidents, House and Senate delegations—the predominant pattern is remarkably consistent. In the 1950s and early 1960s, few elites or citizens recognized women's rights as a legitimate public policy issue, but on the small agenda with which activists and interested elites were concerned, Republicans were slightly more supportive of women's rights compared to their Democratic counterparts. Differences between the parties narrowed across the 1960s. Beginning in the late 1960s and early 1970s, women's rights emerged as a major political issue. Both parties' platforms devoted unprecedented levels of attention to women's rights, and conventions were characterized by extensive debate and controversy over the issue. While the platforms were not greatly differentiated in the early 1970s, differences grew across the decade, culminating in significant divergence at decade's end. After 1980, polarization between the two parties on women's rights, with Democrats relatively more supportive, was the norm. In Congress, the House experienced a dramatic reversal during the 92nd Congress (1971–1972) as Democrats became more supportive of women's rights than Republicans, with polarization generally increasing thereafter. In the Senate, the change was more gradual; beginning with the 92nd Congress, Democrats were more likely to cosponsor pro–women's rights legislation, but differences were not statistically significant until the late-1980s.

This and the following chapter evaluate the empirical evidence in support of the explanation for the evolution of the parties' relative positions outlined in chapter 4. This theoretically grounded explanation identifies those circumstances expected to contribute to a shift in one or both of the parties' positions and in what direction we might expect that shift to occur. Furthermore, the explanation is cross-institutional in that it seeks to explain the relative positions taken by the parties in their various elite forms: organizations, executives, and Congressional delegations. As a result, the analysis calls for a wide-ranging sweep of available evidence.

The model I developed in chapter 4 focused on three variables—the issue, party coalitions, and party elites—and the process of issue equilibrium disruption that brings the issue to the fore and allows change in any one of those three variables to register its impact on party alignment. In this chapter, I focus on issue equilibrium disruption and issue redefinition. First, I investigate the evidence and nature of issue equilibrium disruption in the case of women's rights during this time period. I then examine the manner in which change in the first factor—the issue of women's rights—explains the development of the parties' relative positions. Particular attention is given to the factors that have contributed to shifting issue definition: agenda change, new context, and strategic elites. The ways in which these developments have been meaningful for party positioning on women's rights are then discussed.

EQUILIBRIUM DISRUPTION

Most issues are characterized by stability most of the time (Carmines and Stimson 1989). The scope of participation is circumscribed, alignments are fixed, and understanding of the issue by the few participants is shared and constant. Most elites and members of the public pay little, if any, attention to the issue. From time to time, however, equilibrium is disturbed (Baumgartner and Jones 1993). Such disruption is characterized by a great increase in public and political attention to the issue and a widening of elite participation. Because of the increase in salience, it is during and following periods of equilibrium disruption that we can expect changes in the three factors I have identified (issue, coalition, elites) to register their impact on party alignments. Thus, a change in party positioning is most likely following or accompanying issue equilibrium disruption. In this section, I examine issue equilibrium disruption in the case of women's rights with particular attention to the relative timing of that disruption and party realignment. The argument is first briefly stated here.

Before the late 1960s, the issue of women's rights existed in a generally stable state characterized by limited participation, general agreement over the terms and definitions of the debate, and very little public attention. The politics of women's rights issues centered around the Women's Bureau of the Department of Labor, a few active organized interests, such as the BPW, and a small number of interested members of Congress and various presidential administrations. The limited debate over women's rights was commonly recognized by participants as one of protection versus equality (cf. Costain 1992; Evans 1989; Harrison 1988). For most Americans, however, women's rights did not constitute a meaningful political interest.

Beginning in the late 1960s and early 1970s, this stability of alliances, participation, and issue meaning was disturbed as the issue of women's rights exploded on to the national agenda. For various reasons, discussed in detail in this chapter, public attention to women's rights issues increased sharply as various events and developments educated Americans as to the unique and pressing interests of women. The issue shifted from the purview of a few interested elites on to the broader agenda. The terms of the debate changed from protection versus equality to questions of rights and equality, religious and moral values, and appropriate sex and family roles. The symbolic meaning and substantive content of women's rights politics expanded and diversified, as policies not previously within the scope of public policy making came under consideration. A women's movement and, later, an opposition to that movement, emerged as potent political forces, further contributing to the expansion of the universe of interested participants, as well as shaping the context in which politicians attempted to capitalize on the issue of women's rights.

The result of these various developments was a destruction of the equilibrium that had characterized women's rights politics. Beginning somewhat sharply in 1970 and continuing for much of the decade, the politics of women's rights is characterized by heightened salience, the changing and expanding meaning of the issue, and an expanded population of interested elites. As a result, the parties entered a period of considerable flux. As the decade drew to a close, however, the dust settled, and while continuing to evolve, the new participants, meaning, and alliances associated with the issue of women's rights became somewhat established. Not coincidentally, after 1980, a new alignment of the parties was more or less instituted. While women's rights policy continued to be made, the alignment of the parties around the issue returned to a state of relative stability. A new women's rights equilibrium was established.

Indeed, women's rights not only clearly fits this model of issue disruption but also might be described as an extreme case of such a transformation. As I have emphasized, throughout the first half of the time period examined here, interested groups and individuals were aware of and advocated on behalf of the interests of women. Yet for most Americans, the concept that women have unique interests was literally unthinkable. Thus in 1963, Betty Friedan famously termed the frustrations of white, middle-class, educated women "the problem that has no name." *The Feminine Mystique* informed such women that their dissatisfaction was not individual but was shared, a revelatory, transforming, and, in some cases, galvanizing experience for millions of women. For others, the massive evidence uncovered by the Kennedy Commission (whose first report was also published in 1963) led to the realization that women experience systematic and widespread inequality. For women in the various social movements of the 1960s, firsthand experiences of disparity between the ideals of those movements and the treatment of female activists provided the catalyst. For still others, heightened awareness generated by the women's movement itself, particularly via the multitude of consciousness-raising groups of the late 1960s and early 1970s, transformed their view of gender and society (Davis 1991; Evans 1979; Freeman 1975). Thus, for the majority of the populace, women's rights required a period of discovery—a realization that an interest, cause, or concern existed—that most public policy issues need not experience. In comparison, for example, while attention to the rights of racial minorities has waxed and waned over American history, black Americans did not need to be made aware of racial inequality in the way that women (and men) became conscious of sex discrimination. This is not to suggest that after this period of discovery, all women or men agree that women's status is problematic or in need of public policy solutions. Yet where the issue of women's rights lay largely dormant—unrecognized and ignored—during the 1950s and early 1960s, by the early 1970s, this was clearly no longer the case. While controversial, once recognized, the issue of women's rights eventually came to occupy an acknowledged place in both public and private discourse. In the following sections, I examine various components of the process of women's rights issue equilibrium disruption.

Public Attention

One approach to observing the degree to which women's rights is the subject of public discourse is through the amount of coverage of women's rights in the press. Figure 5.1 presents an annual count of national-level *New York Times* articles, stories, editorials, and letters involving issues of women's rights (see the Appendix for a description of the methodology). As this graph indicates, comparatively little attention was given to women's rights in the press (as represented by the *New York Times*) in the 1950s and 1960s. Beginning rather dramatically in 1970, however, the salience of women's rights increased. Attention, as indicated by level of press coverage, remained high until the early 1980s, then declined. These data provide evidence of a shift for women's rights from relative obscurity to significant presence on the national scene, followed by a return to low levels of attention.

The dramatic increase in news coverage of women's rights beginning in 1970 just precedes the parties' realignment over the issues. Realignment in the House, where we first observe significant change, does not occur until the 92nd Congressional session (1971–1972). While Democrats were more likely to be cosponsors throughout the 1970s, differences in cosponsorship rates in the Senate did not become significant until the mid-1980s. The party platforms are quite similar vis-à-vis women's rights in 1972, with the parties growing apart across the decade. Thus, this piece of

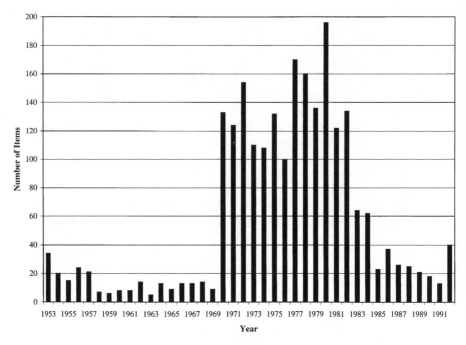

Figure 5.1. *New York Times* Items Relating to Women's Rights, 1953–1992.

evidence supports the expectation that issue equilibrium disruption preceded party realignment.

The cause of the decline in attention to women's rights in the early to mid-1980s can be traced to the institutionalization of women's rights, specifically the emergence of regularized, and less public, relationships between policy makers and feminist interest organizations, as well as the rise of feminist protest within specific institutions[1] (Katzenstein 1998; Costain and Costain 1987). Issues in equilibrium are characterized by low saliency

---

[1] A related change in the indexing of women's rights stories might also have contributed to the observed decline in the number of women's rights items in the *New York Times* after 1983. As women's rights issues became a more accepted and recognized part of political discourse, the *Times* may have established additional index headings related to women's rights, such as abortion, sexual harassment, and child care, so that such items would be found elsewhere than the women heading. Such a shift is difficult to track without a vastly expanded coding scheme; the possibility of such additional headings, however, need not counteract the interpretation of the events offered here. The adoption of additional issue headings and possible general adjustment of the index process suggests that women's rights issues had become institutionalized (or reinstitutionalized) and normalized components of public discourse and political debate, the sort of new equilibrium expected by this model.

and established and institutionalized patterns of decision making. When an issue moves on to the political agenda, saliency increases and those relationships are disturbed. Eventually, a new set of institutions and processes (in addition to the new alliances I am interested in explaining) are adopted, and a new equilibrium is established. Policy making regarding the issue may continue, but the issue's salience decreases (Baumgartner and Jones 1993). The issue of women's rights appears to have followed a comparable process.

These data thus provide evidence of one aspect of this process: the dramatic increases in the salience of women's rights in the early 1970s, followed by a return to lower levels of public attention by the mid-1980s. Level of attention is important because it is during periods of unusually high issue salience that changes in party cleavages are most likely as elites reconsider the electoral utility of the now conspicuous issue. Public attention can draw new individuals and groups into the debate, contribute to a shift in the meaning associated with the issue, and force elites to take stands on issues that they had previously ignored.

Elite Attention

Issue equilibrium disruption involves not only increased public salience but also expanded attention to the issue by policy makers (Baumgartner and Jones 1993). Can we identify such a trend for women's rights across the period? To determine if this has been the case, I examine two types of evidence. The first, the number of House, Senate, and Joint chamber hearings involving women's rights issues, provides a sense of the level of attention to women's rights by elites in Congress. While thousands of bills are introduced each year, a much smaller number of issues are of sufficient interest and import to warrant a hearing. Hearings, initiated by members of Congress, provide both members and interested actors (organized and not) an opportunity to draw attention to an issue, air opinions, and influence the agenda and alternatives considered. Thus, the number of hearings provides a useful measure of the level of elite interest in and attention to the issue. The measure is further recommended as it is employed by Baumgartner and Jones (1993) as an indicator of issue equilibrium disruption. Second, I examine the percent of party paragraphs concerning women's rights issues over this period as a measure of the interest of party elites in women's rights. The percent of party platform paragraphs is employed as an indicator of the degree to which party elites believe women's rights issues are of sufficient import to warrant comment and consideration.

Congressional Hearings. Congressional hearing data are culled from the machine-readable files made available by the Congressional Information Service (see the Appendix for a description of these data). Hearings where a number of issues are discussed, including (but not limited to) an issue or issues relevant to women's rights, are included in the count. For example, if at a hearing before the House Armed Services Committee, testimony is offered on various personnel issues, including the role of women in the military, the hearing is included in the list of women's rights hearings. I graph the total number of women's rights hearings per Congressional session in Figure 5.2. Before 1971, there are fewer than ten hearings on women's rights in every session, except the 84th (1955–1956). The number of hearings per session increases sevenfold from 1969–1970 to 1971–1972 (two to fourteen) and almost doubles again in the next session, 1973–1974, to twenty-five hearings. The number of women's rights hearings increases through 1977–1978, then levels off, with some sharp peaks and evidence of continued growth into the 1990s.

The initial increase in attention beginning in 1971 and continuing through the 1970s indicates a clear divergence from the pattern during the earlier (1950s and 1960s) period. By this measure, the level of elite attention clearly increased, and quite impressively, beginning in 1971. The increase is not as dramatic as that witnessed in the *New York Times* data and, indeed, lags it by a full year. This result suggests that, in the case of women's rights, public attention (to the extent that the editors of the *New York Times* can be considered representative of the public) precedes elite attention, at least attention from elites in Congress in the form of hearings. It should be noted, however, that half of the 1970 *New York Times* items occurred during the four-month period following the August 26 Women's Strike for Equality, which ushered in the modern mass women's movement (Klein 1984), suggesting that much of the dramatic shift in mass salience evident in Figure 5.1 preceded the elite shift (see Figure 5.2) by only a few months. Indeed, it would have been almost impossible for members of Congress to organize women's rights hearings after the August protest, but before the 91st term ended, due to time constraints, the crowded Congressional calendar, and the electoral season. It is thus not particularly surprising that the shift to greater attention in Congress begins during the 1971–1972 session.

While fluctuating, there does appear to be a slight upward trend in elite attention across the 1980s and into the 1990s in contrast to the decline in public attention to women's rights, as measured by *New York Times* coverage. The different patterns can be attributed to the institutionalization of women's rights interest community within the Washington interest universe in the early 1980s (Costain and Costain 1987). While women's rights no longer commanded the public's attention as it had in the 1970s and early 1980s, elite-level decision makers and interest organizations continued to wrestle with questions of public policy related to women's rights.

The sharp increase in elite attention to women's rights beginning in the

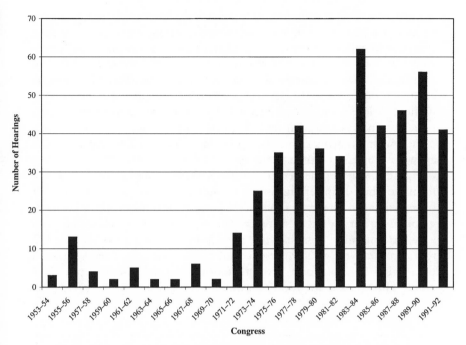

Figure 5.2. Congressional Hearings Relating to Women's Rights, House, Senate, and Joint, 1953–1992.

early 1970s is significant for party realignment because, as I show later, it came at a time when the meaning of women's rights was evolving and the parties' coalitions were shifting. During the period of rapidly increasing Congressional attention in the early and mid-1970s, the parties experienced considerable flux in their relative women's rights positions. After 1980, the parties' relative positions remain largely unchanged, even as attention to women's rights in Congress continued to grow. For various reasons—activist members of Congress, organized feminist activity, and so on—women's rights continued to garner attention from members of Congress. Thus, in the new equilibrium, the parties' relative positions are set and opposing, and women's rights remains an omnipresent part of Congressional debate. The struggle over women's rights occurs, among other ways, in the form of members of Congress holding hearings on various women's rights issues to show their parties' commitment to women's concerns, to afford themselves and their supporters an opportunity to express their views, and to highlight the different positions of the parties' members, all electorally strategic behaviors.

Party Platforms. Another indicator of the level of elite attention to women's rights is the amount of the parties' platforms dedicated to the issue. While party elites have considerable latitude in the size of their platform documents, constraints on time, attention, and effort necessarily provide a limit to the number of public policies, within the vast universe of possibilities, that the parties can address in their platforms. Moreover, as campaign documents, the parties' platforms represent the efforts of the parties to address those issues deemed of greatest interest to voters and, especially, to party constituencies. The portion of the parties' platforms concerned with women's rights thus provides a sense of the active political agenda occupied by women's rights.

Figure 5.3 shows the percent of the Republican and Democratic platforms combined concerning women's rights issues in each year (the unit of analysis is the paragraph). While the percentage of women's rights paragraphs does not rise above six percent in any year, there is a clear shift from very little attention (less than two percent of all paragraphs) before 1972 to a comparatively greater presence after. Attention to women's rights in the parties' 1972 platforms more than doubles from its highest pre-1972 point. The greatest attention to women's rights issues in the party plat-

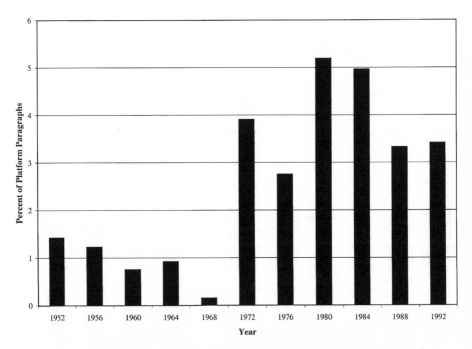

Figure 5.3. Percent Women's Rights Paragraphs, Democratic and Republican Platforms Combined, 1952–1992.

forms occurs in 1980, the year in which the sharp polarization of the parties emerged. Attention drops off slightly after 1980, but as was the case with Congressional hearings, remains at a higher level than that characterizing the period before 1970.

Thus, as with Congressional hearings, elite attention to women's rights as represented by the parties' platforms increases dramatically in the early 1970s (because conventions occur every four years, we are unable to pinpoint any potential increase in party elite attention to women's rights prior to 1972) and while varying, remains high throughout the remainder of the period. Women's rights continues to occupy the parties' agendas, even after their relative positions were established in opposite directions.

Summary

The evidence clearly shows a substantial increase in the general salience of and attention to women's rights by both elites and the public beginning in or around 1970. These findings confirm the general impression suggested by the historical narrative in chapter 2. Women's rights were of little interest to and garnered little attention from either elites or the public prior to 1970. Beginning in the early 1970s, however, we clearly observe a significant increase in interest and attention. Women's rights thus appears to have followed a process of equilibrium disruption, moving from a situation of very little attention from the public or from political leaders to one of widespread interest and heightened saliency. This equilibrium disruption began, depending on the indicator one consults, on or around the year 1970, preceding and accompanying the transformation of the parties' relative positions on women's rights. Equilibrium disruption is potentially consequential because the heightened salience increases the electoral relevancy of the issue. Under such conditions, changes in the issue itself, the parties' coalitions, or the composition of the party elites are most likely to register their impact on party realignment. I turn now to the first of the three factors— issue redefinition—that are expected to contributed to the form of the resulting party realignment.

THE EVOLVING MEANING OF WOMEN'S RIGHTS

When issue equilibrium is disrupted, change in any of the three factors identified (issue, coalitions, or elites) is more likely to lead to party realignment change. While an issue's meaning might evolve, the parties' coalitions may change, and elites may be replaced, these developments are less likely to impact party alignments when an issue is in equilibrium. Because of the low salience associated with such equilibrium, party elites, occupied with myriad other policy concerns, are unlikely to update their positions in reaction to such shifts. When equilibrium is disturbed—as we have seen occurred for women's rights in the early 1970s—the associated higher salience encourages elites to examine, clarify, and promote their position on the issue. Issue meaning change is often associated with issue equilibrium disruption as change in the ideas and meanings associated with an issue represent as one of the major causes of equilibrium disruption (Baumgartner and Jones 1993). In this section, I first present various evidence of how and why the issue of women's rights has evolved during the time period under study. I then describe how these developments has been meaningful for partisan position-taking.

The evolution of women's rights can be divided into three overlapping periods. In the 1950s and 1960s, debate over women's rights focused on protection versus equality. Opposing interests were linked to the opposing viewpoints, particularly social feminists (protection) versus equality feminists, and labor (protection) versus and business (equality) interests. Beginning in the late 1960s, the debate shifted significantly. For various reasons described here, protection disappeared almost entirely from the debate, and during this brief second period—the late 1960s and early 1970s—the debate over women's rights focused almost exclusively on equality issues, particularly basic nondiscrimination policies. The traditional opponents of the equality position either backed down or became supporters and for a brief period, no major organized opposition to women's rights, as now defined, existed. At the same time, the modern women's movement emerged, advocating for policy making on women's rights issues and transforming the women's rights debate. This second period was quite short, however, extending from about 1968 through, at most, 1973. After that time, the agenda for women's rights expanded and diversified dramatically. Opposition to women's rights organized as a political force. The understanding of and alignments over women's rights shifted. As a result, in the third period, women's rights debate took on an almost wholly new character than had the debate thirty years earlier, with important ramifications for party alignments.

Agenda Change

The evolution of women's rights as an issue has both an evaluative and an empirical component (Cobb and Elder 1983). Thus, part of the way in which the issue of women's rights has shifted is symbolic, involving changes in the ways ideas and meanings are associated with women's rights. At the same time, some of the meaningful changes have been empirical or substantive, in the sense that they reflect real changes in the actual policies considered under the heading of women's rights. Symbolic or evaluative change can play a powerful role in shaping the way elites view the electoral utility of the issue. Likewise, changes in the actual policy agenda can mean changes in the real world impact or consequences associated with an issue in a way that causes elites to reevaluate the link between the issue and important constituents. The Republican reversal on race issues, for example, has been attributed in part to the negative reaction to the affirmative action and poverty policies that became part of the civil rights agenda in the 1960s from important Republican constituencies such as employers and the white middle class (Sinclair 1982; but see Carmines and Stimson 1989).

The evolving meaning of women's rights has involved changes in the content of the women's rights agenda, particularly the diversification and expansion of that agenda over time. Prior to the early 1970s, the active women's rights agenda focused on a fairly small set of concerns: the ERA, equal pay, pension and benefits reform, child care, and a few occasional other issues. Over time, however, the agenda for women's rights grew, both in the absolute number and in the diversity of policies under consideration. While unprecedented levels of attention and activity were paid to issues long on the agenda, such as the ERA, myriad new issues were raised: sexual harassment, abortion, women's health, and family and maternity leave, to name just a few.

One indicator of changes in the women's rights agenda is the content of the women's rights bills proposed for the consideration of Congress. While not necessarily indicative of the entire women's rights agenda, the bills introduced can provide a useful window into the Congressional women's rights agenda. While other tools are available for shaping the Congressional agenda, such as offering amendments during committee markup or from the floor, bill introduction is the dominant means by which policy proposals receive consideration in Congress. All women's rights bills were coded into sixteen substantive categories representing the spectrum of women's rights policies considered by Congress during this time (Table 5.1). Coding was designed to be broad enough to delineate general policy areas and narrow enough so that meaningful changes in the content of the agenda would not be obscured. A number of the categories are related. Sexual harassment, for example, is a form of employment discrimination prohibited under Title VII. Sexual harassment bills are given a separate category than employment bills because the policy area touches on issues of workplace behavior and norms in a way that other employment discrimination legislation (removing the marriage bar for women, for example) does not. In addition, a number of the specific categories might be thought of as related to general themes, such as employment or family. Yet a focus on overly broad categories creates further complications. Many policies, for example,

TABLE 5.1
Content Coding of Women's Rights Bills

Category	Sample Title/Abstract
Equal Rights Amendment	A joint resolution proposing an amendment to the Constitution of the United States relative to equal rights for men and women
General discrimination	To prohibit discrimination on the basis of sex or marital status in the granting of credit
Equal pay/comparable worth	Providing that there shall be equal pay for equal work for women
Employment	To provide equality of treatment for married women employees of the Federal Government and for other purposes
Affirmative action	A bill to amend the Small Business Act to assist the development of small business concerns owned and controlled by women
Sexual harassment	To prohibit hazing or sexual harassment in the Coast Guard, the merchant marine, or otherwise at sea, and for other purposes
Maternity/family leave	A bill to entitle employees to maternity leave in certain cases involving the birth or adoption of a child, with protection of the employees' employment and benefit rights, and for other purposes
Child care	A bill to amend the Internal Revenue Code of 1954 to provide a credit against tax for employers who provide on-site dependent care assistance for dependents of their employees
Education	To provide for equal opportunity for women, and for other purposes
Pensions/benefits	To amend Title II of the Social Security Act to reduce from twenty to five years the length of time a divorced woman's marriage to an insured individual must have lasted in order for her to qualify for wife's or widow's benefits on his wage record
Violence against women	A bill to establish a grant program for local rape prevention and control projects

(*continued*)

TABLE 5.1 (*Continued*)

Category	Sample Title/Abstract
Armed forces	To eliminate discriminantion based on sex with respect to the appointments and admission of persons to the service academies
Abortion	To prohibit the use of Federal funds to perform abortions except where the life of the woman would be endangered
Displaced homemakers	To provide for the establishment of multipurpose service programs for displaced homemakers, and for other purposes
Women's health	A bill to amend Title XIX of the Social Security Act to require State Medicaid programs to provide coverage of screening mammography and screening pap smears
International development	A bill to promote the integration of women in the development process in developing countries

Titles/abstracts from the *Congressional Record Index* (1953–1992).

might fall into *either* employment or family: Is child care a family policy because it concerns dependent children or an employment policy because it provides the means for women with children to enter the work force? In general, given the shared underlying focus—women's rights—it is not surprising that the selected issue categories overlap in both concept and consequence. The purpose is not to account for the nuances of every women's rights policy proposal across this forty-year time period, but to discern a general sense of the different policy issues on that agenda and the changing and expanding focus of decision makers—in this case, members of Congress—over time.

Table 5.2 provides a picture of the expansion and diversification of the women's rights agenda in Congress. An "X" indicates that a bill or bills relating to the issue category was introduced into either the House or Senate during the Congressional session; while not reflective of the relative size of the policy on the agenda (i.e., the table does not indicate the number of bills or cosponsorships in each category), Table 5.2 does suggest the number and diversity of issues under consideration. The issue categories are organized in approximate order of least to most sessions on the agenda. While there are single sessions in which other policies are found on the agenda, before the 92nd session (1971–1972), the women's rights agenda is dom-

TABLE 5.2

Women's Rights Agenda, Congress, 1953–1992

Issue	Congress																			
	1953–1954	1955–1956	1957–1958	1959–1960	1961–1962	1963–1964	1965–1966	1967–1968	1969–1970	1971–1972	1973–1974	1975–1976	1977–1978	1979–1980	1981–1982	1983–1984	1985–1986	1987–1988	1989–1990	1991–1992
Sexual harassment																		X	X	X
International development																	X	X	X	X
Maternity/family leave																	X	X	X	
Child care	X																X	X	X	X
Displaced homemakers												X	X	X	X	X	X	X	X	
Health												X	X	X	X	X	X	X	X	X
Education										X	X	X	X		X	X	X	X	X	X
Abortion								X	X	X	X	X	X	X	X	X	X	X	X	X
Violence against women				X					X	X	X	X	X	X	X	X	X	X	X	X
Affirmative action							X			X	X	X	X	X	X	X	X	X	X	X
General discrimination									X	X	X	X	X	X	X	X	X	X	X	X
Armed forces										X	X	X	X	X	X	X	X	X	X	X
Employment		X	X		X	X	X	X	X	X	X	X	X	X	X	X	X	X	X	X
Pensions and benefits		X	X	X	X	X	X			X	X	X	X	X	X	X	X	X	X	X
Equal pay/comparable worth	X	X	X	X	X	X	X	X	X	X	X		X	X	X		X	X	X	X
Equal Rights Amendment	X	X	X	X	X	X	X	X	X	X	X	X	X	X	X	X	X	X	X	X

inated by four concerns: the ERA, equal pay/comparable worth, pensions and benefits, and employment. The ERA is the most constant presence on the agenda—introduced in every year until its passage in 1972, then again after the deadline for state ratification expired in 1982. Its appearance on the agenda in 1977–1978 and 1979–1980 reflects debates over ratification deadline extension and ratification revocation. The issue of equal pay/ comparable worth has likewise been a nearly permanent fixture on the Congressional agenda for women's rights. After a brief break following the passage of the Equal Pay Act in 1963, the issue returned, with proposals for extensions and enforcement of the ideal of pay equity. General employment issues, particularly various forms of discrimination, have also maintained a constant presence on the agenda across this forty-year period. Finally, proposals concerning pensions and benefits—policies dealing with sex inequities, either blatant or related to women's different patterns of wage work, in pensions (including Social Security), taxation, and other benefit programs—likewise have a lengthy history of consideration.

Beginning in 1971–1972, the agenda expands to include many more issues, while attention to the original four continues. Abortion and education enter the agenda for the first time, and the armed forces, affirmative action, and general discrimination, occasional items before the 92nd session, return for the remainder of the period. Across the 1970s and 1980s, additional issues continue to be added. With some exceptions, once an issue is added to the agenda, it tends to remain.

Similar examination of the parties' platforms in Table 5.3 (an "X" indicates that the issue is mentioned in one or both of the parties' platforms) suggests a similar evolution: a small women's rights agenda in the 1950s and 1960s, dominated by the ERA, equal pay and a few other issues, followed by a significant expansion and diversification of the agenda beginning in the early 1970s. While the pattern of agenda change suggested by the parties' platforms differs in some aspects from that reflected in the bill cosponsorship data, both suggest a considerable growth in the size and content of the women's rights agenda after 1970.

Various developments brought about both the substantive diversification of the women's rights agenda evinced here and the more amorphous shifts in the symbols and ideas associated with women's rights described later. Those causes and the shifts in the meaning and agenda of women's rights are detailed next.

New Context

The changing context of women's rights politics has been important for both the meanings associated with women's rights and the substance of the

TABLE 5.3
Women's Rights Agenda, Party Platforms, 1952–1992

Issue	1952	1956	1960	1964	1968	1972	1976	1980	1984	1988	1992
Sexual harassment										X	X
International development											
Maternity/family leave						X				X	X
Child care	X			X		X	X	X	X	X	X
Displaced homemakers											
Health								X		X	X
Abortion							X	X	X	X	X
Violence against women							X	X	X	X	X
Education						X	X	X	X		
General discrimination		X		X	X	X	X	X	X	X	X
Armed forces								X	X		X
Affirmative action			X			X	X	X	X	X	
Employment			X	X		X	X	X	X	X	X
Pensions and benefits		X				X	X	X	X		
Equal pay/comparable worth	X	X	X	X		X	X	X	X	X	X
Equal Rights Amendment	X	X	X			X	X	X	X	X	X

agenda. In this section, I discuss a number of major contextual changes: the evolving role of women in society and the economy, legal developments, the social movements of the 1960s, particularly the civil rights movement, the women's movement itself, and the antifeminist movement that arose in response to it.

Women's Roles and Experiences. It would be difficult to overstate the enormity of change in female experience and expectation across this forty-year time span. Changes in women's labor force participation, educational attainment, marital patterns, and motherhood practices transformed women's experience, the result of developments tracing back to the nineteenth century and before. While some, such as the birth rate, experienced growth following World War II, the long-term trends were for more women in the paid work force, greater educational attainment for women, falling birth rates, and increasing rates of divorce (Klein 1984).

Changing marital patterns, particularly rising divorce rates, resulted in a growing number of single women. These women lacked the financial support of a spouse and necessarily stood outside of the traditional expectation for the pattern of women's lives. At the same time, the Baby Boom was followed by a Baby Bust, as the birth rate steadily declined across the

1950s and 1960s. Women not only had fewer children but also had them closer together, reducing the total amount of a women's lifespan dedicated to caring for small, dependent children. The number of women working outside the home steadily increased. In a dramatic change from previous eras, married women, as well as women with small children, entered or remained in the workplace (McGlen and O'Connor 1998; Klein 1984).

Women's educational attainment steadily increased. In 1950, approximately one-quarter of bachelor's degree recipients were female; by 1960, more than a third were women, and by 1970, that figure was forty-three percent. In 1990, more than half of undergraduate degrees were awarded to women. Women were also earning an increasingly large portion of professional degrees. In medicine, women earned a mere six percent of awarded degrees in 1950; ten years later, that figure had increased only two points. By 1980, however, women earned twenty-three percent of medical degrees, and in 1990, one-third of medical school graduates were female. A similar pattern characterizes the law. Women earned only three percent of law degrees in 1960 and five percent in 1970, but a full thirty percent in 1980. By 1990, forty-two percent of law school graduates were female (McGlen and O'Connor 1995).

These patterns resulted from and complemented various social and economic changes. Technological developments meant that the job of maintaining a household and caring for children—the traditional occupation for women—demanded less of women's time than they had historically. Moreover, as women had fewer children closer together, the amount of each woman's lifespan dedicated to the care of dependent children declined, allowing greater opportunity for alternative occupations. Particularly after World War II, the expansion of the economy and general prosperity permitted and encouraged greater numbers of people, including women, to reach higher levels of educational attainment. Increasingly freed from household responsibilities and better educated, women pursued professional careers in growing numbers. The demands of American suburban household consumption encouraged many women to contribute a second income, while growing numbers of single and divorced women depended on their own income for their, and their children's, survival. Poor and minority women continued to work for low wages and in poor conditions throughout this period and before (Klein 1984; Chafe 1972).

These developments are significant for gender politics because they so altered the life experiences of many American women. In the workplace, women encountered forms of discrimination and inequality to which they had not previously been exposed. For the growing numbers of women for whom an income was necessary for survival, workplace issues, such as job security, discrimination, sexual harassment, and child care, became relevant, pressing concerns. As the numbers of single, divorced, and widowed women grew, greater numbers of women became socially, economically, and psychologically independent, challenging the traditional expectation of female dependency. Attempting to buy a house, eat in a restaurant without a male companion, or earn enough to support a family, these women often faced various forms of discrimination from which dependency had previously shielded them. Finally, as women spent more of their time outside of the home, they were brought into contact with each other, creating networks of shared experience that would form the foundation for feminist consciousness (Klein 1984; Freeman 1975). These changes in the real circumstances of women's lives mattered for women's rights as a political issue by contributing to growing tension between women's traditional roles and the experiences and expectations that characterized the lives of many women and by generating an expanded set of concerns and interests for American women.

Legal Developments. The second contextual change involves developments in the law. One of the most critical changes in the debate over women's rights was the decline of the protection versus equality dimension. A main cause of the eclipse of this dimension has been the evolution of the legal environment. Particularly important have been the interpretation of Title VII of the 1964 Civil Rights Act adopted by the EEOC and the courts and the application of the Fourteenth Amendment's equal protection clause to women. Title VII prohibits discrimination in employment on the basis of various factors, including sex. The sex provision was added by amendment in part as an attempt by Southern conservatives to sink the entire bill. The EEOC initially used the provision's controversial legislative history to justify inaction on sex discrimination. Partly in response to pressure brought to bear by the emerging women's movement, however, EEOC guidelines with regard to sex discrimination were in place by the end of the decade. Both the agency and the courts were applying a broad interpretation of sex discrimination to invalidate most protective legislation, usually by extending such protections to men, by the early 1970s (Davis 1991; Mansbridge 1986).

Concomitantly, throughout the 1960s, feminist lawyers encouraged the courts to apply the Fourteenth Amendment's equal protection clause— originally designed to combat racial discrimination—to discrimination on the basis of sex. In its first report, the Kennedy Commission advocated test cases to establish sex as a suspect category (and thus subject to strict scrutiny) under the Fourteenth Amendment as an alternative to the ERA (Davis 1991). In *Reed v. Reed* (1971), the Supreme Court struck down for the first time a law that treated men and women differently on the basis of the Fourteenth Amendment. In subsequent cases, particularly *Frontiero v. Richardson* (1973) and *Craig v. Boren* (1976), the Court further elucidated and refined its position. While the Court refused to apply the strict scrutiny standard to cases of sex discrimination, as it does for racial discrimination claims, it did adopt a test, heightened scrutiny, that is more stringent than the weakest test, which only requires the state have some rational basis for differential treatment (Epstein and Walker 1995). In creating an intermediate category for sexual discrimination cases, the Court contributed to the invalidation of legislation that distinguished between the sexes. While most cases involved the extension of protections and benefits to men, the result was that most of the little protective legislation remaining was considered unenforceable (Mansbridge 1986).

The erosion of protective legislation shaped the context of the women's rights debate in several ways. First, this development helped eliminate a major division between women's rights groups. The protection versus equality split had divided women since suffrage, and it remained salient into the 1960s. When the EEOC held hearings on the issue of bona fide occupational qualifications (BFOQs) and Title VII in the mid-1960s, the National Consumer's League (an organization with roots in the Progressive Movement and an original supporter of protective legislation), the Young Women's Christian Association (YWCA), and the American Association of University Women (AAUW) were among those lobbying for a broad interpretation of BFOQs that would let protective legislation stand. Traditional equality proponents, such as the NWP and the BPW, were joined by the newly founded NOW in calling for a narrow interpretation that would invalidate protective legislation (McGlen and O'Connor 1998). As late as 1968, the AAUW, YWCA, Women's Bureau of the Department of Labor, and League of Women Voters officially opposed the ERA, the major issue distinguishing equality and protection feminists, while the NWP and BPW continued to support the amendment as they had since the 1930s and 1940s (Boles 1979). In general, second wave feminist organizations sided with the latter on the side of equality and the ERA (Costain 1988; Mueller 1988b). After 1970, the protection versus equality debate no longer divided most women's rights groups; every organization mentioned as an ERA opponent had become a proponent by 1974 (Boles 1979). While some divisions remained, feminists were generally united in their belief that what little protective legislation remained did more harm to women than good. The causes of this change appear to be the elimination of protections, the changing political context, and the transformation of old-line feminist organizations in response to the second wave of the women's movement. This is not to say that support for protective legislation disappeared, only that the controversy was no longer as divisive within the feminist community.

This change in the legal context also had an impact on other interests with links to the parties, particularly the labor movement. Organized labor was a powerful opponent of the ERA and other antiprotection proposals, contributing to the Democratic party's ambivalence on, if not opposition to, the ERA, despite party pledges in support (Costain 1992; Hartmann 1989). More generally, organized labor had long been hostile to women's rights and to women workers. From the onset of national unionization in the late 1800s, the major labor organizations, the American Federation of Labor (AFL) and the Congress of Industrial Organizations (CIO), allowed the membership of few if any women workers and failed to encourage, and in some cases actively discouraged, the unionization of women workers and the industries, such as garment-making, that boasted high proportions of women workers. The relatively short-lived Knights of Labor was more interested in organizing women workers, but it faced considerable opposition from both male laborers and from women themselves (Deckard 1979). Opposition from male labor leaders stemmed from several factors: societywide conceptions of women's presence in the work force as a temporary condition and not central to family survival, desire to protect the family wage ideal used by unions to justify higher wages, and straightforward discrimination against women. In addition, women workers tended to be located in occupations that are notoriously difficult to organize, such as domestic labor. Organized labor favored protective legislation ostensibly as a form of worker benefit, but also because it discouraged employers from hiring women, thus reducing competition for jobs. Even women-only unions, most notably the Women's Trade Union League (WTUL), and unions in which women comprised a large portion of the membership (although rarely of the leadership), such as the International Ladies Garment Workers Union, favored protectionism. The WTUL, in particular, successfully lobbied Congress and the courts for protective legislation for women workers in the early part of this century (Costain 1992; Kessler-Harris 1982).

As women's membership in unions slowly increased, the major unions initially maintained their stance in favor of protective legislation. When the second wave of the women's movement emerged in the late 1960s, however, some of the earliest support came from labor unions. The United Auto Workers (UAW), which had established a Women's Department as early as 1944, supplied NOW with office space and clerical services following NOW's founding in 1966. When NOW voted to include the ERA in its Bill of Rights at its 1967 conference, however, the fledgling organization was forced to relocate. UAW women withdrew from active participation from NOW, but along with women in the other unions, pressed their unions for change on the ERA and for support of the women's movement (Freeman 1975). Within two years, the UAW reversed its position in favor of the ERA. While the AFL-CIO did not follow suit officially until 1974, labor union opposition to the ERA was considered to be unraveling by the early 1970s (Costain 1992). By the end of the decade, labor had adopted a strong position in favor of most feminist demands. As a sign of how much organized labor had changed, in 1979, the AFL-CIO moved its biennial convention from Miami Beach to Washington, DC, to honor NOW's boycott of states that had not ratified the ERA (*NYT* 1/6/79).

There are several apparent reasons for labor's change of position. First are the legal developments I have outlined that generally invalidated protective legislation, thus eliminating labor's main basis for opposition to the ERA. As Davis (1991) points out, however, Congress began extending protections to men as early as the 1938 Fair Labor Standards Act (affirmed by the Supreme Court in 1941), but labor (and some women's organizations) continued to stand pat in opposition for another thirty years. It seems likely that in addition to the changed legal environment, union support for the ERA and the women's movement in general in the 1970s was motivated by changes in its membership (just as I have argued parties are influenced by change in their membership), particularly the growing female presence and the need for a broader appeal in the face of a diversifying work force and shrinking industrial base. Women comprised a fifth of union membership by 1970; by 1984, one-third of unionized workers were women (Women's Bureau of the U.S. Department of Labor 1976, 1985). These aggregate numbers mask the fact that women continued to be greatly overrepresented in some unions, particularly those for teachers and other public employees, and underrepresented in others, such as those for the skilled trades. Yet by taking a more active stance on behalf of women workers, unions were responding to a growing constituency, as well as seeking out new recruits to take the place of a dwindling industrial work force.

The new context created by the dissipation of protective legislation has thus contributed to a shift in the manner in which women's groups as well as organized labor approached women's rights issues. Moreover, the declining relevance of protective legislation contributed to the consensus that generally characterized women's rights politics in the early 1970s. With support for the protection status quo crumbling, little real opposition to proposals such as the ERA and general nondiscrimination policies remained. The result was an unprecedented level of political activity and partisan unity on women's rights (Freeman 1975).

This consensus was short-lived, in large part because of a closely related second legal development that followed: the codification of sexual equality and nondiscrimination. As we have seen, before 1970 the women's rights agenda was dominated by equality concerns, that is, basic nondiscrimination issues such as the ERA, equal pay, and employment discrimination. Those types of policies were a relatively smaller portion of the agenda by the mid-1970s. The causes of this change are several and are discussed throughout this chapter. One of the most important causes was simply the almost thorough accomplishment of legal sex equality.

This achievement was the result of actions on the part of the courts, Congress, and the executive branch, as well as the federal bureaucracy. As noted earlier, the Supreme Court adopted a heightened scrutiny test for claims of sexual discrimination in the mid-1970s. As a result, many provisions that treat women and men differently under the law have either been struck down by the courts or are no longer enforceable. In addition, Congress wrote sex equality into a broad spectrum of areas in the early 1970s. The inclusion of sex in Title VII of the 1964 Civil Rights Act already prohibited sex discrimination in all aspects of employment. In 1972, Congress amended the 1963 Equal Pay Act, extending the spectrum of employers and workers covered and strengthening the enforcement mechanism. That same year Congress passed the ERA, thus temporarily removing, at least from Congress's purview, the major equality item on the women's rights agenda since suffrage. Congress legislated sex equality in education as part of the Educational Amendments Act of 1972 and prohibited discrimination in the provision of credit on the basis of sex or marital status in the 1974 Equal Credit Opportunity Act. In addition to these landmark statutes, Congress also prohibited sex discrimination in military academies, federal pay benefits, Little League baseball, and federal juries, to name a few, during the early 1970s (McGlen and O'Connor 1998; Hartmann 1989; Mueller 1988b).

This flood of anti-discrimination legislation in the early 1970s appears to be the result of several factors. Such legislation benefited from the brief bipartisanship on women's rights during the period. The agenda was dominated by equality concerns, and as the issue of women's rights gained saliency, prohibitions against sex discrimination allowed legislators to show support for the principle of equality, which most Americans supported, at least in theory (Mueller 1998b; Mansbridge 1986). During this period, feminist lobbyists operated almost entirely without opposition, as traditional opponents, such as organized labor, were weakening, and newer foes, such as the New Right, had yet to coalesce (Hartmann 1989). Finally, the extent and breadth of equality legislation is in part attributable to the entrepreneurship of feminist sympathizers, almost exclusively women, in Congress. Representative Martha Griffiths (D-MI) almost single-handedly brought the ERA to the floor of the House by way of a discharge petition, circumventing the Judiciary Committee's long-time chair, staunch ERA opponent Emanuel Celler (D-NY) (Wolbrecht and Martin n.d.; Davis 1991). Representative Bella Abzug (D-NY) carried a standard anti–sex discrimination provision with her to committee meetings and introduced it into nearly every bill considered. She urged like-minded legislators to do the same, resulting in the somewhat stealthy addition of such provisions by "semiautomatic response" (Freeman 1975, 204).

Presidents likewise included women in various anti-discrimination executive actions. As early as 1967, President Johnson issued Executive Order 11375, which added sex to the categories for which discrimination on the part of federal contractors was prohibited by his previous order, 11246 (Freeman 1975). The equality agenda was increasingly accepted within the bureaucracy as well. While slow to act on behalf of sex discrimination, the EEOC eventually took up the cause, moving in the 1970s to enforce a law that had been on the books since 1964. Individuals sympathetic to the cause of women's rights within various government agencies, those whom Freeman (1975) has called "woodwork feminists," helped contribute to increasingly vigilant enforcement (Costain 1992).

The changed context of widespread codification of gender equality was important for several reasons. As equality was achieved (at least in terms of the law), it removed from the agenda those items on which elites of both parties had come to agree. At the same time, the accomplishment of so many nondiscrimination policies created space for other policies to take their place. With interest in and sensitivity to women's concerns heightened by earlier government actions, as well as the advocacy of the women's movement, new public policies could find a place on the agenda. Such issues were raised by enterprising elites seeking to capitalize on interest in women's rights and feminist activists eager to seize the opportunity to attain benefits for women. Furthermore, as nondiscrimination became the de jure, if not de facto, status quo, women's rights supporters became increasingly aware of the limits of such policies in meeting the needs of women. Not only were there few remaining ways for the state to mandate legal equality, but there was increasing evidence that such an approach did not result in equality of outcome, or even opportunity, and that other sorts of policies that addressed the particular circumstances of women were necessary (Costain 1988). The result was increasing attention to other policies, such as child care provision, protections against violence, and reproductive rights.

Thus, the disintegration of protective legislation and the codification of legal gender equality shaped the context in which women's issues were debated and framed. The first contributed to shifting positions on women's rights issues on the part of important debate participants, particularly feminist groups and organized labor. The second, the near achievement of legal gender equality, removed from the agenda those policies on which various interested groups and the parties had largely come to agree, opening the door for new, and as it turned out, controversial, agenda items to take their place.

One of the most controversial items on the expanded women's rights agenda emerged, in part, as the result of another sort of legal development. Legal change vis-à-vis abortion rights occurred rather dramatically with the Supreme Court's 1973 *Roe v. Wade* ruling that certain abortion rights are

constitutionally protected. While activists had been pursuing abortion reform at the state level with some success and NOW had gone on record in
favor of reproductive freedom in 1967, *Roe* placed the issue of abortion on
the national stage, adding an issue to the women's rights agenda that has
elicited passionate opposition and equally passionate defense. While the
subject of abortion was initially controversial, all major women's rights organizations adopted a position in favor of abortion rights by the early
1970s. In doing so, women's rights activists faced a conundrum: On one
hand, feminists argue that reproductive freedom is central to women's
rights generally; on the other hand, feminists have often sought to distinguish the highly controversial issue of abortion from other women's rights
issues. The politics of abortion have colored the debate by linking a controversial medical procedure about which many Americans feel ambivalent
or averse to the spectrum of women's rights issues (Mansbridge 1986;
Conover and Gray 1983). The pro-life and pro-choice movements, like the
antifeminism and women's movements with which they are associated,
have shaped the debate over women's rights, mobilized supporters and opponents, and contributed to a changing political context that party elites
must consider when weighing positions on women's rights.

Abortion has had a major impact on the politics of women's rights for a
number of reasons. While abortion certainly concerns one's views on conception and the nature of personhood, it is also clearly related to notions
of women's role in society, the mythical place of motherhood and the family in our shared consciousness, and various forms of external and internal
control (over one's body, one's life, or one's social system). Save absti-
nence, abortion represents the single most effective rejection of motherhood, a role many believe ordained by God or nature and an institution of
central importance to Western culture. Thus, abortion threatens a social
system built quite fundamentally on the family unit. It challenges the control of men, be they partners, preachers, or political leaders, over not only
women's lives, but men's own lives as well.

It should not be surprising, then, that abortion has been such a touchstone in the women's rights debate. As Luker (1984) has shown, the controversy pits not just two positions on abortion against each other, but two
worldviews that differ fundamentally in their preferences vis-à-vis family,
society, and women's roles. Even for pro-life advocates who do not share
a socially conservative worldview, other women's rights issues have often
suffered a sort of guilt by association with abortion. Thus the Court's decision in *Roe v. Wade* shaped women's rights politics, not simply because
of the addition of a substantive agenda item (reproductive rights), but because of the controversial frame it contributed to women's rights more
generally. The issue of women's rights carries this association, perhaps

alienating some elites and masses who may have been stronger supporters, were they not turned off by the abortion issue.

Other Social Movements. The social movements associated with the 1960s include the civil rights, New Left, student, peace/Vietnam, free speech, consumer rights, and environmental movements. With the exception of the last two, all clearly predate the second wave of the women's movement. While their goals differed, these movements, particularly the civil rights, student, and peace movements, shared a language of revolution, equality, rights, and freedom, tactics that emphasized protest, a commitment to a radical transformation of the institutions and norms of American society, and in many cases, a core overlapping membership (Evans 1979). The older branch of the women's movement, exemplified by NOW, had its roots in traditional forms of political organizing, but the younger branch grew directly out of the New Left and civil rights movements of the 1950s and 1960s (Freeman 1975). Many of the women's movement's earliest activists had been participants in one or both of those movements, and brought the skills, tactics, and language they had gained through those experiences to their advocacy of women's rights (Evans 1979). While NOW lobbied government officials for implementation of Title VII and sued on behalf of victims of sex discrimination, early press coverage of women's rights often focused on the more colorful actions of the younger branch, such as the hexing of Wall Street and protests at the 1968 Miss America Pageant (see Morgan 1970). Such actions associated feminism and women's rights in the minds of many Americans, including party elites, with the perceived radicalism and extremism of the earlier movements that so alienated the Silent Majority (Miller and Levitin 1984).

The issue of women's rights has been particularly linked to civil rights. The grouping of the cause of rights for racial minorities and those for women involved shared language and tactics, as well as changes in the nature of the pursuit of racial equality and awareness of women's rights. The association of the oppression of blacks and women has a long tradition in American history. As touched on in chapter 2, the first wave of the women's movement developed, in large part, out of the abolitionist movement and borrowed much of its tactics, language, and organization from that cause. The links between the pursuit of racial and sexual equality weakened across the nineteenth century, however. Many feminists were disappointed when women were not granted the vote along with black men following the Civil War. During Reconstruction and the subsequent onset of Jim Crow, feminist activists focused almost exclusively on suffrage, often adopting racist and elitist strategies in their pursuit of that goal (O'Neill 1969), which further distanced the cause for women's rights from that for blacks.

In the early postwar period, the civil rights movement focused on segregation, lynching and other violence, and the systematic denial of blacks' political rights. While certainly distinct, analogies can be drawn between these concerns and those of American women. While most women live with men, sex segregation characterized most paid occupations, and those women who did not work outside the home were likewise segregated into communities comprised entirely of women and children for considerable durations of time. Where public violence against blacks served to intimidate and control the lives of African Americans, private violence against women, in the form of sexual assault and domestic abuse, similarly constrained and hindered women's lives. While not facing the obstacles of Jim Crow, women in the 1950s lacked political representation of their interests and were denied certain political rights, such as systematic exclusion from jury service. Again, the oppression of blacks and women clearly differ in both form and consequence. Yet as many women in the civil rights movement eventually came to conclude, the condition of blacks and that of women were comparable on many levels (Evans 1979). The difference was that while the issue of racial discrimination was widely debated in the 1950s, discrimination against women remained almost entirely unacknowledged, except by a small number of elites. Comparisons between racial minorities and women were simply not recognized or voiced.

By the mid-1960s, however, analogies were increasingly drawn between the condition of women and that of African Americans. Personal experiences with discrimination led women in the New Left and civil rights movements to identify parallels between race and sex discrimination (Evans 1979). The shift in the focus of the civil rights movement from ballot access and segregation to economic and employment discrimination further contributed to comparisons with women's rights. The view that racial and sexual discrimination are related phenomenon, and that both call for government action, was increasingly adopted by elites (Costain 1992). The inclusion of sex in Title VII of the 1964 Civil Rights Act provided a powerful statement of the connection between the discrimination endured by blacks and women. While the law was clearly designed to address the needs of racial minorities, particularly African-Americans, the sex provision meant that sexual employment discrimination would be handled within the law and by government agencies, at least theoretically, in the same manner as was discrimination against blacks. The application of the Fourteenth Amendment's equal protection clause—like the Civil Rights Act, intended to benefit blacks—to women in 1971 further forwarded the linkage between the two forms of discrimination. In 1967, President Johnson signed an executive order adding sex to the classifications requiring affirmative action programs on the part of federal contractors. The addition of sex was the result of one of NOW's first lobbying efforts and reflected the general feminist strategy of advocating government address women's discrimination in the same manner and with the same commitment as they did blacks' (Freeman 1975). By 1978, the federal government had expanded its de facto definition of minority to include women, thus providing the opportunity for women to benefit from various federal anti-discrimination and affirmative action programs and policies (Reinhold 1978).

The emergence of a context in which women's rights was linked to the social movements of the 1960s and particularly to the struggle for civil rights for African Americans was meaningful for the relative positions adopted by the parties for several reasons. First, while war protesters clashed famously with the Democratic leadership at its 1968 convention in Chicago, many (if not most) of the protest movements of that era were clearly associated with the Democratic party by the early 1970s. Nixon promised "peace with honor," but it was Democrats—Eugene McCarthy and Robert Kennedy in 1968, George McGovern in 1972—who were embraced by activists as genuine antiwar presidential candidates. The McGovern-Fraser reforms opened up the Democratic party to blacks and young people (especially students), as well as women, increasing the association of that party with related movements. The alliance of Democrats with the women's movement and feminism was thus encouraged by the association of that party with other social movement groups and organizations (Freeman 1975).

Second, as Carmines and Stimson (1989) show, by the late 1960s, the Democratic party had established itself as the party of civil rights. As the issue of women's rights became increasingly linked with that of race, opposition to women's rights appeared increasingly incompatible with the Democratic position on civil rights. Likewise, Republicans were forced to reevaluate their position as the ERA and other women's rights issues became viewed as part of a larger movement to use the tools of government to eradicate discrimination. For reasons related to both a strategy of symbolic racism and a tradition of limited government, Republicans had come to oppose that policy regarding race and thus favoring it for women seemed increasingly inconsistent.

Women's Movement. As the preceding discussion suggests, foremost among the causes of changes in the women's rights context was the advent of the second wave of the women's movement in the late 1960s. The emergence of the women's movement helped move women's rights into the public spotlight, shape the symbols and meaning associated with women's rights, and draw attention to the latent political power of women voters.

The terms first and second wave are often employed to describe the women's movements of the nineteenth and twentieth centuries, respectively. In the prevailing account, the first wave originated at the 1848 Women's Rights Convention in Seneca Falls, New York, and concluded with the accomplishment of national women's suffrage in 1919. The second wave of the women's movement began in the late 1960s and emerged as a mass movement in 1970 (Klein 1984). Whether and when the second wave concluded largely depends on one's definition of a social movement and interpretation of recent historical facts.[2] While feminism declined as a mass protest movement in the early 1980s, a number of women's rights organizations have become institutionalized members of the policy-making community in Washington, and feminists have continued to press for reform within various institutions (Katzenstein 1998; Costain and Costain 1987). The wave terminology is intended to describe the cyclical rising and falling of women's movement activity, emphasizing that a degree of organization and activity has persisted between the waves. Thus, while conventional wisdom holds that women's rights activism disappeared after 1920 (for a challenge to that wisdom, see Andersen 1996), organizations such as the NWP, the BPW, and the AAUW continued to advocate various women's rights concerns, albeit with smaller membership and less publicity than they formerly enjoyed. As is often true for social movements, many first wave organizations were active participants in the second wave, alongside the newer organizations (Boles 1979).

The modern women's movement has its roots in the changing socioeconomic experiences of women described earlier (Klein 1984), political opportunities (Costain 1992), and the existence of networks of women with similar gender-based experiences (Evans 1979; Freeman 1975). In its early stages, the women's movement was characterized by an older and a younger branch. The older branch, of which NOW is the preeminent organization, was generally comprised of upper-income, well-educated, white women with political connections and experience. NOW was founded in 1966 at a convention of state commissions on the status of women by women who sought a women's civil rights organization to advocate women's concerns in the political sphere. The younger branch, on the other hand, consisted largely of younger women from the student, civil rights, and peace movements (Freeman 1975). This branch of the women's movement grew out of the inconsistency perceived by many women activists between the rhetoric and ideals of the civil rights and student movements and the treatment of women within those movements (Evans 1979). While NOW was (and is) a highly structured, national-level organization, the younger branch was characterized by a conscious rejection of formal structure, emphasis on participatory democracy, and an inclination toward radical protest action. In the early days of the modern women's movement, the political theater and protest actions of the younger branch received ex-

[2] Books and articles in the mid-1990s have announced and described a third wave, so while there is little consensus on when or if the second wave receded, another wave may have arrived (cf. Heywood and Drake 1997).

tensive press coverage (Freeman 1975). Sensationalist coverage linked feminism with the radicalism many associated with the civil rights, student, and peace movements.

Both branches of the women's movement emerged simultaneously and independently in the mid- to late-1960s. While each initially viewed the other with suspicion, by the early 1970s, the branches were increasingly indistinguishable in their organization, methods, and demands. The younger branch gave up most of its more outrageous tactics, while NOW, and other older branch organizations like the Women's Equity Action League (WEAL) and the NWPC, increasingly emphasized protest, where once they had limited their activities to lobbying and legal maneuverings (Costain 1992). Women's rights organizing was widespread as literally thousands of groups formed across the country (Freeman 1975). In addition to these new groups, many long-standing women's organizations such as the NWP, AAUW, and BPW were inspired to adopt increasingly stronger, even radical, stands and expand their activism (Boles 1979). Small, local groups often began with consciousness-raising and moved on to efforts such as rape crisis centers, publishing collectives, community daycares, and feminist book stores (Davis 1991). National, policy-inclined organizations such as NOW, WEAL, and the NWPC lobbied political institutions on behalf of an ever-expanding feminist agenda (Costain and Costain 1987).

Given the amorphous nature of the phenomenon and the many types of activities they encompass, identifying and measuring social movements are difficult tasks. In an effort to map shifts in the level of women's movement activity over this period I produce an event count series of women's movement activity. The methodology employed is adopted from that used by McAdam (1982) to trace the activities of the civil rights movement, and has been utilized by others to study the women's movement (Rosenfeld and Ward 1996; Costain 1996; Costain and Majstorovic 1994). This methodology is described in the Appendix.

Figure 5.4 displays the event count series of national-level pro–women's rights activity from 1953 to 1992. Women's movement activity is comparatively circumscribed in the 1950s and 1960s. Consistent with previous research, this analysis suggests that the women's movement emerged as a mass movement in 1970, as reflected in the dramatic increase in events (Klein 1984). After a decade of considerable activity, the women's movement appears to peak in 1980. By 1985, feminist activity drops off considerably, falling to levels slightly exceeding those of the 1950s and 1960s.

This pattern is quite similar to that found in Figure 5.1, the graph of *New York Times* coverage of women's rights issues—a not surprising result, given that both are derived from the annual *New York Times* index. More fundamentally, the relationship derives from the fact that attention to issues in the media is event-driven and the press is attuned to change

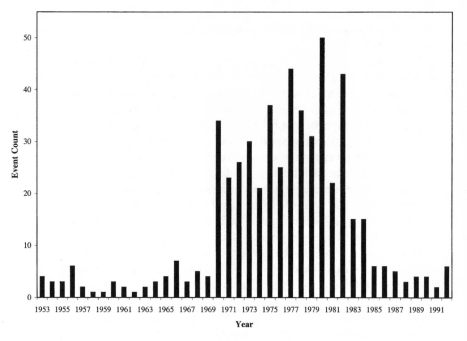

Figure 5.4. Women's Movement Event Series, 1953–1992.

and action. This does not mean that the measures of public attention to women's rights and women's movement activity presented here are not meaningful separately. Public attention matters theoretically for the explanation offered here and is of significance independently. The women's movement is of similar independent significance. The similarity of the two series simply suggests that women's movement events contributed to, if not caused, the variation in public attention to and salience of women's rights evinced in Figure 5.1.

The women's movement has mattered for party politics vis-à-vis women's rights for several reasons. First, as I argued earlier, the language, tactics, and origins of the women's movement led to comparisons and connections with other, earlier movements, particularly the civil rights and student movements. This association affected how the issues linked to the women's movement were received and perceived by both the public and elites.

The women's movement also contributed to the change in the policy agenda on women's rights by drawing attention to concerns that had not previously been part of the political debate. Prior to the late 1960s, the political agenda for women's rights was almost entirely limited to the ERA, sex discrimination in employment, equal pay, and pension and benefit reform, with occasional attention to child care, violence against women, and the armed forces. NOW's earliest actions focused on equality concerns, which for the most part meant demanding that the EEOC enforce sex discrimination legislation. By the time NOW held its first national conference in 1967, however, its concerns were already expanding to reflect the interests of its broadening membership. At that meeting, NOW adopted a Bill of Rights calling for action on eight points, four of which concern equality—the ERA, employment discrimination, equality in education, equality in job training—and four of which, while having equality as their goal, focused on unique needs of women (what some term difference policies): maternity leave benefits and rights, tax deductions for home and child care expenses, child care centers, and reproductive freedom (Costain 1992; Freeman 1975; Morgan 1970).

While ERA ratification dominated much of the movement's resources during the 1970s, the women's movement's agenda continued to diversify and expand beyond the early focus on equality. By 1973, NOW, WEAL, and the NWPC had established national offices in Washington, DC, where they engaged in full-time, increasingly professional lobbying efforts for various women's rights. The women's lobby, joined by many established women's groups such as the AAUW, BPW, and League of Women Voters, successfully fought not only for basic nondiscrimination, but also for issues such as abortion reform, protections for pregnant workers, and child care (Ferree and Hess 1985). While initially experiencing the greatest success with equality issues, these organizations pressed for an expanded agenda. Indeed, at its first national conference in 1973, the NWPC committed itself to work for such issues as daycare and welfare reform directed at women "and not solely for the narrower objective of achieving equal legal status for women" (Shanahan 1973, 38).

Just how expansive the feminist agenda had become is reflected by the proposals that emerged from the 1977 National Women's Conference in Houston, organized by an act of Congress in honor of the United Nation's International Women's Year. The 2,000 delegates adopted a decidedly feminist National Plan of Action addressing twenty-five different policy areas. The Plan included equality proposals covering everything from education and employment to insurance, media, and arts and humanities programs. Yet the growing focus of the movement on issues beyond basic equality was reflected in the number of other types of policies. Proposals covered such issues as child care, women's health, the needs of homemakers and older women, rape, and domestic violence. The Plan called for affirmative action programs for disabled and minority women, to foster women-owned businesses, and to advance the representation of women in elected and appointed office. Finally, the Plan supported reproductive freedom, including abortion rights (Evans 1989; Bird 1979).

In sum, the women's movement has drawn attention to many issues not previously part of the women's right agenda. While the movement has continued to focus on equality issues, it has called attention to "a host of new issues . . . thereby substantially enlarging the public-policy [sic] agenda" (Hartmann 1989, 99). Clearly, not every new issue on the women's rights agenda during this time period was the exclusive product of feminist activism. Yet, the women's movement has often been crucial in, as the feminist slogan goes, making the personal political by moving matters once considered private, inappropriate for public discussion, or unrelated to politics onto the political agenda. This change is significant because the new issues often entailed a set of assumptions or consequences related to the appropriate role of government in eradicating inequality and to women's position in society, the economy, and the family. This shift in the types of policies being considered under the women's rights rubric contributed to a rethinking by party elites of the linkage between women's rights issues and the parties' electoral constituencies.

Finally, a central theme of feminist rhetoric has been to draw attention to the latent political clout of women as well as to encourage women's political activism. As fifty-one percent of the population, women comprise a potentially powerful voting bloc. From the beginning, the second wave has sought to claim representation of all women in an effort to establish the strongest possible bargaining position. As NOW and other women's rights organizations shifted toward a greater emphasis on electoral and party politics in the late 1970s, this strategy was increasingly employed (Costain and Costain 1987). The emergence of the so-called gender gap in 1980 helped activists appeal to political elites on the basis of the women's vote. In particular, NOW's leadership, faced with the imminent defeat of the ERA and the election of a president opposed to most of its agenda, seized on the gender gap as evidence of the power and relevance of feminism. Feminists Eleanor Smeal (former NOW president) and Bella Abzug both authored books asserting that the gender gap would be the key to women's political dominance, while NOW pushed the gender gap in monthly updates to the press. Gender gap arguments were directed at the parties and elected officials. The term "gender gap" was first used in a policy paper written by NOW for presentation at the Democratic party's general meeting in 1981 and was also employed as a strategy for convincing legislators in states that had not ratified the ERA of the electoral consequences of opposing the feminist agenda (Mueller 1988a; Bonk 1988; Smeal 1984; Abzug 1984).

Despite the claims of women's movement activists, scholars have argued that women do not behave as a traditional voting bloc. Unlike traditional ethnic or racial voting blocs, women do not overwhelming recognize their gender as a meaningful part of their identity or as politically relevant and they do not necessarily support female candidates (Bennett 1986). Others have pointed to myriad other issues and factors that contribute to the gender gap in voting and public opinion, many of which are not directly related to women's rights issues or feminism (cf. Cook and Wilcox 1991; Erie and Rein 1988; Miller 1988; Conover 1988; Mansbridge 1985).

Yet perceptions are often as influential as reality. By sensitizing political elites to the potential influence of women's votes and by forwarding the idea that women voters are influenced by women's rights issues, the women's movement has contributed to the changing context of women's rights politics. Before the emergence of the modern women's movement, both parties and their candidates limited their few appeals to women voters to symbolic actions, such as the appointment of a few token women to positions within the party and its administrations (Costain 1991). The establishment of the Kennedy Commission is often viewed as the first break in this model and as a shift toward actual policy proposals as a strategy for appealing to women voters (Harvey 1998; Costain 1991), although it is not at all clear that this was the intent of the Kennedy administration given that commissions are generally designed to create the appearance of action rather than action itself; indeed, Women's Bureau Director Esther Peterson proposed the Commission as a means of deflecting attention from the ERA as a policy proposal (Hartmann 1989). Regardless of Kennedy's intentions, the publicity afforded the Commission and the extent of the data on sex discrimination it produced created a political climate in which Kennedy faced considerable pressure to take real action on women's rights policy. In the following presidential elections of 1964 and 1968, however, neither party's candidates particularly appealed to women voters by way of commitment to women's rights public policy.

The first post–second wave electoral campaign—1972—marked the beginning of significantly different strategies vis-à-vis women voters on the part of both parties. While neither party made women's issues a particular feature of their campaigns in the 1970s (Davis 1991), it is significant to note that efforts to attract women voters were more likely to emphasize women's rights issues, rather than symbolic actions such as appointments, than had been the case in previous campaigns. In the 1980s, the parties' approaches to appealing to female voters diverged. Democrats emphasized their commitment to feminism and women's rights. This approach was particularly evident during the 1984 campaign, when candidates for the Democratic nomination publicly courted feminist organizations and the party's nominee, Walter Mondale, chose a female running mate at the suggestion-cum-demand of NOW. Republicans, on the other hand, adopted the position that women voters were neither a monolithic group nor uniformly committed to feminist ideals. Using advanced polling and focus group techniques, Republicans focused non-gender-specific appeals toward the women voters they believed the GOP (with its emerging antifeminist position on many issues) was most likely to attract (Costain 1991; Mueller 1988a; Bonk 1988).

Yet the gender gap remains a potent political issue for both parties. While Republicans have largely maintained their opposition to many women's rights policies, their emphasis on child care and other economic and work-related issues of interest to women in later elections reflects their continuing efforts to appeal to women voters (Sanbonmatsu 1996). As Witt (1985) points out, the strategy adopted by the GOP in the early 1980s to basically cede some demographic groups of women, such as single working women, to the Democrats suffers from the inherent flaw that it is the ceded groups that are experiencing the greatest relative growth, while other groups of women, such as married women who do not work outside of the home, make up an ever-smaller portion of the population. After 1984, Democrats, on the other hand, sought a more mainstream image by distancing themselves from feminist organizations and the perception of a party controlled by so-called special interests. Both parties, however, remain committed to seeking out women voters.

Thus, the effect of the women's movement on the context of women's rights has been threefold: connect women's rights to the other social movements of the time, expand the political agenda for women's rights, and alert the parties to the potential power of women voters. The first linked women's rights to a set of characteristics, ideals, and people to which various groups of Americans were differently predisposed to favor or oppose. The second helped create a political agenda that was of differing appeal to each party's coalition. The third shaped the links perceived by elites between the parties' relative positions on women's rights and their electoral fortunes vis-à-vis a group that had been largely disregarded in the past, the more than half of the electorate that is female.

Organized Opposition. Finally, the countermobilization against women's rights, the antifeminist movement, has had a major impact on how elites and the public view women's rights. This movement came about in response to the passage of the ERA in 1972 and the Supreme Court's establishment of abortion rights in 1973 (*Roe v. Wade*) and is linked more broadly to the social conservatism of the New Right, which emphasizes traditionalism and religious values. While the earlier conservative movement represented by the 1964 Goldwater candidacy included traditionalist aspects (Brennan 1995), social conservatism is in many ways antithetical to the economic, libertarian conservatism of that movement (Klatch 1987). Social conservatism has its roots in the backlash against what many Americans perceived as the excesses of the 1960s—lack of social order, lawlessness, sexual promiscuity, and civil unrest (Miller and Levitin 1984). However, what Richard Nixon termed the Silent Majority did not emerge as a full-scale movement until the ERA and abortion provided the impetus (Himmelstein 1990).

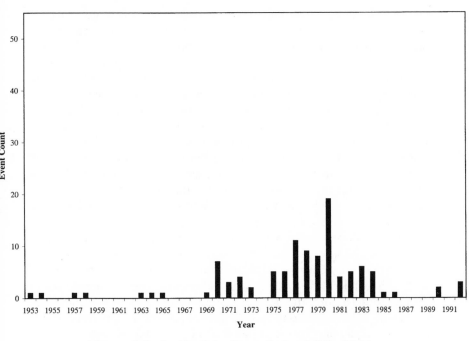

Figure 5.5. Antifeminist Event Series, 1953–1992.

Figure 5.5 provides a sense of the presence of the antifeminist movement (see the Appendix for a description of the event count methodology) on the national political scene. While there is a noticeable increase in antifeminist activities in 1970, the real growth is largely found over the late 1970s, culminating in 1980, and like the women's movement (see Figure 5.4) falling off across the early 1980s. As the graph shows, national-level antifeminist activity never approached the level of activity of the women's movement. The opposition's efforts tended to be focused at the subnational level (although Conover and Gray [1983] find the impact and power of antifeminism to have been exaggerated at the state level as well), where ERA ratification was opposed state by state. The women's movement, on the other hand, was notoriously late in organizing state and local efforts to support the ERA and other women's rights policies (Davis 1991). Furthermore, a focus on events may understate the impact of prominent antifeminists such as Phyllis Schlafly and others in the national debate. The press, focusing on conflict, often turned to Schlafly to provide a counter to pro-ERA and pro–women's rights positions, even when no actual opposition event occurred.

Like the women's movement, the opposition contributed to a restructuring of the debate over women's rights. During the surge of women's rights legislative activity in the early 1970s, feminists were largely successful in their efforts to frame women's rights as beneficial to all women. As traditional opponents, such as organized labor and protection feminists, backed off or changed sides, the women's movement was able to almost unilaterally define women's rights issues, and they did so by emphasizing their universal appeal and benefit to women and society as a whole.

The emergence of a countermovement changed that context. Instead of a boon to women, the antifeminist movement framed women's rights as an attack on the traditional family, a threat to more traditional and dependent women, especially housewives, a perversion of the natural order, and an intrusion of government into the private lives of Americans. Led by Schlafly, the antifeminist movement insisted that the ERA, and more generally, feminism, would lead to such unpopular outcomes as unisex toilets and pregnant women in military combat. Schlafly succeeded in touching on the fears of housewives, who felt their position and security eroding in the midst of widespread societal change; religious fundamentalists, who believed the nuclear family with a dependent and subservient wife to be divinely commanded; and Catholics and others who opposed abortion and contraception (Mansbridge 1986). The ERA and *Roe* provided the impetus, but the New Right continued its active opposition to women's rights for the remainder of the period of study in a variety of organizational forms that were alternatively issue specific, generally antifeminist, or broadly New Right, such as the Moral Majority and the Christian Coalition.

The antifeminist movement has thus been a major counterbalance to the effect of the women's movement, contributing to a change in the alignment of interests around the issue. Support for gender equality grew rapidly across the 1970s, yet while Americans tended to favor the general principle of equality, support for the specific consequences of that equality elicited less uniform responses, particularly when the status quo was called into question (Mansbridge 1986). The antifeminist component of the New Right changed the debate by articulating consequences of women's rights that many Americans found distasteful, uncomfortable, or undesirable. Women's rights opponents successfully persuaded many Americans that feminism destroyed the family, was in opposition to religious values, and would lead to societal breakdown. As a result, the emergence of an antifeminist movement created lines of cleavage where once (if briefly) few had existed.

While the women's movement politicized some women, the antifeminist movement politicized others, particularly religious women and those who do not work outside the home. More broadly, antifeminism was part of an emerging socially conservative Right, consisting in large part of religious fundamentalists, who opposed what they saw as a breakdown of societal norms and traditions. While social conservatism had existed prior to the women's movement, the salience of women's rights issues brought new individuals—male and female—into the movement and galvanized those already sympathetic (Himmelstein 1990). Antifeminism was thus important not only in its impact on the political debate over women's rights, but also by its effect in creating a new constituency for party elites to factor into their position-taking calculus. The role of social conservatives as party coalition members in shaping the evolving response of the parties, particularly the GOP, to women's rights is considered in chapter 6.

Summary. Clearly, contextual changes have been central to the evolution of meaning associated with women's rights. The forty-year period examined here includes an unprecedented transformation in women's roles, important developments in the law, the social and political upheaval brought about by the movements of the 1960s, the emergence of a mass movement for women's rights, and the countermobilization against that movement. As a result, when citizens and elites thought about women's rights in 1980 they did so with a very different set of assumptions, frames, and associations than they had just twenty years earlier. Women's rights and feminism became associated with concepts and ideas in ways they had not been before; indeed, some of that with which women's rights became associated did not exist or had not been named in the 1950s. The ERA in 1980, for example, was not a fairly straightforward amendment that many believed would mainly eliminate various protective employment laws (the prevailing view in 1952), but was considered by many to be a fundamental rejection of women's traditional roles, an attempt at government intervention in the family, and a sign of general moral and spiritual decay (Klatch 1987; Mansbridge 1986). When an issue is understood in new ways, the politics surrounding it almost certainly shift, and the result, as I discuss later, can be quite significant for the relative positions that parties take.

Strategic Elites

An underlying assumption of this research is that elites behave strategically; that is, they make choices to achieve their goals, based on their beliefs about relevant other actors and variables. One way elites act strategically is by using issues as a means for attaining publicity, expanding their (or their party's or allies') base of support, or bettering their position vis-à-vis other elites. Elites have an incentive to attempt to shape debate over the issue in an advantageous manner or shift attention away from issues that do not advantage themselves, their party, or allies. Their issue-related efforts affect the politics of the issue both by their association with a side of the debate and by their efforts to shape the issue to their advantage. These individuals may be well-known, such as presidents and presidential candidates, members of Congress, and other prominent elites. The association, often purposeful, of the likes of Ted Kennedy, Jesse Jackson, or Newt Gingrich with a certain issue positions provides powerful cues to other elites and the public about the nature of the issue. At times, strategic action has unexpected effects. Kennedy's attempt to woo women voters with the establishment of the President's Commission on the Status of Women, for example, resulted in the unearthing of extensive evidence of sex discrimination had consequences far beyond Kennedy's expectation: increased salience of women's rights, the creation of a network of politically active women sensitive to women's rights concerns, and eventually, the founding of NOW (Freeman 1975). Alternatively, individuals with little clout may use the issue to achieve greater political prominence. In their effort to use issues to gain political advantage, such individuals may introduce arguments and frames that can influence the debate over the issue.

Given the prominence of women's rights during the latter half of this forty-year period, it is not surprising that a number of elites have sought to use the issue to their advantage and shaped issue definition as a result. Perhaps the best known and most influential person in this category is Phyllis Schlafly. As noted in the discussion of the antifeminist movement earlier, Schlafly's efforts have had an important effect on the debate over women's rights and on the parties' evaluations of the electoral advantage of favoring or opposing women's rights. For Schlafly, opposition to women's rights resulted in nationwide exposure and impressive, if temporary, influence within the Republican party in a manner that had eluded her previously.

Before she took on feminism, Schlafly was a long-time Republican party activist and an unwavering anticommunist who focused almost exclusively on foreign affairs. She has been a delegate, alternative, or in attendance at every Republican convention since 1952, the same year she ran unsuccessfully for Congress. Perhaps her greatest claim to fame before the ERA was penning *A Choice Not an Echo* in 1964. In this thin volume, Schlafly decried the control of the mostly eastern liberal Republican establishment over the GOP presidential nomination and urged her party to adopt a strident conservative position as both correct and strategic. The book's title was a rallying cry for Goldwater Republicans, and Schlafly was a major Goldwater supporter. The Goldwater movement, however, was (temporarily) discredited by his disastrous showing in the 1964 presidential election, and Schlafly's prominence in the party suffered. In 1967 she ran in a divisive race for the presidency of the National Federation of Republican Women and was denounced as an extremist. She lost the election narrowly amid claims of vote fraud on the part of her opponent. Following the election, she launched a newsletter, *The Phyllis Schlafly Report*, in which she expounded her views on current events, particularly foreign affairs (Felsenthal 1981).

In February 1972, Schlafly first mentioned the ERA in her *Report*.

Schlafly's criticism of the ERA was framed in a more general condemnation of feminism; it was in this first article that Schlafly famously noted that women who did not like their position in society should "take up your complaint with God" (quoted in Mansbridge 1986, 110). After the ERA passed the Senate, Schlafly took on the ERA in earnest. She founded StopERA in October 1972 and soon devoted herself full-time to opposing ERA ratification (Felsenthal 1981). She formed state chapters, ran systematic training conferences on all aspects of political organizing, and was ubiquitous in every available forum to denounce the evils of feminism and the ERA. Her impact on ERA ratification was enormous, as a result of both the extent and discipline of her organization in the states and her ability to shape the debate. Her efforts were not in vain; many scholars and activists share Jane Mansbridge's view that "the Amendment would have been ratified by 1975 or 1976 had it not been for Phyllis Schlafly's early and effective effort to organize potential opponents" (1986, 110). When the ERA failed in 1982, Schlafly remained active in the Republican party and in the New Right, continuing to oppose feminist policy initiatives as the head of the Eagle Forum, which focuses on family issues, and as the leader of the Republican National Coalition for Life, which she founded in 1990 (Freeman 1993).

Schlafly's opposition to women's rights, like her belief in strong defense against the communist threat, is by all accounts a sincere reflection of her true convictions, despite the contradiction many have noted between her own life as an accomplished woman who travels widely pursuing her chosen profession as a political activist and her advocacy of traditional female roles (Felsenthal 1981). Yet there is little doubt that Schlafly is also a careful political strategist who has sought to shape the political debate over feminism in a way that increases her own power and influence, as well as that of her allies in the conservative movement. In doing so, she contributed to a transformation of the manner in which both elites and the public view the issue of women's rights with important consequences for the alignment of interests around the issue. She is, of course, not alone. The New Right generally has used women's rights to mobilize supporters and create a power base. In their attempt to do so, they have characterized feminism as selfish, antifamily, antireligious, and radical. By articulating a multitude of specific and general reasons to oppose feminism, Schlafly shaped the way in which Americans, both elites and the public, view women's rights.

Other elites have influenced the evolution of the issue of women's rights as well. By their association with the issue—chosen or ascribed—and in their characterizations of the problems at hand, these individuals have cast the women's rights debate in particular light. For example, the labeling of McGovern as the Triple A candidate (acid, amnesty, and abortion) in 1972 helped associate women's rights with radical demands. Fellow Democrat

Walter Mondale's 1984 presidential campaign contributed to the association of women's rights with dreaded "special interests," despite the fact that such issues are ostensibly of interest to more than fifty-one percent of the population as well as to the men who are their fathers, husbands, and sons. In neither case were these associations adopted by the candidates themselves, but encouraged by their opponents as campaign strategy. As this discussion and the historical overview in chapter 2 suggest, such short-term candidate-specific attacks can have a lasting effect on how an issue is viewed and understood.

Elites more sympathetic to women's rights have likewise employed such issues strategically as part of a broad electoral appeal or attack against the other candidate. Reagan's opponents seized on his approach to women's rights as campaign fodder. Carter's campaign, for example, repeatedly pointed to the Republican party's rejection of the ERA as symptomatic of the party's, and particularly Reagan's, insensitivity to women's concerns, linking opposition to women's rights to the so-called conservative revolution, and thus, the left-right dimension in American politics. Democratic strategy in 1980 involved painting Reagan as an extremist, and highlighting his opposition to what Carter called the "mainstream" ERA was part of this approach (Costain 1992, 95). Interestingly, while Carter emphasized his support of various women's issues as part of a more general electoral effort to discredit Reagan, the NOW board very publicly chastised Carter vis-à-vis his women's rights record in early 1980, claiming that while he might favor the ERA, he had not directed sufficient resources to the ratification effort (Clymer 1979). This too was clearly strategic on the part of feminist leaders. By taking the dramatic step of attacking Carter, even in the face of an opponent, Reagan, who was widely considered hostile to women's rights, the NOW board sought to demonstrate the independent power of the women's movement. While feminists were quite successful in their efforts to obtain concessions from Democrats at the 1980 convention (Germond and Whitcover 1981), these actions, along with similar highly public squabbles, contributed to a sense that women's rights issues were not mainstream at all, as Carter argued, but controversial and even extreme. While in all likelihood not the intention of the NOW board (and indeed, while refusing to endorse any candidate, the NOW convention retracted *opposition* to Carter in the fall of 1980), strategic action taken to achieve one goal—greater political clout—can have unintended consequences for issue meaning and association.

Issue Redefinition and the Politics of Women's Rights

From 1952 to 1992, various developments transformed the substantive and symbolic meaning of women's rights. The context in which women's rights issues were understood and debated changed dramatically. Women became more likely to work outside the home, had fewer children closer together, and were increasingly independent both financially and psychologically from men (Klein 1984). As a result, many American women came face-to-face with the reality of discrimination in ways they had not previously, as well as developing new interests and needs that often suggested public policy solutions. Legal developments helped move some items off the political agenda, dissolving old divisions and providing space for new agenda items. The Court's establishment of abortion rights helped add a new and controversial issue to the women's rights debate. Social movements introduced powerful and contentious symbols and concepts into American political discourse. The reemergence of the women's movement in the late 1960s connected women's rights issues to the broader spectrum of rights-based movement demands. This was particularly the case for women's rights and civil rights, where legal developments, similarities in appeals, tactics, and language, and the shared experiences and roots of many activists made the linkage between expanded rights for women and racial minorities salient (Evans 1979). The second wave of the women's movement, and the antifeminist movement that emerged to oppose it, contributed to the expansion of the women's rights agenda; shaped the meaning and symbols associated with women's rights; politicized and mobilized citizens, many of whom were previously apolitical; and alerted party elites to the potential electoral impact of their adherents. Strategic elites used women's rights to enhance their own political position, shaping the meaning and agenda of women's rights in the process.

As a result, the issue of women's rights changed in ways that were consequential for the relative positions adopted by the parties. Before the late 1960s, the agenda for women's rights was largely (but not entirely) limited to a few equality concerns such as the ERA, discrimination in employment and benefits, and equal pay. The dominant women's rights cleavage distinguished between those who favored protection and those who favored equality. This division was generally, although not completely, reflected in the parties' positions. The equality position was compatible with the Republican party's preference for individualism and free markets. More importantly, the equality perspective fit with the interests of important members of the Republican coalition. In particular, employers favored the elimination of many regulations expected as a consequence of the major equality provision, the ERA. Furthermore, pro-equality businesswomen were active in the Republican grassroots, and also urged their party to support the equality position. For Democrats, on the other hand, the protectionist status quo was more consistent with both that party's ideological predisposition and its coalition of interests. Laws that sought to protect women from the negative impact of the free market were in keeping with the Democratic party's New Deal tradition of an active government looking out for the less powerful and oppressed. Important Democratic party constituencies, particularly organized labor, favored protectionism. Labor opposed equality, particularly the ERA, because it would remove protections they had fought to obtain for women workers. Not incidentally, protective legislation held down the competition for jobs since such legislation provided a powerful disincentive to hire women workers. In addition to labor unions, many of the women's groups that favored protectionism had ties to the Democratic party and encouraged its stance (Costain 1992).

The developments described in this chapter contributed to an important redefinition of women's rights. By the early 1970s, changes in the law had largely eliminated the protections being fought over, and most of the traditional proponents of protectionism, including women's rights organizations and eventually organized labor, adopted new positions in favor of legal equality for women. The second wave of the women's movement emerged, championing women's rights to both the general public and political elites within the context of the other rights-oriented movements that preceded it. The women's rights agenda of the second period (late 1960s/early 1970s) was initially dominated by equality concerns, including the ERA and prohibitions against sex discrimination in various areas of the law. In that context, what difference existed between the two parties' relative positions on women's rights largely faded as both parties sought to show their support for now largely noncontroversial women's rights agenda. Republicans continued to favor legal equality for women, while Democrats' reasons for opposing it had been eliminated.

This bipartisanship was short-lived. In the third period (roughly post-1973), the women's rights agenda quickly expanded beyond equality through the accomplishment of many equality goals and the addition of many new items to the agenda. Women's rights issues were increasingly linked to controversial movement politics and a general anti-traditionalist counterculture that alienated many Americans. An organized opposition to feminism emerged, creating substantial controversy over the issue of women's rights.

These developments shaped the parties' relative positions on women's rights. For the Republican party, the association of women's rights with what some perceived as radical movement and counterculture politics clashed with the party's established stance in defense of tradition. Many of the new items on the women's rights agenda implied nontraditional roles for women in the economy, society, and family, further contributing to this tension. Moreover, while the equality agenda had been largely limited to prohibitions against discrimination (policies that call for little government action or expenditure), a number of new items on the agenda entailed intervention or action on the part of the federal government (e.g., federally financed child care, displaced homemaker programs, affirmative action).

Such policies are generally antithetical to the Republican preference for limited government. Finally, women's rights was linked to civil rights by a shared movement tradition, language of rights, and in particular, similar public policy demands. Republicans had come to oppose a policy of government intervention on the part of racial minorities (Carmines and Stimson 1989), so to favor government activism to ensure women's rights seemed increasingly inconsistent.

For Democrats, the changing women's rights agenda fit well with the party's position in favor of an activist government and sympathetic posture vis-à-vis the oppressed and marginalized. The Democratic party had become linked to the social movements of the 1960s, particularly the peace, student, and civil rights movements, so the conception of women's rights as part of that lineage and tradition encouraged a positive response from Democratic elites; women's rights were part of a general Democratic party position on the side of those seeking to establish and defend their political and economic rights (Freeman 1987). As the party of civil rights (Carmines and Stimson 1989), the analogies between racial and sexual discrimination further fostered a connection between feminism and the Democratic party.

Most importantly, changes in the symbols and agenda of women's rights as an issue have led to changes in the perceived links between women's rights issues and important constituencies within both parties. For Democrats, the new symbols and agenda made a pro–women's rights stance an obvious strategy for appealing to the various social movement–related, rights-oriented groups that had come to identify with the Democratic party in the late 1960s and early 1970s. At the same time, many of the new programs and policies (such as child care, sexual harassment, and pregnancy discrimination) were viewed as attractive to the party's base of working-class women and to the growing number of professional women, once the province of the Republican party, who were moving toward the Democratic party at this time and whom the party sought to cultivate.

For Republicans, on the other hand, the identification of the new agenda with the women's movement alienated many of the traditionalist and socially conservative adherents who were becoming an ever larger and more powerful portion of that party's constituent base. The association of the women's rights agenda with social liberalism and the civil rights and other movements transformed the frames with which Republican elites evaluated women's rights policies. As women's rights were incorporated into the general category of oppressed or marginalized groups seeking policy benefits, they came in conflict with Republican positions on other issues, such as civil rights, labor, welfare, and so on. Unlike the equality policies that dominated the women's rights agenda in the 1950s and 1960s, the diversified agenda of the 1970s and 1980s included many more policies that required government action or outlay and interference in the economic and social structure, anathema to general conservative small government philosophy. Thus, the new definition of and agenda for women's rights was increasingly odious to important Republican constituencies. Traditional business interests objected to the interference with business practices that affirmative action, sexual harassment, pregnancy discrimination, and other women's rights employment policies represented. Socially conservative constituents opposed the progressive social, economic, and political roles for women that many of these new policies were viewed as codifying and affirming. In short, Republican party elites had to evaluate their position on women's rights issues with new frames and understandings as to the impact on their coalition of interests, leading to transformed GOP positioning vis-à-vis the Democratic party on women's rights.

It is important to note that substantive agenda change is only one aspect of the evolution of the issue of women's rights and is only partially responsible for the changing party positions we have observed. Even when the agenda remained the same, changes in the symbols and meaning of women's rights shaped the parties' responses. I have argued that Republi-

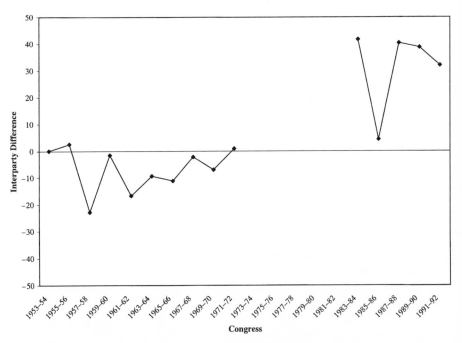

Figure 5.6. Interparty Difference in Cosponsorship of the Equal Rights Amendment, House, 1953–1992.

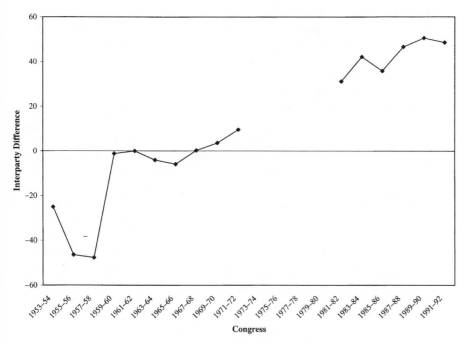

Figure 5.7. Interparty Difference in Cosponsorship of the Equal Rights Amendment, Senate, 1953–1992.

cans were less comfortable with the new women's rights agenda than they had been with the previous equality-dominated agenda. Yet the transformation of the parties' relative positions extended to equality issues as well. The ERA provides a case in point; Figures 5.6 and 5.7 show the interparty difference in ERA cosponsorship (percent Democrats cosponsoring any ERA bills minus percent Republicans doing so) during this period (with a ten-year gap following the passage of the ERA in 1972). Clearly, there has been a significant partisan shift on the ERA, the major equality issue for much of this period. The language of the amendment is virtually invariable across this forty-year period; what changed were the meanings associated with the ERA specifically, and feminism generally, as well as the composition of the parties' coalitions and the manner in which elites evaluated the utility of women's rights support for their goals. The ERA meant one thing in the 1950s and something very different by the 1980s, and that different meaning contributed to very different position-taking by both parties.

The symbols and meanings associated with women's rights have been transformed across this period. Women's rights once pitted equality feminists against protection feminists and employers against labor. While the concept of women's rights contains an aspect of a challenge to traditionalism throughout this entire period, the various developments I have described here have made that dimension far more salient. Women's rights issues came to be seen as part of a broader culture war. Even the ERA did not escape this transformation; indeed, it was one of the main instigators of the change. In the 1950s, it had been the prime battleground for protection versus equality; by the early 1970s, it was widely seen as a means to insert into the Constitution a principle with which few disagreed. Yet as the decade progressed, the ERA became associated with a whole set of symbols and ideas that appealed to some groups of people and repelled others. The result was the partisan realignment witnessed in Figures 5.6 and 5.7.

The developments described in this chapter brought about a transformation in party elites' perceptions of the connection between women's rights and party constituencies. It is these two additional variables—the parties' constituency bases and the party elites themselves—that provide the rest of the story vis-à-vis the causes of partisan transformation on women's rights. The impact of those factors on women's rights party realignment are examined in chapter 6.

CHAPTER SIX

Shifting Coalitions and Changing Elites

CHAPTER 5 reviewed the evidence of substantial disruption of the women's rights issue equilibrium and the redefinition of women's rights. Both contributed to the realignment of the parties' relative positions on women's rights. In this chapter, I examine two additional factors proposed as possible contributors to the transformation and polarization of the parties' positions on women's rights: changes in each party's coalition of interests and in the composition of the elites themselves. Much of what I consider here is related to, or meaningful because of, the issue-specific developments described in chapter 5. Other aspects are independent of those developments, but with complementary effects on the direction of party positioning.

This chapter is divided into two major sections. First, I consider changes in the composition of the parties' coalitions relevant to the parties' positions on women's rights. Second, I examine the role of party elite membership change, membership turnover generally and specifically the increasing numbers of women, in accounting for the observed partisan transformation on women's rights. For the most part, I focus on Congress in an effort to track both effects. Doing so allows me to most systematically relate coalition and elite changes to the parties' positions on women's rights. I note comparative expectations and examine other types of evidence when appropriate.

COALITIONS: THE CHANGING COMPOSITION OF THE PARTIES' BASES

The interest coalitions of both the Democratic and Republican parties have experienced changes relevant to women's rights during this time period. In this section, I focus on two important and related shifts in the composition of the parties' coalitions. First, I examine the interrelated devolution of the Democratic Solid South and rise of social conservatism within the GOP and their impact on party alignment over women's rights. Second, I investigate the effects of the increasing ideological polarization of the parties at a time in which support for women's rights became ideologically structured.

Broadly, the hypothesized effect of party coalition change is as follows:

When the interests associated with one or both parties change in some manner that is relevant to the issue in question, party elites, particularly following issue equilibrium disruption, will shift their position on the issue in response. If a party's coalition changes, but there is no relationship between the interest(s) in question and the issue, then we do not expect to observe party issue position change. If an issue is of concern to a component of a party's coalition, but that part of the coalition remains stable, change in the party's issue position is again not predicted. Thus, the party coalition hypothesis requires (1) that a shift occur in the coalition of one or both of the parties and (2) that the coalition change involve interests with preferences vis-à-vis women's rights. An alternative type of coalition development can be consequential as well. As I have indicated, for party coalition change to be meaningful for the parties' alignment over an issue it must involve a component or aspect of the parties' coalition with preferences vis-à-vis the issue. Yet, as chapter 5 demonstrates, the connections between issues and interests can evolve over time. Thus, an alternative requirement of the party coalition hypothesis is (3) that an aspect of the party's coalition revises or establishes its perspective on the issue. Thus, while the focus of this chapter is on the ways in which coalition *change* can contribute to party realignment, we will also continue to explore how a change in the connection between issue and coalition can affect the parties' relative positions.

It is important to distinguish conceptually between party elites, such as members of Congress and party leaders, and the parties' coalitions of interests. Party elites are the individuals who comprise the party in government and as an organization. In general, party elites are identifiable in a straightforward manner. While there may be a few prominent partisans who do not hold elected office or serve in an official position of party leadership—for example, a Jesse Jackson or a Rush Limbaugh—by and large it is possible to define who the elites are and to formulate a research design to observe their behavior and infer their positions.

When we talk of party coalitions, on the other hand, the concept is more ambiguous and the identification and measurement issues more complicated. By party coalition I mean the general array of interests associated with each political party. This association is reflected in various ways and takes on many possible forms: identifiers, voters, convention delegates, funding sources, activists, and organized allies. What these various actors have in common is that the parties rely on their support, whether it be in the form of votes, money, effort, or time. Moreover, the parties are distinguished by the particular set of interests that generally provide that support to each party. Said another way, Democratic identifiers, voters, delegates, funding sources, activists, and organized allies tend to differ from their Republican counterparts on the basis of various demographic characteristics and policy preferences (cf. Kessel 1988; Monroe 1983; Page 1978). Business interests are generally associated with the Republican party, while organized labor is associated with the Democratic party, to provide just one example. These differing interests are important because they comprise the broad coalitions of support on which each party depends for electoral success. This is not to say that Democrats are indifferent to at-tracting support from business interests—on the contrary!—or that Re-publicans do not attempt to appeal for the support of unionized workers, sometimes quite successfully. It is simply to recognize that the parties' sources of support differ, not absolutely, but systematically enough to dis-cern tendencies. As a result, each party represents a particular coalition of interests.

How then to go about the task of identifying the composition of each coalition, observing any change over time, and linking those interests to women's rights? For this time period—1952 to 1992—we are confronted with more than a few measurement challenges. The most critical is our lack of surveys or other similar instruments to determine the preferences of var-ious interests vis-à-vis women's rights prior to the 1970s. While we might be able to infer the preferences of organized groups from statements and actions, there are few available surveys of party activists or delegates prior to the early 1970s, reliable data on fundraising sources do not exist prior to the establishment of the Federal Election Campaign Administration in 1974, and while the voter surveys conducted by the National Election Studies cover the entire period examined here, there are no consistent items related to women's rights prior to 1970. Thus, the crucial task of linking parties to interests, and those interests to women's rights, is some-what confounded.

To observe coalition change across the entire period of study and to re-late those interests in question to women's rights, I focus on a number of indicators. In addition to measures that tap the concept directly, I also em-ploy an indirect approach to tracking changes in the parties' coalitions. Specifically, because direct measures of the parties' sources of support and their preferences vis-à-vis women's rights (e.g., fundraising sources, con-vention delegates) are difficult to come by prior to the early 1970s, I use the composition of the parties' delegations in Congress to approximate the composition of the parties' coalitions. Members of Congress are party elites, but in the aggregate they can provide some indication of the composition of the party's coalitions. As one interest begins to comprise a larger portion of the party's coalition, we can expect to see this shift re-flected in the composition of the party's Congressional delegation, which represents the coalition. The relationship is not direct, given the local vari-ation in party character, the role of electoral factors not related to policy (most notably, incumbency), and the vagaries of the federal election system. Thus, in looking at the parties' Congressional delegations in an attempt to track the composition of the parties' coalitions over time, it is important to keep in mind the disparity between measurement and concept. With that caveat, it is possible to attain a sense of the composition of the parties' coalitions with the Congressional data. Comparative statistics from sources more equivalent to the coalition concept and other evidence are discussed as well.

Social Conservatism and the South

A number of scholars have both noted various party coalition shifts across this time period and attributed party realignment on women's rights to certain of these shifts, particularly the rise of conservatism generally, and social conservatism specifically, within the Republican party (cf. Melich 1997; Costain 1991; Hartmann 1989). Relatedly, after a period of declining party unity, Democrats and Republicans in Congress became increasingly polarized beginning in the early 1970s. Figures 6.1 and 6.2, which show the median party unity scores for Republicans and Democrats in both chambers over time, provide evidence of this development. Party unity votes are those on which a majority of voting Democrats oppose a majority of voting Republicans. A member's party unity score indicates on what percentage of those votes she voted with the majority of her party. The median score for each session provides a sense of the level of unity within the party. The greater the extent of member agreement with their fellow partisans, the higher the unity.

This increasing cohesion and polarization have been attributed to increasing intraparty homogeneity within both parties, brought about by declines in the relative sizes of the conservative Southern wing of the Democratic party and of the liberal/moderate wing of the Republican party (Rohde 1991; Kessel 1988). The causes of these shifts are myriad and include the enfranchisement of Southern blacks, deliberately race-based appeals to Southern whites by the Republican party in an effort to drive a wedge into the Democratic Solid South (the so-called Southern Strategy, first embodied by Goldwater's 1964 campaign), the aging and straining of the New Deal coalition, and various institutional and electoral reforms (Rohde 1991; Carmines and Stimson 1989; Petrocik 1981).

While intraparty homogeneity increased, the parties' coalitions have also become more ideologically distinct in ways that have been meaningful for their positions on women's rights. In the Republican party, the growing power and presence of social conservatives (or the New Right) have been particularly consequential (Melich 1997; Costain 1991; Hartmann 1989). Social conservatives have been a part of the conservative movement within

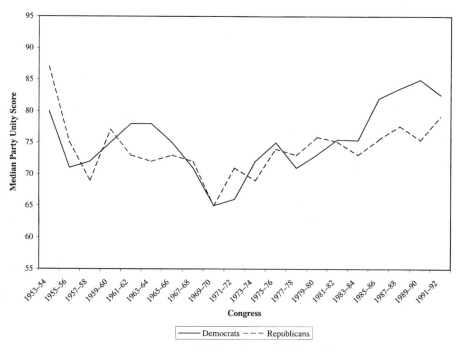

Figure 6.1. Median Party Unity Score, Democratic and Republican
Parties, House, 1953–1992.

the Republican party since Goldwater's 1964 candidacy (Brennan 1995)
and are linked to what Nixon called the Silent Majority of the late 1960s
and early 1970s—citizens alienated and dismayed by the perceived lawlessness, radicalism, and anarchism of the 1960s (Miller and Levitin 1984).
Social conservatism first emerged as a full-fledged movement in reaction to
women's rights, especially the ERA and abortion rights in the early 1970s,
although its agenda is broader, including such concerns as the separation
of church and state, social welfare, and states' rights (Himmelstein 1990).
Social conservatives clearly oppose the vast majority of feminist proposals,
viewing feminism as an attack on the family, religiously ordained sex roles,
and social order (Klatch 1987). As social conservatives became increasingly
important to the electoral strategy of Republican elites and made up an increasingly active part of that parties' constituent bases, the GOP was forced
to adjust and develop its positions on women's rights issues accordingly.

In addition—and not unrelated—the disintegration of the once Solid
South has had implications for the composition of both parties (Rohde
1991). At the presidential level, the South can no longer be considered a

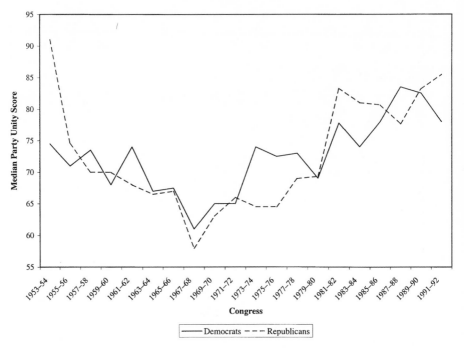

Figure 6.2. Median Party Unity Score, Democratic and Republican Parties, Senate, 1953–1992.

surety for Democratic candidates as greater numbers of Southern voters throw off tradition to vote Republican. In Congress, the Democratic delegation, once dominated by Southerners, particularly in positions of seniority, has become more moderate, liberal, and Northern since 1958. As time progressed, Southern states and districts began to slowly elect Republicans for the first time since Reconstruction. These developments are linked to the increasing identification of blacks (and civil rights) with the Democratic party and the weakening connection between white Southerners and the Democratic party. Here again the causes are rooted in the resolution of long-term tensions within the Democratic New Deal coalition (particularly between white Southerners and blacks) as well as a deliberate strategy on the part of Republicans to use racial and social conservatism to pry white voters away from the Democratic party. These changes have been both a cause of and reaction to the transformation of the parties' relative positions on civil rights (Carmines and Stimson 1989).

This regional shift is important for women's rights as well; to the extent that Southerners represent a distinct set of policy preferences and attitudes—specifically social conservatism and traditionalism, as well as an inclination toward states' rights and a mistrust of the federal government— the decline of the strength of Southern conservatives (voters, delegates, and so on) in the Democratic party has been meaningful for the calculus of party elites vis-à-vis women's rights. Furthermore, as I have argued, the establishment of the Democratic party as the party of civil rights in the 1960s (Carmines and Stimson 1989) was also significant for women's rights. As the issue of women's rights became linked with that of race, opposition to the former appeared increasingly incompatible with the Democratic party's position on the latter. Likewise, Republicans were forced to reevaluate their position regarding women's rights as it became increasingly seen as part of a larger effort to use government to eradicate forms of discrimination. Republicans, especially conservatives, had come to oppose that policy with regard to race, and thus extended that opposition to women's rights.

Measuring social conservatism across this forty-year time period is a difficult task. The phenomenon itself did not exist in any politically meaningful way prior to the early 1970s. Measures of general ideology do not tap into the subtle distinction between social conservatism and general ideology that is important to understanding women's rights politics and are generally not available in studies (e.g., the National Election Studies) prior to the early 1970s. Few surveys ask the sorts of religiosity or relevant policy questions consistently, or at all, that would allow us to identify social conservatives and link them to parties across this time period. As is common with surveys, topics are not included until they become salient; as a result, the National Election Studies and other long-term surveys do not include items related to social conservatism until the mid-1970s. This measurement deficiency thus tells us something about the phenomenon; apparently pollsters and other political observers did not consider social conservatism particularly important prior to the mid-1970s.

With these limitations in mind, I focus on a rough indicator that represents social conservatism. The indicator is the portion of each party's coalition that is from the South, providing a measure of the regional composition of each party's coalition. As is always the case with what amounts to dummy variables for the South, such a gauge provides the simplest possible representation of myriad social, economic, religious, and historical characteristics. However, the South has displayed a clear predisposition with regard to social conservatism and particularly women's rights during this period; for example, nine of the fifteen states that failed to ratify the ERA were Southern, and of the ten states of the Solid South, only one (Texas) ever ratified (Mathews and De Hart 1990). More generally, evangelical Christian strength, a central component of social conservatism, tends to be concentrated in the South (Wald 1987). The South can thus be conceived of as a way to observe the dual phenomenon of increasing social conservatism within the GOP, and concomitant declining relevance of Southern conservatives within the Democratic party. While the Republican Southern strategy relied initially on racial conservatism, it certainly involved an appeal to social conservatism as well, and the success of that strategy is reflected in the growth of Southern Republicanism (Himmelstein 1990). The use of the South dummy thus allows me to incorporate several related developments into one indicator.

I observe the regional composition of the parties' coalitions two ways. First, I examine the portion of each party's presidential coalition drawn from the Solid South.[1] Figure 6.3 shows the percentage of each party's electoral college votes that are from Southern states (Scammon, McGillivray, and Cook 1998). While these series clearly reflect the vagaries and idiosyncrasies of each election, a pattern can be discerned through the noise. In the 1950s, when Eisenhower defeated Democrat Adlai Stevenson, not once, but twice, some eighty percent of Democratic support came from Southern states. Seven and six of the ten Southern states gave their support to the Democratic ticket in 1952 and 1956, respectively. In the election of 1960, the portion of the Democratic coalition that was Southern dropped to twenty-nine percent. Still, seven of ten Southern states supported John Kennedy, and the portion of the GOP presidential coalition that was Southern continued to hover around ten percent, as it had for Eisenhower in the 1950s. Recall as well that 1960 was an extremely close election, suggesting that every coalition member was highly valued.

A dramatic shift occurs in 1964. Goldwater, the Republican candidate, captured only six states, but five of those were from the South (the other being his home state of Arizona). Thus, a full ninety percent of the Republican presidential coalition, such that it was, was Southern, while only fourteen percent of Lyndon Johnson's enormous winning coalition was drawn from Southern states. Only half of the Southern states went to Texan Johnson. While the large Southern GOP coalition in 1964 is something of an artifact of the complete rejection of Goldwater in every other region of the country, the fact that Goldwater was able to win five Southern states is attributed in large part to his overtly racist, states' rightist, and traditionalist campaign (Brennan 1995; Carmines and Stimson 1989).

In 1968, sixteen percent of Republican Nixon's victorious coalition was Southern, while thirteen percent of Democrat Hubert Humphrey's coalition was from the South. Like 1960, the 1968 election was relatively close, yet in 1960 twenty-eight percent of the Democratic coalition was Southern, a dramatic decline from the 1950s, but more than twice the portion

---

[1] Southern states: Alabama, Arkansas, Florida, Georgia, Louisiana, Mississippi, North Carolina, South Carolina, Texas, Virginia.

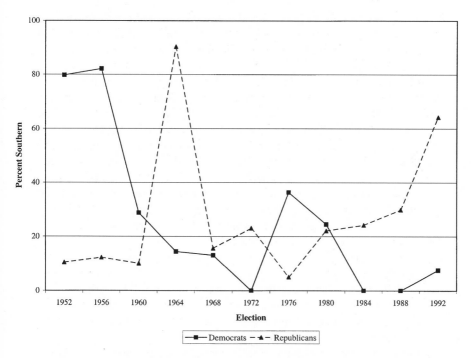

Figure 6.3. Percent Electoral College Votes from Southern States, Democratic and Republican Party Candidates, 1952–1992.

in 1968. Clearly, the degree to which Democratic candidates could depend on Southern states was on the decline. In 1972, every Southern state went Republican, making the South a fifth of the large Republican coalition. Following Watergate and with a fellow Southerner on the ticket, Democrats rebounded in 1976, taking all but one Southern state. More than a third of the Democratic presidential coalition in 1976 was Southern, while only five percent of the GOP presidential coalition was from the South. Yet 1976 appears to be the last gasp of the Democratic Solid South. In 1980, 1984, and 1988, Southern states always made up more than one-fifth of the successful Republican presidential coalitions; by 1988, Southern states are a full third of the GOP coalition. In 1992, Southerner Bill Clinton was the first Democrat to receive *any* Southern electoral college votes since 1980, but unlike fellow Southerner Carter, Clinton carried only three Southern states. Despite an entirely Southern ticket of Clinton and Al Gore, a full sixty-four percent of the GOP presidential coalition in 1992 was Southern.

Clearly, then, there has been a realignment of the regional composition of the parties' coalitions, a development that has meant that the South has been increasingly important to Republican presidential coalitions. It is not lost on Democratic strategists that the only successful Democratic presidential candidates in the last three decades—Carter and Clinton—are Southerners. At the same time, it is clear that the South is in no way as central to the Democratic presidential coalition as it was forty years ago. I do not mean to suggest that Democrats have written off the South as part of the party's coalition. However, the Democratic strategy for appealing to the South has largely taken the form of Southern candidates—Carter, Lloyd Bentsen as the vice presidential nominee in 1988, Clinton—rather than policy. Republicans, on the other hand, have not been particularly dependent on Southern candidates (unless one counts Texan George Bush), but have concentrated instead on issue appeals to Southern—and socially conservative—voters (Black and Black 1992).

A similar realignment of regional composition characterizes the parties' Congressional coalitions. Figures 6.4 and 6.5 show the percent of each party's House and Senate delegation that is from the Solid South. As these graphs show, Southern presence in the Democratic party delegation has been declining during this time period, while the Southern portion of the Republican delegation has been growing.

Historical narrative suggests a trajectory for social conservatism within the parties' organizations, particularly the GOP, similar to that reflected in these series. In the Republican party, the struggle between conservatives and moderates traces to the early postwar period and before. Goldwater's successful candidacy in 1964 involved a clear rejection of the mostly eastern seaboard moderate branch of the party. It is just this segment of the party that Phyllis Schlafly derides as "kingmakers" who brought the GOP to ruin in her 1963 book *A Choice Not an Echo*. The title itself calls for the Republican party to represent a real (read: conservative) choice against comparatively liberal Democrats, rather than only an echo.

The conservative movement within the GOP was briefly discredited after Goldwater's overwhelming defeat in the 1964 general election. Yet his very nomination and the reaction to it shaped the future paths of both parties, particularly with regard to their positions on race, a shift with consequences for the entire political system (Carmines and Stimson 1989). In 1968 and 1972, Richard Nixon reached out to Americans alienated by the perceived social anarchy and anti-traditionalism of the 1960s—the so-called Silent Majority (Miller and Levitan 1984). In the early and mid-1970s, members of the right wing of the Republican party sought out and developed alliances with religious leaders, particularly evangelicals and fundamentalists, over such issues as abortion and the ERA. In doing so, the right wing of

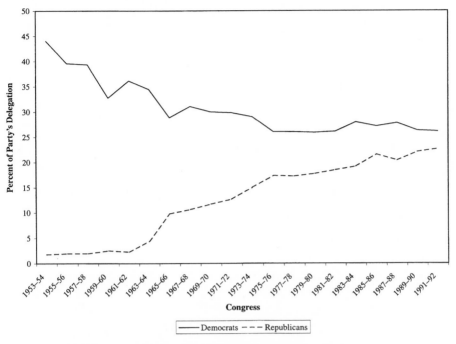

Figure 6.4. Decline of the Solid South in the House: Percent Democrats and Republicans from the South, 1953–1992.

the GOP shifted away from foreign affairs issues, such as anticommunism, toward social issues, including, but not limited to, women's rights. This shift was politically useful for those on the right as it mobilized new supporters to the cause (Baer and Bositis 1988).

Organizationally, Phyllis Schlafly's StopERA, founded in 1973, was one of the earliest opponents of feminism. She was joined by several other anti-ERA and antifeminist groups through the decade. In 1979, the Moral Majority was founded by evangelical minister Jerry Falwell at the encouragement of Republican activists. Along with other organizations that followed, such as the Christian Voice and the National Christian Action Coalition, the Moral Majority provided an organized expression of social conservatism. These organizations were developed by strategists for overtly political purposes—to mobilize a growing evangelical and socially conservative constituency into political action. From the beginning, this political activity was clearly intended by organizers to take place within the Republican party. The entrepreneurs responsible for creating these organizations

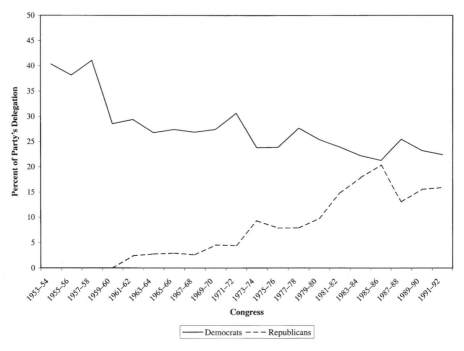

Figure 6.5. Decline of the Solid South in the Senate: Percent Democrats and Republicans from the South, 1953–1992.

were themselves active within the Republican right wing and viewed the organization of social conservatives as a means to increase the right's power within the GOP (Baer and Bositis 1988)

After a series of victories (e.g., Reagan's election, successful challenge of liberal Senators, ERA defeat), the New Right experienced something of a backlash in the mid-1980s, resulting in the dissolution of the Moral Majority as an organizational entity after the 1984 election (Baer and Bositis 1988). Social conservatives did not by any means disappear from the Republican scene, however. In 1988, television evangelist Pat Robertson campaigned for the Republican nomination. While ultimately unsuccessful, Robertson's candidacy was viewed as a sign of evangelical activism and relevance within the GOP. Roberston used the list of supporters from his run as the original market for the organization he founded after the 1988 election, the Christian Coalition. At the 1992 Republican convention, the Christian Coalition claimed to have three hundred delegates (some journalists, however, put the number closer to two hundred), including twenty members of the Platform Committee (Freeman 1993). This considerable presence—even only two hundred Christian Coalition delegates comprised ten percent of the total—suggests that social conservatives had become a major force in the Republican party.

Opposition to the ERA and abortion were major rallying events for organized social conservatism (Himmelstein 1990) and general antifeminism has been a consistent tenet of the New Right (Klatch 1987). Thus, the rise of social conservatism within the Republican coalition can be expected to have had direct bearing on that party's approach to women's rights. Social conservatives have expressed strong preferences on major women's rights issues, and have made such issues central to their activism in the GOP, with clear consequences for that party's positioning.

On the Democratic side, the decline of the Solid South has contributed to increased intraparty homogeneity. During the 1940s and 1950s, senior Southerners dominated the party leadership and often voted in opposition to the rest of their party; indeed, this practice was so common that the Republican and Southern Democratic voting bloc was given a name, the Conservative Coalition (Rohde 1991; Sinclair 1982). The growing number of moderate northern Democrats, the impact of the 1965 Voting Rights Act (i.e., the enfranchisement of black Southerners), and other institutional changes led to the decreasing presence and power of traditional Southern Democrats in the late 1960s and 1970s (Rohde 1991; Carmines and Stimson 1989). The remaining Democratic presence in the South tends to be concentrated in urban and other areas where blacks comprise a large portion of the population. Thus, even where Democratic support in the South remains, it is often of a very different nature than that twenty to thirty years ago.

For women's rights, this development has meant the decline of strength of a portion of the party's coalition likely to oppose women's rights, particularly in the issue's post-1970 form. A prime example is Senator Sam Ervin (D-NC) who campaign fervently against the ERA, offering numerous amendments to protect women's traditional roles during the 1972 Congressional debate, extolling the virtues of true womanhood, and extending his franking privilege to Phyllis Schlafly (Mathews and De Hart 1990). In 1972, Ervin had been in the Senate for almost twenty years, a not unusual tenure for a Southerner. While Ervin represents perhaps an extreme example, he is indicative of the general approach of most traditional white Southerners to women's rights, particularly in light of the emergent association of women's rights with civil rights. As Mathews and De Hart point out in reference to Ervin: "In historical perspective . . . it is not surprising that Sam Ervin should have opposed the Equal Rights Amendment. He had, after all, fought every piece of civil rights legislation presented when he was in the Senate. If he did not believe that black Americans had grievances that should be redressed by federal legislation, he could not be expected to concede the same to women" (1990, 40). Their analysis could be extrapolated more generally: If women's rights were analogous to civil rights, then most traditional white Southerners could be expected to oppose them. The declining power of such forces within the Democratic party was thus consequential for that party's evolving position on women's rights.

I have argued that the increasing social conservatism of the Republican party and the related decrease in the size of the Southern contingent of the Democratic party have contributed to the realignment of the parties' positions on women's rights. While social conservatism did not emerge as an organizational force until the 1970s, beginning, it should be emphasized, with antifeminist organizations, there is evidence that the Republican party has considered appeals to that emergent constituency an important strategy since at least the late 1960s, if not as early as 1964 (Melich 1996; Baer and Bositis 1988). The assumption is that social conservatives have been consistently opposed to women's rights across this time period, although it was only when a real movement on behalf of those rights emerged that social conservatism became organized (Himmelstein 1990).

Continuing to use the South as a crude indicator of social conservatism, I examine the relationship between social conservatism and women's rights across this time period in Table 6.1. This table shows the percent of Southern and non-Southern members of the House and Senate, respectively, who cosponsored any pro–women's rights bills for each session from 1953 to 1992 and the significance of the difference between the two groups. In every session in both chambers, non-Southern members are more likely to cosponsor women's rights bills than are Southern members. This finding is consistently significant in the House, with only three exceptions, all in the 1950s. There is some evidence in the House, then, that social conservative/Southern opposition to women's rights became stronger after the 1950s. This development still clearly precedes the parties' realignment. While the findings are not as consistently significant in the Senate, Southerners are significantly less likely to cosponsor women's rights legislation in more than half of the sessions across the entire time span. In short, then, this analysis supports the contention that social conservatives, as measured by the South, have generally been less supportive of women's rights. Thus, as the Republican party's coalition has become more socially conservative, and the Democratic party's less so, this development can be expected to have contributed to a movement of the parties in new and opposing directions on women's rights issues.

Significantly, the shift in Southern/social conservative loyalties clearly predates the shift in the parties' women's rights positions. The Southern

TABLE 6.1

Percentage of Southern and Non-Southern Members Cosponsoring Any Pro–Women's Rights Bills, House and Senate, 1953–1992

Congress	House			Senate		
	Southerners	Non-Southerners	Difference	Southerners	Non-Southerners	Difference
1953–1954	3.0 (100)[a]	5.6 (340)	−2.6	4.4 (23)	27.8 (90)	−23.4*
1955–1956	6.2 (97)	12.4 (340)	−6.2	23.8 (21)	53.0 (83)	−29.2*
1957–1958	33.7 (98)	60.5 (344)	−26.8***	17.4 (23)	41.0 (83)	−23.6*
1959–1960	15.5 (97)	15.7 (344)	−0.2	0.0 (20)	8.0 (88)	−8.0
1961–1962	15.5 (103)	37.6 (346)	−22.1***	0.0 (21)	3.4 (88)	−3.4
1963–1964	17.4 (98)	28.5 (344)	−11.1*	30.0 (20)	44.8 (87)	−14.8
1965–1966	17.0 (100)	31.4 (341)	−14.4**	13.6 (22)	36.1 (86)	−22.5*
1967–1968	26.5 (98)	40.8 (341)	−14.3*	10.0 (20)	41.9 (86)	−31.9**
1969–1970	45.9 (98)	65.6 (349)	−19.7***	25.0 (20)	42.5 (87)	−17.5
1971–1972	28.0 (100)	45.0 (342)	−17.0***	22.7 (22)	40.7 (86)	−18.0

(continued)

TABLE 6.1 (Continued)

Congress	House Southerners	Non-Southerners	Difference	Senate Southerners	Non-Southerners	Difference
1973–1974	26.7 (101)	43.4 (341)	−16.7**	5.0 (20)	16.1 (87)	−11.1
1975–1976	14.7 (102)	35.7 (339)	−21.0***	5.0 (20)	33.7 (86)	−28.7*
1977–1978	42.2 (102)	64.0 (339)	−21.8***	36.4 (22)	76.8 (82)	−40.4***
1979–1980	13.9 (101)	34.2 (339)	−20.3***	5.0 (20)	29.6 (81)	−24.6**
1981–1982	45.5 (101)	66.8 (343)	−21.1***	25.0 (20)	82.7 (81)	−57.7**
1983–1984	61.1 (108)	82.8 (331)	−21.7***	65.0 (20)	93.8 (81)	−28.8***
1985–1986	60.6 (109)	73.0 (330)	−12.4*	42.9 (21)	75.0 (80)	−32.1*
1987–1988	57.8 (109)	76.1 (331)	−18.3***	40.0 (20)	71.6 (81)	−31.6**
1989–1990	60.9 (110)	76.0 (333)	−15.1***	60.0 (20)	75.0 (80)	−15.0
1991–1992	60.6 (109)	81.6 (332)	−21.0***	85.0 (20)	89.0 (82)	−4.0

Note: N in parentheses.
* $p \leq 0.05$, ** $p \leq 0.01$, *** $p \leq 0.001$. Significance indicated by Z-test for the difference in rates between two sets of binomial data described in the Appendix. Membership totals may exceed 435 (House) or 100 (Senate) because of turnover during the session.

shift can be traced to the late 1950s/early 1960s in Congress and to 1964 specifically with regard to presidential coalitions. Republican strategists clearly regarded social conservatives and the South as important parts of the party's overall electoral strategy by the late 1960s (Melich 1996; Black and Black 1992; Baer and Bositis 1988; Phillips 1969).

Why did the changing social conservative/Southern composition of the two parties not register an impact on the parties' women's rights positions prior to the 1970s? A few processes appear to be at work, the most important of which is the issue equilibrium disruption described in chapter 5. As I argue, issue equilibrium disruption brings an issue to the attention of a wide spectrum of elites, accompanied by high saliency that increases the electoral relevance of the issue. Thus, while various developments may be occurring that might be expected to affect the parties' positions, it is not until the issue comes to the fore that the parties' relative positions are dramatically affected. Second, the parties did appear to be moving together in the 1960s, when the shift in the Southern composition of the parties' coalitions began.

General Ideology

More generally, the two parties' coalitions have long been distinguished ideologically (cf. Kessel 1988; Miller et al. 1986; McClosky, Hoffman, and O'Hara 1960). As I have argued, it is important to distinguish between general ideology and social conservatism in our understanding of women's rights politics. However, women's rights has been integrated into the left-right continuum to an increasing degree across this period. Before the early 1970s, traditional economic conservatives had reason to *favor* women's rights, as the issue was partly conceptualized as antiregulation. This relationship was not particularly strong, however, mostly because of the low salience and small agenda for women's rights during the earlier period. One of the effects of the issue changes described in chapter 5, however, was to link women's rights to liberalism generally. The evolution of the women's rights agenda, especially the expansion of the agenda to include items that necessitate government intervention or expenditure, was part of the cause. Another important factor was the connections established between race and women's rights. Before the mid-1960s, racial policy constituted a unique second dimension in Congressional decision making, but after that time it was largely subsumed into the left-right dimension (Poole 1997). Following that time, women's rights were linked to race, and thus by transitivity, to the left-right dimension as well.

Continuing to observe the parties' coalitions via the parties in Congress, I employ the D-NOMINATE scores developed by Poole and Rosenthal

(1997, 1991).[2] Poole and Rosenthal's algorithm estimates a unique position in two-dimensional space for each member in each session based on all nonunanimous (and non-near-unanimous) roll call votes. The first dimension, employed here, can be conceived of as representing placement on the left-right spectrum and has been shown to explain virtually all variation in roll call behavior throughout American history. The second dimension delineates major divisions within the parties. It has contributed only a small amount of additional explanatory power throughout American history and has been of declining importance since the late 1960s. The first dimension D-NOMINATE score is bounded by -1 and 1, with a positive D-NOMINATE representing a more conservative position (Poole 1997; Poole and Rosenthal 1997, 1991).

Figures 6.6 and 6.7 show the median D-NOMINATE score (first dimension) for each party in the House and Senate from 1953 to 1992. As expected, Republicans are consistently more conservative than are Democrats. Republicans were becoming less so, as represented by the party median, across the earlier portion of the series, but they began to move in a more conservative direction again in the latter half. In the House, this shift begins after 1977–1978, while in the Senate, the move is earlier, changing directions after 1971–1972. Democrats show less of a striking shift, but do appear to be moving in a more liberal direction in both chambers around the same time as Republicans are becoming more conservative.

For the general ideological polarization of the parties' coalitions, two factors appear to be at work vis-à-vis women's rights. First is change: There is evidence that polarization increased, particularly as represented by the Republican median. In the Senate, this shift begins in the early 1970s; in the House, the late 1970s. As such, the timing of these shifts does not exactly correlate with the shift in party positioning on women's rights, especially in the House, where we observed a dramatic shift in positioning in 1971–1972, but with a decline in ideological polarization until the late 1970s. Moreover, the consistent ideological divergence of the parties swamps the comparatively small increases in polarization. Yet, ideology has been important, for reasons related to the second factor: the development of a connection between the left-right spectrum and women's rights. While the degree of ideological divergence has varied somewhat over time, the Democratic and Republican coalitions are consistently and significantly distinguished by ideology. However, women's rights does not map onto the left-right spectrum particularly well before 1970, but does after that time, with consequences for the parties' positioning on women's rights.

[2] For the final two sessions, the 101st and 102nd, Poole and Rosenthal provide coordinates estimated by a slightly different algorithm, W-NOMINATE, making comparisons of those sessions' medians with the rest of the series inappropriate. Within the session, the scores provide a comparable indication of placement on the left–right spectrum.

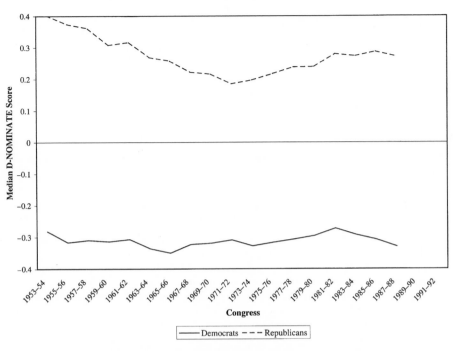

Figure 6.6. Median D-NOMINATE Scores, Democratic and Republican Parties, House, 1953–1988.

To examine the relationship between general ideology and women's rights support across this period, I compare the rate of pro–women's rights cosponsorship of liberal and conservative members of Congress in Table 6.2. Liberal and conservative members are classified by positive (conservative) and negative (liberal) D-NOMINATE scores. Obviously, this broad categorization misses a great deal of variation, but it does provide a basic delineation of the two groups.

This analysis generally confirms the expected relationship between general ideology and women's rights across this time period. Turning first to the House, liberals are more likely to cosponsor women's rights legislation than are conservatives in the first two sessions, but in the session immediately following those (1957–1958), conservatives are more likely to cosponsor than are liberals. In the next four sessions (1959–1966), conservatives and liberals are not significantly distinguished in their cosponsorship activity, and the direction of difference is inconsistent. In 1967–1968, liberals are significantly more active cosponsors, but in the next session (1969–1970), the difference between the two groups is statistically

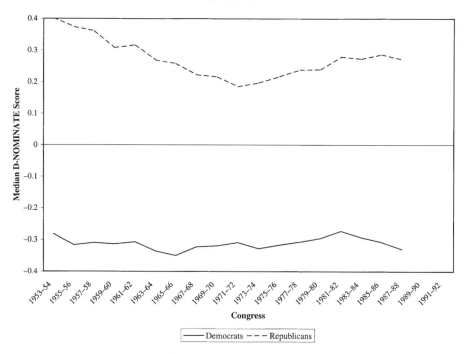

Figure 6.7. Median D-NOMINATE Scores, Democratic and Republican Parties, Senate, 1953–1988.

insignificant. This mixed pattern and lack of significance supports the contention that women's rights did not map particularly well onto the ideological spectrum before the early 1970s. Beginning in 1971–1972, however, the pattern changes sharply. With the notable exception of 1984–1985, liberals are always significantly and considerably (more than twenty-five points) more likely to cosponsor women's rights legislation than are conservatives after 1970. The significant finding in 1967–1968 suggests that the association of women's rights with liberalism may have been evolving since the late 1960s, but certainly after 1970, women's rights are clearly and strongly related to the left-right spectrum, in keeping with the arguments put forth in chapter 5.

The Senate findings further confirm the basic pattern. Before 1969, conservatives and liberals are either not significantly distinguished in their cosponsorship of women's rights bills or, as is the case in 1955–1956 and 1957–1958, conservatives are more active cosponsors. Beginning in 1969, liberals become significantly more likely to cosponsor women's rights bills than conservatives. There are a few exceptions to this rule; in 1973–1974

TABLE 6.2

Percentage of Liberal and Conservative Members Cosponsoring Any Pro–Women's Rights Bills, House and Senate, 1953–1992

Congress	House			Senate		
	Liberals	Conservatives	Difference	Liberals	Conservatives	Difference
1953–1954	8.5 (177)[a]	2.7 (258)	5.8***	16.3 (49)	31.0 (58)	−14.7
1955–1956	15.1 (192)	7.8 (244)	7.3*	36.0 (50)	57.4 (54)	−21.4*
1957–1958	49.2 (197)	59.0 (244)	−9.8*	19.2 (47)	51.8 (56)	−32.6***
1959–1960	15.1 (232)	16.7 (204)	−1.6	7.7 (65)	4.7 (43)	3.0
1961–1962	31.6 (215)	33.6 (229)	−2.0	3.3 (60)	2.0 (49)	1.3
1963–1964	28.7 (209)	24.0 (229)	4.7	43.1 (65)	40.5 (42)	2.6
1965–1966	29.4 (248)	26.7 (191)	2.7	33.3 (63)	29.6 (44)	3.7
1967–1968	45.6 (202)	31.1 (235)	14.5***	36.9 (65)	34.2 (41)	2.7
1969–1970	65.9 (205)	59.2 (235)	6.7	47.5 (61)	28.3 (46)	19.2*
1971–1972	57.8 (213)	26.3 (224)	31.5***	45.8 (59)	27.1 (48)	18.7*

(continued)

TABLE 6.2 (Continued)

Congress	House			Senate		
	Liberals	Conservatives	Difference	Liberals	Conservatives	Difference
1973–1974	54.0 (215)	26.1 (226)	27.9***	10.9 (64)	19.1 (42)	−8.2
1975–1976	44.4 (257)	12.3 (179)	32.1***	34.8 (69)	17.1 (42)	17.7
1977–1978	71.1 (256)	43.1 (179)	28.0***	79.1 (67)	50.0 (36)	29.1***
1979–1980	44.6 (249)	10.0 (190)	34.6***	34.4 (61)	10.5 (38)	23.9**
1981–1982	86.2 (217)	39.6 (220)	46.6***	83.3 (48)	59.6 (52)	23.7**
1983–1984	89.2 (241)	63.3 (196)	25.9***	93.7 (48)	84.3 (51)	9.4
1985–1986	73.0 (233)	67.2 (204)	5.8	77.6 (49)	58.0 (50)	19.6*
1987–1988	89.6 (240)	50.3 (199)	39.3***	81.0 (58)	44.2 (43)	36.8***
1989–1990	86.4 (286)	46.5 (155)	39.9***	91.9 (62)	39.5 (38)	52.4***
1991–1992	87.4 (269)	58.8 (170)	28.6***	96.9 (65)	72.2 (36)	24.7***

Note: N in parentheses.

*$p \leq 0.05$, **$p \leq 0.01$, ***$p \leq 0.001$. Significance indicated by Z-test for the difference in rates between two sets of binomial data described in the Appendix. Membership totals may exceed 435 (House) or 100 (Senate) because of turnover during the session.

conservatives are slightly more likely, but this difference is not significant. In the 1975–1976 and 1983–1984 sessions, liberals are more likely to cosponsor, but the difference is not statistically significant. Overall, in all but one case, liberals are more likely cosponsors after 1969, and the differences are significant in all cases but two. Once again, these data support the argument that women's rights became associated with liberalism after the late 1960s. As the parties are distinguished by ideology, and have become more so since the 1970s, this mapping of women's rights onto the left-right spectrum can be expected to have had considerable consequences for the alignment of the parties on these issues.

Conclusion

Driven by electoral goals, party elites take positions on issues that they believe will best satisfy and expand their coalition of interests. As the party's coalition changes in ways that are relevant to the issue in question, or as the relationship between the coalition and the issue evolves, we can expect the party or parties to adjust their position on the issue in response as part of strategic and purposeful electoral appeals. In this section, I identified two components or aspects of the parties' coalitions with distinct preferences vis-a-vis women's rights: social conservatism (measured roughly by the South), which while unorganized prior to the 1970s, is generally opposed to women's rights across this period of study, and general ideology, which has been consistently related to women's rights since the late 1960s and early 1970s. The predispositions of these groups with respect to women's rights are important because of the place of each in the parties' respective coalitions. The Republican party's coalition became more socially conservative during this time, while the Democratic coalition became less so. The parties' coalitions have also become slightly more ideologically polarized at a time when women's rights came to be associated with the left-right spectrum.

Three final points deserve note. First, the coalition changes detailed here came about in large part as a result of developments unrelated to women's rights. The decline of the Democratic Solid South, for example, has its roots in racial politics (Carmines and Stimson 1989). The growing ideological polarization of the parties is likewise attributed to various institutional and political developments (cf. Rohde 1991). At the same time, the politics of women's rights has contributed to the parties' changing coalitions as well. Social conservatism emerged as an organized force in large part in opposition to women's rights developments, specifically the ERA and *Roe v. Wade* (Himmelstein 1990). Thus, the processes have contributed one to another. The Republican party's coalition became more socially conservative for a number of reasons, which led it in a particular direction vis-à-vis women's rights, which further contributed to its social conservatism, and so on. While I am interested in the contribution of social conservatism to Republican opposition to women's rights, the causal arrow also moves in the other direction.

Second, this analysis emphasizes the interdependent nature of the three factors—issue, coalition, and elites—that form the center of the model I have put forward. Specifically, the ideological polarization of the parties mattered for women's rights in part because of changes in the issue detailed in chapter 5. As a result of various developments, women's rights took on left-right dimensionality in how they were and are understood and approached by elites and masses. This change in the issue of women's rights was important for the parties' positioning because the parties' coalitions are distinguished by ideology and became more so during the latter part of the period in question. Party coalitions and issue meaning are tightly related; one matters because the other does.

Finally, I have focused here on the major ideological cleavage between the parties' coalitions and the emergence of social conservatism. As discussion in earlier chapters shows, other specific coalition developments (many linked to issue redefinition; see chapter 5) have been important as well. While its influence may be declining somewhat, organized labor's shift on the ERA and other issues has contributed to the Democratic party's position taking. The civil rights and other social movements that became associated with the Democratic party during this era have increasingly viewed feminists as allies and helped feminists pursue policy goals within the party. Chapter 2 highlights the emergence of organized feminism and its eventual embrace as a recognized Democratic constituency with obvious effects on that party's position taking. The GOP chose to court antifeminists and social conservatives instead. More generally, the ways in which the parties viewed certain groups of women as their natural allies and pursued their votes have been consequential as well (Witt 1985).

ELITES: MEMBERSHIP REPLACEMENT
AND PERSONAL PREFERENCES

I hypothesize that variation in the parties' positions on issues can be explained by changes in the issue itself, the parties' coalitions, and the party elites whose actions, statements, and decisions create the parties' issue position. In this section, I consider the impact of the last factor—the elites themselves. Elite change can bring about shifts in the parties' positions in two main ways. First, new elites may have a different understanding of the relationship between the issue and the parties' electoral fortunes; that is, new elites may view the electoral utility of certain issues and positions differently than do previous elites of the same party. Given the considerable consistency of elite behavior over time, membership replacement is a likely mechanism for translating the transformed issue debate or new coalition politics in to new party positions. On the other hand, when issue redefinition occurs, change in the behavior of established elites is possible, potentially allowing established elites to serve as a conduit for the effects of issue change. Second, new elites may have different personal preferences regarding the issues. While electoral considerations are foremost in the minds of party elites, personal policy preferences and interests may also play a role in determining members' positions and activities on an issue, particularly during a period in which constituent and other cues are unclear. In this construction, the introduction of certain new elites may serve as a means for introducing members whose preferences differ systematically from their former colleagues. In this section, I first consider the alternative hypotheses of elite replacement or conversion as the mechanism for party change. I then consider the impact of a specific subset of elites—women— on the parties' evolving positions.

Replacement and Conversion

Changes in the actual elites who represent the party can be consequential by bringing in individuals with different understandings or beliefs about the relationship between issues and the parties' constituencies. This possibility represents the replacement expectation for party change. New elites can contribute to party change because they are in some manner systematically different from old elites, for example, by representing different constituencies. In this case, we expect new elites to play a role related to the impact of coalition change in that new elites matter when they represent the newer interests of the party's coalition. New elites can also be a mechanism for transmitting changes in issue meaning, definition, or agenda as their views are more likely to be affected by changes in issue meaning and to reflect an evolving understanding of the relationship between the issue and electoral constituencies. This argument simply assumes that elites that enter politics at different times may reflect different understandings and beliefs about the strategic value of certain public policies. In either case— whether new elites behave differently from old because of their different constituent bases or because they represent changed understandings of the strategic utility of the issue—the result is a change in the issue preferences of newer elites vis the older, which can contribute to change in the party's positioning. These sorts of explanations are consistent with the over- whelming evidence of consistency of elite behavior over time (Poole and

Rosenthal 1991; Carmines and Stimson 1989; Sinclair 1982; Asher and Weisberg 1978). Because elites tend to maintain consistent policy positions, membership replacement is a likely mechanism for party realignment.

Yet despite the general finding of consistent behavior, an alternative mechanism could be at work. The same work that finds elite behavior overwhelmingly consistent also suggests that change in policy definition or debate can lead to conversion, that is, a change in the behavior of existing members (Poole and Rosenthal 1991; Sinclair 1982; Asher and Weisberg 1978). We have seen that a change in the policy debate surrounding women's rights has occurred. It is possible that long-term elites reacted to those changes with new behaviors, and thus new positions, on women's rights; in short, they may have converted to new positions. In both cases—replacement and conversion—issue and coalition change matter. The question is what the mechanism for that impact has been. This is not a small concern—it is of central interest to our understanding of the process of party issue position change. A vast literature shows individual political elites to be overwhelmingly constant in their policy preferences over time, as expressed by their actions, with very few exceptions. Those deviations, however, are typically associated with issue change. The question, then, is whether the politics of women's rights are characterized by replacement or conversion.

To evaluate the role of new elites on the parties' evolving positions on women's rights, I again turn to the Congressional cosponsorship data introduced in chapter 3. As a basic test of the replacement and conversion hypotheses, I have divided House and Senate members into two groups, those elected before and after 1970. The 1970 cutoff is a crude demarcation of the kinds of issue equilibrium disruption and redefinition I have described. If the process is characterized by a replacement mechanism, members who entered office before 1970 should be more likely to evaluate and act on women's rights based on earlier conceptions of the issue and its relationship to their party's coalition of interests. As a result of the disruption of the equilibrium beginning around 1970, those elected after that year are expected to reflect the various issue and coalition changes detailed earlier. To evaluate this hypothesis, I compare the cosponsorship behavior of the two groups in both the Democratic and Republican parties for each session after 1970. For Democrats, if replacement is the mechanism, the expected difference is negative; newer elites (post-1970) should be more likely to cosponsor any pro–women's rights bills than those elected before 1970. For Republicans, on the other hand, if replacement characterizes this process the expected difference is positive, as newer elites (post-1970) are less likely to cosponsor than Republican elites who entered office before 1970. If replacement is not the mechanism, suggesting conversion, than the period in which elites took office should not distinguish the rates of cosponsorship of pro–women's rights bills between members of the same party.

The results of this analysis are presented in Tables 6.3 and 6.4 for the House and Senate, respectively. In general, the evidence that members elected after 1970 behave systematically differently vis-à-vis women's rights than do those elected before 1970 in either party or chamber—the replacement hypothesis—is quite weak. The strongest evidence of replacement is for Democrats in the House (see Table 6.3). With only one exception (1971–1972), the difference for House Democrats in every session is negative, as predicted, although only four of the ten negative differences are statistically significant. For House Republicans, however, the difference is also consistently negative, contrary to what the replacement model predicts. In only three sessions are Republicans elected before 1970 more likely to cosponsor pro–women's rights bills than Republicans elected after 1970, and the differences are not statistically significant in any of those cases; indeed, there are *no* statistically significant differences in the cosponsorship behavior of Republicans elected before and after 1970. House Republicans thus do not follow a pattern consistent with the replacement hypothesis.

The Senate findings (see Table 6.4) are even less supportive of the replacement hypothesis. With only three exceptions, differences for Senate Democrats are positive, in contrast to replacement expectations, and in no session are the differences between Democrats elected before 1970 and those elected after 1970 statistically distinguished from zero. Differences between Senate Republicans are also almost always positive, as predicted by the replacement model, with one exception. Yet differences in cosponsorship activity between Republicans elected before and after 1970 are not statistically significant in any session except 1981–1982.

Thus, these results generally run counter to the expectations of the replacement hypothesis. A possible explanation is that these findings are a function of the particular cutoff chosen. While 1970 represented a significant turning point for gender politics, the issue changes described in the preceding chapter evolved over a considerable period of time, with particularly rapid change in the late 1960s and 1970s. The coalition changes just examined likewise unfolded gradually, rather than abruptly. As a result, an exclusive focus on the 1970 demarcation may miss possible replacement effects. To consider that possibility, I compare the pro–women's rights cosponsorship rates of members elected before and after the gamut of elections from 1968 to 1978. Summaries of the results for each chamber and party are presented in Tables 6.5 and 6.6. A negative sign denotes a significant and negative difference between the cosponsorship rates of members elected before and after the indicated date. A positive sign means the

TABLE 6.3

Percentage of Members Elected Pre-1970 and Post-1970 Cosponsoring Any Pro-Women's Rights Bills, House Democrats and Republicans, 1971–1992

	Democrats			Republicans		
Congress	Elected pre-1970	Elected post-1970	Difference	Elected pre-1970	Elected post-1970	Difference
1971–1972	50.4 (228)[a]	50.0 (30)	0.4	29.3 (157)	24.0 (25)	5.3
1973–1974	41.9 (191)	54.4 (57)	-12.5	30.7 (127)	37.9 (66)	-7.2
1975–1976	31.4 (172)	42.7 (124)	-11.3*	16.3 (80)	25.0 (64)	-8.7
1977–1978	58.5 (130)	68.1 (166)	-9.6	43.8 (64)	53.1 (81)	-9.3
1979–1980	31.3 (99)	41.0 (183)	-9.7	11.3 (53)	17.1 (105)	-5.8
1981–1982	74.3 (70)	75.4 (179)	-1.1	35.7 (42)	47.7 (153)	-12.0
1983–1984	76.2 (63)	82.3 (209)	-6.1	59.3 (27)	74.3 (140)	-15.0
1985–1986	55.0 (60)	73.7 (198)	-18.7**	57.1 (21)	72.5 (160)	-15.4
1987–1988	74.6 (55)	86.5 (208)	-11.9*	33.3 (18)	55.4 (159)	-22.1
1989–1990	74.4 (43)	88.3 (223)	-13.9*	40.0 (15)	52.5 (162)	-12.5
1991–1992	79.5 (39)	88.8 (233)	-9.3	66.7 (15)	57.5 (153)	9.2

[a]*Note:* *N* in parentheses.

*$p \leq 0.05$, **$p \leq 0.01$, ***$p \leq 0.001$. Significance indicated by Z-test for the difference in rates between two sets of binomial data described in the Appendix. Membership totals may exceed 435 because of turnover during the session.

TABLE 6.4

Percentage of Members Elected Pre-1970 and Post-1970 Cosponsoring Any Pro–Women's Rights Bills, Senate Democrats and Republicans, 1971–1992

Congress	Democrats			Republicans		
	Elected pre-1970	Elected post-1970	Difference	Elected pre-1970	Elected post-1970	Difference
1971–1972	41.4 (58)[a]	25.0 (4)	16.4	32.6 (43)	0.0 (2)	34.9
1973–1974	7.7 (52)	9.1 (11)	−1.4	27.0 (37)	0.0 (6)	27.0
1975–1976	34.7 (18)	16.7 (49)	18.0	33.3 (30)	0.0 (7)	33.3
1977–1978	71.1 (38)	66.7 (27)	4.4	66.7 (24)	71.4 (14)	−4.7
1979–1980	36.7 (30)	20.7 (29)	16.0	29.4 (17)	12.5 (24)	16.9
1981–1982	80.0 (20)	73.1 (26)	6.9	92.3 (13)	61.0 (41)	31.3*
1983–1984	00.0 (16)	86.2 (29)	13.8	86.7 (15)	85.4 (41)	1.3
1985–1986	86.7 (15)	65.6 (32)	21.1	72.7 (11)	63.0 (43)	9.7
1987–1988	92.3 (13)	69.1 (42)	23.2	77.8 (9)	48.7 (37)	29.1
1989–1990	90.0 (10)	91.1 (45)	−1.1	57.1 (7)	47.4 (38)	9.7
1991–1992	88.9 (9)	98.0 (49)	−9.1	100.0 (6)	73.7 (38)	26.3

[a]*Note: N* in parentheses.

*$p \leq 0.05$, **$p \leq 0.01$, ***$p \leq 0.001$. Significance indicated by Z-test for the difference in rates between two sets of binomial data described in the Appendix. Membership totals may exceed 100 because of turnover during the session.

difference is significant and positive. No sign means the difference was not statistically distinguished from zero or that the analysis was not applicable (the difference between members elected before and after 1978 in 1969– 1970, for example). Recall that the replacement hypothesis predicts a negative sign for Democrats and a positive sign for Republicans.

This extended analysis does not particularly strengthen the case for replacement. Turning first to Democrats in the House (see Table 6.5), the replacement effects are generally sustained, but weaker. Where the predicted negative sign characterizes four sessions using the 1970 cutoff, it characterizes three using the 1972 cutoff, and two with all other cutoffs. The significant findings are generally grouped in the late 1980s. Republicans in the House, on the other hand, continue to contradict the replacement hypothesis: While the 1972 cutoff results in insignificant findings, as is the case for 1970, the 1968 and 1974 cutoffs produce two significantly significant negative findings apiece, while 1976 and 1978 show one negative finding each. Thus, for House Republicans, not only are newer members not less likely than longer-term members to cosponsor pro–women's rights legislation, but at times they are actually significantly more likely.

Turning to the Senate, the findings for Democrats (see Table 6.6) lend a very small degree of support to replacement. Using the 1972, 1974, and 1978 cutoffs results in one statistically negative difference for each. The 1968 cutoff, on the other hand, shows one positive difference, in opposition to the replacement hypothesis. The findings are thus extremely weak for replacement as a mechanism for party change among Senate Democrats. Finally, Senate Republicans provide somewhat stronger support for replacement. For the 1968, 1970, and 1976 cutoffs, the difference is significantly positive (as predicted) in one session, in two sessions for 1972 and 1974, and in three for 1978. On the other hand, there is also a significant negative finding in 1979–1980 for the 1976 cutoff. Like the supportive findings for House Democrats, the positive findings are concentrated in a particular period—in this case, the late 1970s and early 1980s, particularly 1981–1982.

Overall, then, this extended analysis provides only weak support for replacement as a causal mechanism. House Democrats and Senate Republicans show signs of a replacement process, but even in those cases the findings are not particularly strong or consistent. For House Republicans and Senate Democrats, the results are either the opposite as predicted, rarely as expected, or nonexistent. Replacement does not characterize a particular party, chamber, or time, but the limited support for the replacement mechanism comes from one party in one chamber during one time period (Democrats in the House in the late 1980s, for example) and the other party in the other chamber at another time (Republicans in the Senate in the late 1970s and early 1980s). Important caveats vis-à-vis this analysis should be

TABLE 6.5

Comparing Rates of Pro–Women's Rights Cosponsorship by Democrats and Republicans Elected Pre– and Post– Various Years, House, 1969–1992

Congress	Democrats						Republicans					
	1968	*1970*	*1972*	*1974*	*1976*	*1978*	*1968*	*1970*	*1972*	*1974*	*1976*	*1978*
1969–1970												
1971–1972												
1973–1974												
1975–1976		−										
1977–1978												
1979–1980												
1981–1982							−					
1983–1984							−					
1985–1986	−	−								−	−	−
1987–1988		−	−							−		
1989–1990	−	−	−	−	−							
1991–1992												

Note: A negative sign denotes a significant and negative difference (binomial Z-test) between the cosponsorship rates of members elected before and after the indicated year. A positve sign denotes a significant and positive difference between the cosponsorship rates of members elected before and after the indicated year. No symbol indicates no significant difference or not applicable.

TABLE 6.6

Comparing Rates of Pro–Women's Rights Cosponsorship by Democrats and Republicans Elected Pre– and Post– Various Years, Senate, 1969–1992

Congress	Democrats						Republicans					
	1968	1970	1972	1974	1976	1978	1968	1970	1972	1974	1976	1978
1969–1970												
1971–1972												
1973–1974												
1975–1976	+											
1977–1978				−								
1979–1980							+		+	+	−	+
1981–1982								+	+	+	+	+
1983–1984												
1985–1986												
1987–1988												+
1989–1990												
1991–1992			−									

Note: A negative sign denotes a significant and negative difference (binomial *Z*-test) between the cosponsorship rates of members elected before and after the indicated year. A positive sign denotes a significant and positive difference between the cosponsorship rates of members elected before and after the indicated year. No symbol indicates no significant difference or not applicable.

noted, however. Particularly in the Senate, but also in some years in the House, the subdivision by party and period elected results in small Ns in the cells, often below that at which the central limit theorem can be depended on. Thus, because of the small number of members meeting certain criteria in certain sessions, our confidence in the representativeness of those characterizations of members' behavior is weakened.

With this caveat in mind, the analysis here suggest that conversion, rather than replacement, may have characterized party realignment on women's rights. That is, the realignment of the parties' relative positions on women's rights resulted from changing behavior on the part of elites, rather than membership turnover. This conclusion emphasizes the important role of issue change, as detailed in the preceding chapter. While the replacement hypothesis is supported and suggested by other studies of Congress (Poole and Rosenthal 1997; Carmines and Stimson 1989; Sinclair 1982; Asher and Weisberg 1978), many of these authors have allowed that issue redefinition, especially a change in the mapping of an issue onto the left-right spectrum that structures so much of American political debate, can lead to conversion. These results may also be attributed to the responsiveness of established elites to changes in the parties' electoral coalitions. As the distribution of preference vis-à-vis women's rights among important party constituencies shifted, strategic elites may have responded by adjusting their behavior regarding women's rights in response. At the same time, some replacement processes have affected women's rights. The changing regional composition of the parties via replacement has led to racial and ideological polarization in Congress (Carmines and Stimson 1989; Rohde 1991). As womens's rights became linked to civil rights and mapped on to the left-right spectrum, these shifts have surely contributed to the parties' realignment. Thus racial and ideological polarization have been important for women's rights in large part due to issue redifinition.

This is also not to say that this analysis is necessarily at odds with the findings of great consistency on the part of elites. By attributing the shift in large part to issue change, the assertion is that the elites did not change, the issue did. It is quite likely that conservative elites in 1962 were still conservative in 1982, but while women's rights were not viewed as antithetical to that conservatism in 1962, they were in 1982. Poole and Rosenthal, perhaps the most prominent proponents of the consistency thesis, point out that "how specific issues map onto the dimensions may change over time" (1991, 232). Thus, knowing where to place individual legislators in a generalized space does not tell us "how specific issues get defined in terms of the structure . . . [but] once the positions of the alternatives have been defined, a spatial model can predict the outcome" (Poole and Rosenthal 1991, 229). It is the defining, and redefining, of the issue that appears to have been so determinative for the spatial mapping of women's rights. As the issue changed, so did elites' behavior, with consequences for the parties' relative positions.

Female Elites

The major expectation vis-à-vis elite change is that incoming elites will be more likely to represent new understandings of the issue and its relationship to the possibly evolving party coalition. The previous analysis did not provide much direct support for the role of replacement as the mechanism in the case of women's rights. In this section, I consider the possibility that a subset of new elites held distinct personal preferences vis-à-vis the issue that affected the relative positions adopted by the parties. Electoral concerns are primary for party elites. At the same time, it is entirely possible, if not probable, that elites have personal preferences on policy issues as well (Wittman 1990). While too much action on behalf of one's own issue preferences when in opposition to constituent preferences will in all likelihood lead to the loss of elite status, there are circumstances under which elites might be expected to act on their own preferences. For example, there is evidence that when public and constituent opinion is not clear, and other cues are not forthcoming, members of Congress rely on their own personal judgment and preferences in making decisions (cf. Fenno 1973; Kingdon 1973). If an issue is not of central concern to one's constituents, an actor may be able to even go against the preferences (weak, if any) of her constituents and make decisions on the issue based on her personal preferences.

In the case of women's rights, women in particular embody a group of elites who might be expected to have unique and strong personal preferences. As a result of personal experiences, female elites may be predisposed to personal and professional interest in issues specific to women, sympathetic to the needs of women vis-à-vis public policy, and cognizant of the unique ways in which government action impinges on women's lives. Additionally, female elites may include women in their conception of their representative duty, that is, women in office may feel an obligation to represent women generally, in addition to their responsibility to their individual district. While evidence that women legislators are more likely to vote for pro–women's rights policies than are their male counterparts is mixed (Burrell 1994; Thomas 1989; Leader 1977), there are indications that women are more likely to introduce women's rights legislation, particularly when their proportion of the legislature has reached a certain level (Thomas 1991; Saint-Germain 1989), include representing women's interests in their role conception (Thomas 1994; Reingold 1992), and consider their efforts on women's rights bills significant accomplishments or priorities (Mezey 1994; Thomas and Welch 1991; but see Mezey 1978).

Female elites may have contributed to the parties' changing positions on women's rights in a number of ways. Before 1970, women elected to office often succeeded their husbands (usually following his death in office) and were thus viewed as simply continuing his policies and positions. After 1968, what Burrell (1994) has termed the "feminist era," the onset of the women's movement and the politicization of women contributed to the emergence of a new class of female representatives, few of whom owed their position to their husbands and many of whom recognized their gender as politically relevant. At the same time, the number of women in the House began to increase at a faster rate than it had historically, albeit still quite slowly. This development was not replicated in the Senate, where the number of female members did not exceed two until 1994 (see Figures 6.8 and 6.9). Yet, this new coterie of female elites may have been more likely to support feminist policy, thus shaping their parties' positions. In particular, the new class of Democratic women may have been particularly supportive of women's rights. Having found little evidence for replacement as a mechanism for party change on women's rights, and given the small proportion of female elites, it is unlikely that the behavior of new women elites provided the major impetus for party realignment. However, it is possible that women elites, particularly Democrats, acted differently than their male counterparts, and in doing so, shaped the direction taken by their parties.

Cosponsorship. As Figure 6.8 shows, while Democrats initially experienced greater growth, the small increase in the proportion of women in the House (I concentrate on the House here as there are so few women in the Senate) soon characterized both parties. Thus, again, at first glance, gender alone does not appear to be a probable cause of the disparity in the parties' positions, as both parties have experienced similar changes in the gender composition of their elites. This, of course, assumes that Democratic and Republican women were equally likely to favor and advocate women's rights. Table 6.7 compares the cosponsorship rates of Republican and Democratic women against both men and women of the same and opposing parties. Overall, female elites rarely differ significantly from each other in their advocacy of women's rights, as measured by cosponsorship, despite the fact that the two parties differed significantly across this period. Republican women are significantly more active in 1959–1960, and Democratic women's rates of cosponsorship significantly exceeds that of Republican women in 1975–1976 and 1977–1978, but the two groups are otherwise statistically indistinguishable. At the same time, women in both parties are significantly more likely than their male counterparts to cosponsor women's rights legislation in a substantial number of sessions, both before and after 1970. On their face, these two results—little difference between Republican and Democratic women and consistently higher rates of cosponsorship by women of both parties as compared to men of the same

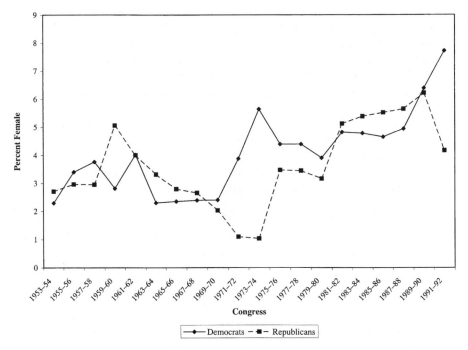

Figure 6.8. Women as a Percentage of Each Party's Membership, House, 1953–1992.

party—do not provide much support for a central role for female elites in the parties' realignment. Democratic and Republican women were equally active cosponsors, and were more active than their fellow partisans, but their parties moved in divergent directions on women's rights after 1970. On the other hand, there is some evidence that while not statistically distinguished from Republican women, Democratic women were comparatively more active cosponsors. In the 1970s, Democratic women were more likely to cosponsor than both Democratic and Republican men in every session, but Republican women were more active than Republican men in only two sessions and were not more active cosponsors than Democratic men, as they had been during number of pre-1970 sessions. Overall, it appears that at least during the crucial decade of the 1970s, Republican women cosponsored at rates significantly equivalent to Democratic men, while Democratic women exceeded men of both parties, thus perhaps playing a leadership role and contributing to the association of feminism with the Democratic party.

For the most part, however, this analysis provides little support for the

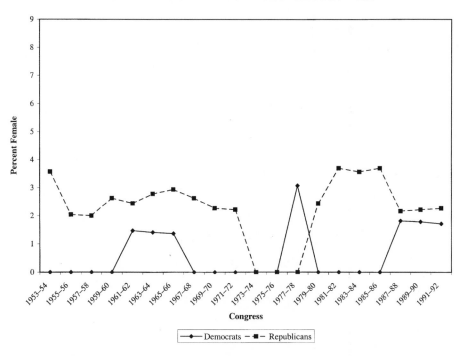

Figure 6.9. Women as a Percentage of Each Party's Membership, Senate, 1953–1992.

hypothesis that the post-1970 new breed of women elites were a central part of the realignment of the parties' positions on women's rights. In fact, the finding that women were more active cosponsors of pro–women's rights legislation than their fellow partisans both before and after 1970 is quite intriguing. Students of women in Congress have often focused exclusively on those in office after about 1970, in part because women in office during that period were not be expected represent the interests of women, as they primarily gained their positions through their husbands (cf. Gertzog 1995, Burrell 1994). The findings here suggest that despite their different paths to office and the absence of an active women's movement, women in office in the 1950s and 1960s were indeed distinctively active for women's rights. Based on this analysis, it is thus difficult to attribute realignment to a new radical class of pro–women's rights female legislators in the Democratic party after 1970.

Initiation. Women may have influenced their parties' relative stances on women's rights in other ways. I have concentrated on the cosponsorship act as a measure of support for women's rights by party elites in Congress.

TABLE 6.7

Comparing Rates of Pro-Women's Rights Cosponsorship by Democratic and Republican Women, House, 1953–1992

Congress	Democratic Women	Democratic Women Compared to			Republican Women	Republican Women Compared to		
		Democratic Men	Republican Women	Republican Men		Republican Men	Democratic Women	Democratic Men
1953–1954	60.0 (5)	+		+	50.0 (6)	+		+
1955–1956	25.0 (8)				33.3 (6)	+		
1957–1958	66.7 (9)				83.3 (6)			+
1959–1960	37.5 (8)	+	−	87.5 (8)	+		+
1961–1962	63.6 (11)	+			71.4 (7)			+
1963–1964	83.3 (6)	+		+	50.0 (6)			
1965–1966	42.9 (7)				50.0 (4)		+	
1967–1968	33.3 (6)				36.6 (5)			
1969–1970	66.7 (6)				64.3 (4)			

1971–1972	90.0 (10)	+		+	50.0 (2)	+	
1973–1974	100.0 (14)	+		+	100.0 (2)	+	+
1975–1976	92.3 (13)	+	+	+	40.0 (5)	+	−
1977–1978	100.0 (13)	+	+	+	60.0 (5)	+	−
1979–1980	81.8 (11)	+		+	60.0 (5)	+	
1981–1982	66.7 (12)				80.0 (10)	+	
1983–1984	92.3 (13)				100.0 (9)	+	
1985–1986	91.7 (12)				100.0 (10)	+	
1987–1988	100.0 (13)			+	100.0 (10)	+	
1989–1990	94.1 (17)			+	100.0 (10)	+	
1991–1992	100.0 (21)			+	100.0 (7)	+	

Note: Figures indicate rate of pro–women's rights cosponsorship. *N* in parentheses. A negative sign (−) denotes significantly less likely to cosponsor (binomial *Z*-test); a positive sign (+) indicates significantly more likely to cosponsor. No symbol indicates no significant difference.

All cosponsorship activity may not represent equal interest or support for a policy, however. In particular, we might expect the initiators of the legislation to be more interested or committed to the policy in question. Members who add their names to the legislation later in the process (as is allowed in the Senate throughout this period and to varying degrees in the House since 1968), while indicating support for the policy, are often performing a less costly act that may not reflect the degree of support shown by the initiators of the legislation. Furthermore, by introducing the bill, initiators furnish the opportunity for other members to support the policy, as well as provide cues to their colleagues about the nature and appeal of the legislation. If women of either party are more active in introducing legislation, they may provide incentive, or disincentive, for others to jump on board. If, for example, Democratic women were particularly active as initiators of women's rights legislation they may have provided cues that encouraged cosponsorship on the part of Democrats, but discouraged participation by Republicans.

To consider this possibility, I examine the first cosponsors of all pro–women's rights legislation during this period. As before, I limit this examination to the House because of the scarcity of women in the Senate. In the period before multiple cosponsorships were permitted in the House (pre-1968), I focus on the first individual to introduce the bill, treating members who introduce the same bill after the first is introduced as cosponsors of the original. This approach is potentially problematic in that I use the bill title and short description alone to identify identical bills, when in fact, bills may have the same title and descriptions but differ in their specific provisions. Furthermore, examining the first cosponsor only provides a rough estimate of the initiation effect I am interested in. When a bill features several cosponsors in its originally introduced form, there is no guarantee that the individual listed first was the initiator of the policy or the author of the bill. Some bills are introduced and reintroduced in each Congress, so that the first cosponsor is simply the member who got around to introducing it before any others; such an action, while not evidence of authorship or expertise, might still suggest greater interest. Moreover, some bills represent the work of several members, either in an ad hoc fashion or more formally, such as on behalf of the Congressional Caucus for Women's Issues, in which case the first cosponsor listed may simply reflect seniority or a sign of honor afforded by other members.

With these caveats in mind, I turn to the data. Table 6.8 shows the difference between the percent of all members who are Democratic or Republican women, the percent of all first cosponsors who fall into either category, and the significance of the difference. Women from both parties are, with the exception of Republican women in a few instances, more likely to be the first cosponsor of pro–women's rights bills than would be expected if this behavior was distributed randomly without regard to gender or party. Democratic women are consistently significantly more likely to be the first cosponsor than their numbers suggest (with one exception), and often by a wide margin. Republican women, on the other hand, are less consistently more likely to be first cosponsors; the differences are significant in seven of twenty, or only thirty-five percent, of the sessions. In four of the other cases, Republican women are actually less likely to be initiators, although the differences are not statistically significant.

This analysis of first cosponsors provides some support for the contention that Democratic women contributed to the realignment of the parties on women's rights issues. Democratic women have clearly played a major role in initiating women's rights legislation. Their level of initiative on women's rights legislation exceeds their numbers in office throughout the entire time period and is higher than forty percent as early as 1961–1962, so it is difficult to link this behavior directly to the dramatic emergence of realignment in the House in the early 1970s. On the other hand, the number of Democratic women did increase in the early 1970s when the Democratic shift to greater women's rights support in the House occurred. Democratic women, too small in number to determine their party's position on women's rights issues, might have, by their initiative, played a small role in encouraging their fellow partisans to shift their positions. Republican women, on the other hand, while more likely than their numbers suggests to initiate women's rights bills, were not nearly as dominant as their Democratic sisters, and indeed, declined in relative activism after the 1950s. For various reasons, then, Democratic women's activism on behalf of women's rights may have played a role in shifting their party's relative position.

Activism. Finally, there is anecdotal evidence of the role of female elites, particularly those associated with the Democratic party who entered into office in the late 1960s and 1970s, in shaping women's rights politics. Democratic congresswomen, such as Bella Abzug (NY, 1971–1976), Elizabeth Holtzman (NY, 1973–1980), Shirley Chisholm (NY, 1969–1982), Patricia Schroeder (CO, 1973–1992), and Martha Griffiths (MI, 1953–1974), were active in the women's movement, advocating women's rights not only in their capacity as elected officials, but also by giving speeches, organizing and mobilizing supporters, and lobbying their colleagues for women's rights. Abzug and Chisholm, for example, were founding members of the NWPC, and many female party elites allied themselves with feminist organizations and campaigned for ERA ratification. In doing so, they contributed to the restructuring of the debate around the issue of women's rights and provided cues to other elites and to mass identifiers about the

TABLE 6.8
Democratic and Republican Women as a Percentage of House Membership and of First Cosponsors, House, 1953–1992

Congress	Democratic Women			Republican Women		
	Members	First cosponsors	Difference	Members	First cosponsors	Difference
1953–1954	1.1 (440)[a]	25.0 (4)	−23.9***	1.4 (440)	25.0 (4)	−23.6***
1955–1956	1.8 (437)	8.0 (25)	−6.2*	1.4 (437)	4.0 (25)	−2.6
1957–1958	2.0 (442)	6.3 (16)	−4.3	1.4 (442)	25.0 (16)	−23.6***
1959–1960	1.8 (442)	14.3 (7)	−12.5*	1.8 (442)	14.3 (7)	−12.5*
1961–1962	2.5 (449)	42.9 (7)	−40.4***	1.6 (449)	14.3 (7)	−12.7*
1963–1964	1.4 (442)	44.4 (9)	−43.0***	1.4 (442)	0 (9)	1.4
1965–1966	1.6 (441)	25.0 (4)	−23.4***	0.9 (441)	0 (4)	0.9
1967–1968	1.4 (439)	14.3 (7)	−12.9*	1.1 (439)	14.3 (7)	−13.8***
1969–1970	1.3 (447)	50.0 (4)	−48.7***	0.9 (447)	0 (4)	0.9

1971–1972	2.3 (442)	38.3 (47)	−36.0***	0.5 (442)	0 (47)	0.5
1973–1974	3.2 (442)	33.3 (102)	−30.1***	0.5 (442)	6.9 (102)	−6.4***
1975–1976	3.0 (441)	52.2 (67)	−49.2***	1.1 (441)	1.5 (67)	−0.4
1977–1978	3.0 (441)	34.5 (87)	−31.5***	1.1 (441)	1.8 (87)	−0.7
1979–1980	2.5 (440)	31.6 (19)	−29.1***	1.1 (440)	10.5 (19)	−9.4***
1981–1982	2.7 (444)	33.3 (18)	−30.6***	2.3 (444)	11.1 (18)	−8.8*
1983–1984	3.0 (439)	21.8 (55)	−18.8***	2.1 (439)	3.6 (55)	−1.5
1985–1986	2.7 (439)	20.0 (55)	−17.3***	2.3 (439)	5.5 (55)	−3.2
1987–1988	3.0 (440)	18.9 (37)	−15.9***	2.3 (440)	5.4 (37)	−3.1
1989–1990	3.8 (443)	23.2 (56)	−19.4***	2.5 (443)	14.3 (56)	−11.8***
1991–1992	4.8 (441)	33.9 (62)	−29.1***	1.6 (441)	19.4 (62)	−17.8***

[a]*Note*: N in parentheses.

*$p \leq 0.05$, **$p \leq 0.01$, ***$p \leq 0.001$. Significance indicated by Z-test for the difference in rates between two sets of binomial data described in the Appendix. Membership totals may exceed 435 because of turnover during the session.

connection between the Democratic party and women's rights issues. In Congress, these women often led the way on women's rights legislation, both as initiators of bills, as we have seen here, and in encouraging other members to join their effort. The most noteworthy case of such action was Martha Griffiths's extensive efforts to secure the discharge petition signatures necessary to bring the ERA to the floor of the House for consideration in 1970 (Wolbrecht and Martin n.d.; Davis 1991; Freeman 1975).

A number of prominent Republican women have also championed women's rights, such as First Lady Betty Ford, one-time Republican party chair Mary Louise Smith, Representatives Margaret Heckler (MA, 1967–1983) and Millicent Fenwick (NJ, 1975–1983), and Senator Nancy L. Kassebaum (KS, 1979–1996), to name a few (Cummings 1983; Bennetts 1980b; Shanahan 1976; Lelyveld 1976; *NYT* 10/13/81). These women have been less strongly identified with the women's movement than the aforementioned Democratic women, however, and particularly in later years, their pro–women's rights stances, especially those on the ERA and abortion, have been viewed as exceptions to the Republican rule. Thus, while a number of Democratic women are considered prominent feminists, this has been less so the case for Republican women. The different perception of the feminism of Republican and Democratic women is in some ways a result of the parties' realignment, but may have contributed to that outcome as well.

Summary. In general, the data on women in the House examined provide mixed support for the influence of women elites in contributing to their parties' realignment on women's rights. Both in terms of simple cosponsorship and bill initiation, Democratic women have been more active than their counterparts in either party throughout this forty-year time period. While their numbers did indeed grow slightly beginning in the early 1970s, the fact that they have been *consistently* active limits the amount of responsibility for the dramatic party shifts in the 1970s we can attribute to Democratic women. On the Republican side, women have likewise generally been women's rights proponents across this period, and actually remained more supportive than their male counterparts after 1970 (possibly more attributable to the lack of support from male Republicans than any increased activity on the party of female Republicans), but they have not been able to keep their party from adopting a general anti–women's rights stance. On the other hand, a number of Democratic women have been prominent feminists, possibly contributing to the association of women's rights with the Democratic party. While a number of Republican women have also been feminist activists, such women have generally kept, or been granted, a lower profile. As their party has become increasingly hostile to women's rights, these few women are increasingly likely to be viewed as exceptions to the rule, unable to stem the antifeminist tide.

CONCLUSION

Party elites, I have argued, adopt positions on issues in an effort to attract and expand the party coalition. Thus, variation in one or several of the three factors—the issue itself, the parties' coalitions, and the parties' elites—is hypothesized to bring about an observed change in the positions associated with each party. In the case of women's rights, there is evidence that two of the factors—the issue and the parties' coalitions—have been consequential, while the analysis has suggested less support for the third factor, change in the elites themselves.

The composition of the parties' coalitions have clearly evolved in ways that have affected the parties' relative positions on women's rights. One aspect of the parties' coalitions—ideological polarization—has been meaningful because of the issue changes that caused women's rights to map onto the left-right spectrum, while others have involved changes in the party alliances of groups—social conservatives/Southerners—that have been generally consistent in their opposition to women's rights. On the other hand, the evidence for the impact of elite turnover is decidedly mixed. The analysis here suggests that conversion, a change in the behavior of the elites in power, rather than replacement, may characterize women's rights realignment. Here again, the other factors come into play. As the issue of women's rights evolved and the interests associated with each party shifted, elites, both new and old, responded in particular ways to the issue of women's rights. The result was a significant transformation and eventual polarization of the parties' relative positions vis-à-vis women's rights.

CHAPTER SEVEN

The Politics of Women's Rights

FUNDAMENTALLY, this research concerns change. Moreover, it examines change in an issue area—women's rights—that has involved some of the most momentous social transformations of the twentieth century. Not long ago it was commonly held that women's place was in the home, that women who did work outside the home should earn less than men, and that women lacked the emotional fortitude to serve as political leaders (see McGlen and O'Connor 1998). That these beliefs have generally, if not entirely, been dismissed stands as "one of the biggest social changes of our times" (*The Economist* 1997, 87). This transformed societal mindset has been accompanied, and in many cases preceded, by a major revolution in the participation of women in social, economic, and political life. By a wide margin (although not as wide as many may prefer), more women today work outside the home, achieve advanced levels of educational and professional attainment, and hold elected and appointed office than did a mere forty years ago. With changes of this magnitude, it is perhaps not surprising that there has been a transformation of political alignments as well.

In the 1950s and 1960s, women's rights politics was limited to a few interested individuals—activists, interest groups, and interested members of Congress and the various presidential administrations—and a few policy issues, mainly concerning equality and nondiscrimination. Institutionally, activity centered around the Women's Bureau of the Department of Labor (Harrison 1988). The nexus of the debate—protection versus equality—was recognized by participants and had characterized women's rights politics since before suffrage. Organized labor and social feminism preferred the protectionist status quo, business interests and equality feminists favored greater legal equality for women. Women's rights thus fit Baumgartner and Jones's (1993) description of an issue in equilibrium: limited participation, general agreement as to the terms of the debate, and stable alliances. The Republican party was generally perceived as more supportive of women's rights, a perception confirmed by an examination of cosponsorship activity in Congress. Party platforms reveal less of a difference between the parties' positions, although observers characterized the GOP as more supportive. Across the 1960s, partisan differences declined. In general, neither party devoted much attention to women's rights.

In the late 1960s and early 1970s, the women's rights equilibrium was greatly disrupted. Many Americans, both elites and the public, confronted, for the first time, the very idea that women have unique interests, interests largely overlooked and disregarded by policy makers. Women's rights moved from a situation of limited participation and little public scrutiny to one of considerable public attention and expanded involvement on the part of national political leaders and organized interests. The agenda for women's rights grew and diversified, new meanings and symbols became associated with women's rights, and alliances shifted and developed as a mass movement for women's rights, and later, an opposition to that movement, emerged. Both parties' platforms devoted unprecedented levels of attention to women's rights, with extensive debate and controversy characterizing both parties' conventions throughout the 1970s. The parties' platforms were generally similar with regard to women's rights in the early 1970s, but grew increasingly divergent across the decade, culminating in 1980 with the Republican rejection of the ERA and embrace of the pro-life abortion position, contrasted with Democrat's expanded support for the ERA, abortion rights, and other pro–women's rights positions. In the House, the Democratic delegation emerged as significantly more supportive of women's rights in the early 1970s, while divergence between the parties in the Senate grew more slowly across the decade.

After 1980, women's rights politics returned to an equilibrium, albeit a considerably different one than had characterized the issue area prior to 1970. Public attention to women's rights declined, and a new set of actors—far larger than the small set of the 1950s and early 1960s—dominated debate over women's rights, with the alignment of interests on each side substantially fixed. Party alignment could, for the most part, also be described as fixed after 1980. Democrats stood on the pro–women's rights side, while Republicans took up a number of opposition positions. These divisions are discernable in the considerable polarization of cosponsorship and roll call behavior in both chambers, as well as the differences in the parties' platforms. While women's rights issues still sparked occasional debate at the parties' conventions, the outcomes were no longer in any real doubt as each party largely maintained the positions it had adopted by 1980.

A few characteristics of party transformation with regard to women's rights deserve emphasis. First, in order to appreciate the shift from issue equilibrium to disruption and back, it is important to distinguish between real intraparty controversy over an issue, and debate in which the outcome is virtually certain. In the 1970s, both parties' conventions were characterized by genuine debate over women's rights. Feminists encountered both successes and failures in their dealings within the Democratic and the Republican parties. As a result, the parties' platform positions shifted and evolved across the 1970s. After 1980, however, while women's rights were occasionally debated and discussed, the outcomes were never really in any doubt; while new issues continued to be added to the women's rights agenda, the parties' platforms went unchanged on major women's rights issues after 1980. In that sense, a new equilibrium was achieved. Thus, while elite attention to women's rights continued into the 1990s, a new set of alliances and understandings as to the meaning and definition of women's rights has clearly been in place since the 1970s.

Second, the role of issue equilibrium disruption in contributing to the opportunity for shifts in the parties' positions should be underscored. When great amounts of attention are directed toward an issue, party elites have an incentive to consider how they might exploit that issue for the benefit of themselves and their party. While the potential for a realignment of alliances, and thus parties, around an issue is heightened when the issue moves onto the political agenda, it is not always the case that realignment occurs; issues, party coalitions, and elites are generally stable and consistent so for many issues, party elites simply continue to align themselves as they had previously. If the issue, the parties' coalitions, or the elites have evolved, however, the calculations of those elites as to how to best utilize the issue for electoral gain may change as well, leading to a realignment in the parties' relative positions.

Women's rights represents an extreme case of this process. While a small number of citizens recognized the unique concerns of women in the 1950s and early 1960s, the discovery of discrimination against women in the late 1960s and early 1970s was a dramatic revelation for most Americans that disrupted social, economic, and political relationships. The various developments described in chapter 5 drew widespread attention to a set of concerns—the rights of women—that in the minds of most citizens, both elites and the public, had not merely been off the active political agenda—they had simply not existed. When women's rights moved to the center of national political debate, elites in both parties responded to the ways in which the issue was framed and defined, and to the developments in the composition of their coalitions, both of which had evolved over an extended period of time. The disruption of issue equilibrium—perhaps better described as issue discovery in the case of women's rights—forced elites to evaluate the issue in light of issue and coalition change which had been in the works for some time before the issue appeared on the political agenda. The result of their evaluation and reaction was a realignment of the parties on women's rights.

Finally, this work has emphasized the importance of real politics—the interplay of events, actors, and circumstance, and how they are interpreted—in the shaping of parties' responses to issues. Long-term systematic developments, such as changes in the composition of the parties' coalitions, have clearly been important in bringing about the transformation of the parties' positions on women's rights. Yet as highlighted particularly in chapter 5, the politics of women's rights and the impact of those politics on elites' evaluation of the issue (particularly its link to their constituents) have been crucial as well. In an attempt to be systematic concerning phenomenon such as these, scholars have a tendency to downplay more erratic circumstances such as individual activism (a Phyllis Schlafly, for example) or external events (a mass rally in 1970 that moves women's rights into the mainstream of political discourse). Yet these factors are not incidental to this process, but central and causal, as we have seen.

ON PREDICTABILITY AND DETERMINISM

From the vantage point of the late 1990s, the parties' present alignment on women's rights can appear inevitable. Republican opposition and Democratic support seem quite obvious outcomes, begging the question of whether there is really a puzzle to be solved in the first place. Yet it is not at all clear that a Republican shift away from women's rights support was a foregone conclusion, nor that the Democratic embrace of feminism was predetermined by any one factor or combination of factors. If nothing is certain but change, can we predict the shape and nature of future party issue alignments?

As with any human phenomenon, little can be predicted with certainty, except, of course, death and taxes. An infinite number of factors can alter the course of events in such a way as to lead to an unexpected outcome. In 1960, one would not have expected that Kennedy's appeal to female voters in the form of an innocuous President's Commission would help usher in a second wave of the women's movement or that Congress would add sex to the 1964 Civil Rights Act, linking gender to race and, when the EEOC initially refused to enforce the law, further contributing to the initiation of the modern women's movement. As late as 1970, few would have predicted that the Supreme Court would issue a major decision on abortion as early as 1973 (certainly those petitioning the court did not expect a victory so soon), thus placing abortion on the national agenda and linking a contentious and emotional issue to women's rights politics; that Cold Warrior Phyllis Schlafly would so effectively take up the banner of opposition to feminism; or that conservatives, so badly discredited in 1964, would come to dominate the Republican party. Each of these developments was consequential for the evolution of the parties' positions with regard to women's rights.

Thus, the arguments presented here provide an explanation for past developments, not a prediction of future party alignments or positions. What we can expect is that when elites perceive women's rights to be salient and strategically important, they will evaluate their policy positions in light of the evolving understanding of the issue and the relationship to their party's coalitions in an attempt to best advantage themselves and their parties.

WOMEN'S RIGHTS AND THE AMERICAN PARTY SYSTEM

The case of women's rights demonstrates the extraordinary power of the American parties to mediate conflict. The women's rights revolution did not simply entail policy demands, but represented a fundamental challenge to, and transformation of, social, economic, and political institutions. Few aspects of American life were left untouched. That the American parties were able to translate this conflict into electoral choice is testament to their relevance and ability to structure important social cleavages. Many feminist activists resisted association with one or the other political parties, believing that doing so would threaten feminist political independence and unnecessarily inject divisiveness, weakening the movement's bargaining power (Costain and Costain 1987); still others resist incorporation into traditional political institutions at all. Yet contrary to feminist rhetoric, it is clear that significant numbers of citizens fundamentally disagree with not only the means, but also the ends pursued by the women's movement. While partisanship vis-à-vis policy issues is often portrayed negatively (and accurately) as contributing to unnecessary stalemate and suboptimal outcomes, the association of opposing issue positions with the opposing political parties may alternatively attest to the healthy functioning of a democratic system. Because political parties structure electoral choice, they represent a central mechanism by which citizen preferences are translated to government in a republican system. On the critical issue of women's rights, the American parties together provide representation of opposing positions, and in doing so fulfill their responsibility to offer American citizens real and meaningful choice on the central issues of the day.

As discussed in chapter 1, parties serve as effective mediating institutions within American democracy. To do so, parties must offer real and clear alternatives, particularly in terms of the policy positions put forward by their candidates; if they do not, the vote—a choice between two parties—is rendered meaningless. Examination of the parties' platforms, the statements and actions of their presidents and presidential candidates, and the behavior of their delegations in Congress clearly demonstrate that the parties have come to represent divergent viewpoints regarding women's rights, thus offering Americans a considerable degree of choice regarding women's rights at the ballot box.

Yet it is not enough that parties declare opposing positions; for the divergent policy alternatives offered by the parties to be meaningful for the democratic process, citizens must be aware that differences between the parties exist. Evidence of citizens' awareness of the divergence between the parties on women's rights is mixed. Since 1972, the National Election Studies has occasionally asked respondents to place each party on a seven-point scale ranging from "Some people feel that women should have an equal role with men in running business, industry, and government" on one end of the spectrum to "A women's place is in the home" at the other. The item is not perfectly analogous to public policy; even individuals who concede that women should participate in the world outside of the home may have very different views on specific policy questions. On the other hand, debates over women's rights policy have often involved opposing views on the appropriate role of women in society (Klatch 1987) and the item's generality advantages it over questions focused on one or another specific policy, rather than women's rights generally. For these reasons, as well as its availability over time, the equal role scale has been used by others alone, or in combination with other items, as a general measure of support for feminism (Cook 1989; Cook and Wilcox 1991). Figure 7.1 shows the percent of voters describing the Democrats as comparatively more supportive of women's rights, the percent who view the GOP as relatively more supportive, and the percent who placed the parties at the same place on the equal role scale in those years in which the item was employed.

In 1972, a full sixty percent of voters described the parties as occupying the same place on the equal role scale, a perception we might describe as accurate given that the parties' platforms were generally indistinguishable on women's rights. The seeds of party polarization were already sown; Democrats in the House, for example, were already far more supportive of women's rights than their Republican colleagues. Thus, it is perhaps not surprising that more than thirty percent of voters considered the Democrats more supportive, and less than ten percent placed the Republican party in a more supportive position. What is striking about Figure 7.1 is that despite the dramatic polarization of the parties in all their institutional forms across the next two decades, the percentage of voters who view the parties as indistinguishable on women's rights remains above forty percent throughout the remainder of the period, with the exception of 1980. Moreover, the percentage of voters who view the Republican party as more supportive of women's rights—an increasingly inaccurate view—does not decline over time, but in fact, increases slightly. The portion of voters correctly describing the Democrats as the party more supportive of women's rights does grow across this period from approximately thirty percent in 1972 to almost fifty percent by 1988, with a sharp increase to over sixty percent in 1980. The events of 1980 apparently amplified the parties' polarization over women's rights, but even in the midst of considerable press coverage, only sixty-four percent of voters accurately described the parties' relative positions on women's rights. Once a new equilibrium was estab-

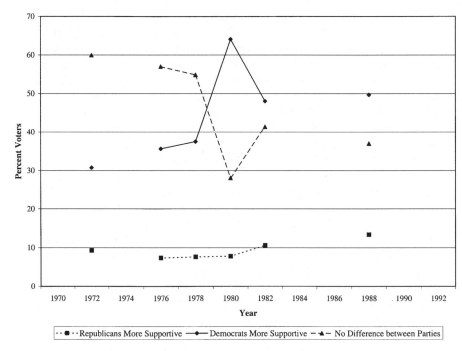

Figure 7.1. Voters' Knowledge of Parties' Relative Positions on Women's Rights (Equal Role Scale), 1972–1988.

lished and public salience decreased, the public's awareness of the differences between the parties appears to have faded, despite the fact that on most major women's rights issues the parties' platforms remain unchanged after 1980, and the parties in Congress actually grow more divergent. On the other hand, in the available observations after 1980, more voters describe the Democrats as comparatively more supportive of women's rights than either other category. Moreover, these findings are consistent with other research suggesting the inaccuracy of Americans' perceptions of party positions; only fifty-nine percent of voters correctly described the Democratic party as pro-choice and the Republicans as pro-life in 1992, for example (Abramowitz 1995).

Thus, there is evidence that the increasing polarization of the parties on women's rights was accompanied by increasing awareness of the parties' divergent positions. Yet, the reality that a sizable percentage of voters either fail to discern a difference between the parties or incorrectly assign greater support to Republicans (even in 1980, a full third of voters fall into one of these two categories) might be viewed as an impediment to the sort of democratic linkage between policy choices and the citizenry that parties are expected to provide. Caveats regarding question wording and the mass of accumulated evidence regarding citizens' propensity to incorrectly answer basic civics questions helps put these findings in perspective. Moreover, it should be noted that neither party's presidential candidate particularly emphasized women's rights in 1988, but the election is still characterized by the highest percentage of voters viewing the Democrats as more supportive outside of 1980; one wonders what percentage of voters would have recognized differences in 1992, when women's rights were more salient, had the question been posed. Still, the connection between the policy choices offered by the parties and the degree of choice recognized by voters remains less strong then one might hope.

This is not to say that the parties' positions on women's rights have not been meaningful for voters and the party system more generally. Parties' issue positions can be expected to shape the distribution of policy preference and partisanship in the electorate as well. This relationship is complex, warranting considerable research of its own. Awareness, political sophistication, and activism are just some of the factors that affect the relationship between elite action and mass response (Carmines and Stimson 1989). Moreover, the casual links are considerably complicated: Do citizens (particularly new entrants) identify with parties based on the proximity of each party's positions on key issues to their own (cf. Carmines and Stimson 1989; Franklin and Jackson 1983; Jackson 1975), or are citizens' preferences shaped, in part, by the cues they receive from party elites (cf. Gerber and Jackson 1993; Zaller 1992; Campbell et al. 1960)? Figure 7.2, showing the difference between the mean self-placement of Democratic and Republican identifiers and strong partisans on the equal role scale (positive score indicates Democratic respondents more egalitarian), does suggest that elite level divergence is accompanied by polarization at the mass level, particularly for strong partisans. In general, as the parties have polarized on women's rights, their adherents have become increasingly differentiated on the issue as well, although with considerable variation.

The link between the parties' polarization on women's rights and mass behavior that has received the most attention is the emergence of the gender gap in which women favor the Democratic candidates and the Democratic party at greater rates than do men. Said another way, it has not escaped the attention of social scientists and activists that greater relative Democratic party support from women has occurred concomitant to the realignment of the parties over women's rights (Freeman 1999). In terms of party identification, the shift in party loyalty actually precedes the elite alignment. As Figure 7.3 shows, a larger portion of men than women identified with the Democratic party before 1964, but after 1964, women were more likely to identify with the Democratic party than were men. Signifi-

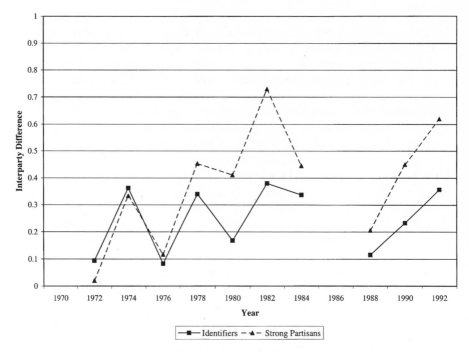

Figure 7.2. Party Polarization on the Equal Role Scale, Identifiers and Strong Partisans, 1972–1992.

cantly, female identification is actually quite stable from 1970 to 1992; it is male Democratic party identification that falls off considerably. These data, however, are merely suggestive; myriad factors appear to contribute to the gender gap, of which the parties' polarization on women's rights is only one potential factor (cf. Clark and Clark 1999; Carroll 1988; Conover 1988; Erie and Rein 1988; Miller 1988; Mansbridge 1985). I leave the delineation of the relationship between party realignment, partisanship, attitudes, and gender to future research.

Parties' role in structuring democratic choice requires that parties offer voters actual policy alternatives and that at least some voters recognize those divergent options. Regarding the latter, this brief perusal of available evidence suggests that while not overwhelming, voters are more likely to describe Democrats as the party associated with women's rights than they are Republicans, and this tendency has increased as the parties have grown more polarized. Women's rights preferences among the citizenry appear to be increasingly structured by partisanship, while a pro-Democratic gender gap has emerged. The democratic linkage, however, requires a final step:

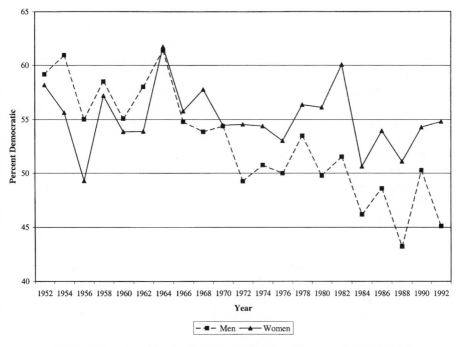

Figure 7.3. The Gender Gap in Party Identification, 1952–1992.

Voters' selection between the options offered by the political parties is only meaningful if those choices are translated into public policy. Thus, for parties to play the role of mediating institutions within the American democratic system, divergent issue positions must be connected to the functioning of government. The evolution of the parties' positioning vis-à-vis women's rights has had clear consequences for public policy outcomes. In the early 1970s, a confluence of factors contributed to an unprecedented level of policy making with regard to women's rights, including the brief consensus between the parties on the general concept of legal equality for women. The result was the passage of the ERA and major federal nondiscrimination legislation covering education, credit, and employment, as well as the federal pay scales, military academies, jury duty, and so on (Mueller 1988b). These laws extended to and transformed many areas of American life. Title IX of the 1972 Educational Amendments Act, for example, was recently lauded on its twenty-fifth anniversary for its major impact on women in sports. While only five percent of colleges were estimated to be in full compliance with Title IX in 1996, the level of women's participation in sports has grown impressively. In 1972, fewer than 300,000 girls participated in high school sports; by 1996, more than two million girls did so (McGlen and O'Connor 1998). While its impact on sports has received much of the attention and controversy, Title IX also covers admissions, employment, and academic procedures, and it has been a crucial part of the revolution in gender and education these past twenty-five years. Similarly, prohibitions against credit discrimination have helped open the door to financial independence for millions of American women, the opening of the military academies and induction in the armed forces to women has provided alternative opportunities for careers and professional advancement, and so on.

In some ways, feminist activists were correct that injecting partisanship into the women's rights debate would hinder policy making. Since the brief period of partisan consensus in the early 1970s, the pace of gender-related legislating, particularly of the import of the early laws, has slowed considerably. Part of the reason is that with the major areas of discrimination legislated, problems faced became more difficult and complicated, and solutions more controversial and divisive. Yet the emergence of party polarization over women's rights and feminism contributed to this stalemate as well. Clearly, important legislation pertaining to women's rights has emerged from Congress since the early 1970s, but it has generally been few and far between, the outcome of protracted, often partisan, battles, and significant compromise. Struggles for the extension of the ERA deadline and prohibitions against pregnancy discrimination in the late 1970s foreshadowed the emergent partisan nature of those fights. The failure of the effort for ERA ratification can be in part attributed to the emergence of partisan divisions; as Mansbridge writes, "a constitutional amendment needs an overwhelming majority, so once it becomes a partisan issue its chances of passing are minimal" (1986, 19).

In a broader conception, however, the lack of activity on women's rights can be viewed as reflecting the reality of divergent preferences vis-à-vis women's rights public policy. In other words, in some cases, lack of federal action may be the preference of certain segments of the population—preferences being represented by one of the two major political parties. The Family and Medical Leave Act provides one example of the way in which party polarization on women's rights has affected the outcome of policy making. As first proposed by Democratic Representative Patricia Schroeder (CO) in 1985, the bill required all businesses to provide between four to six months of job-protected leave for responsibilities related to childbirth, adoption, and the care of ill and elderly relatives. The bill also established a commission to study and make recommendations within two years on the issue of *paid* parental and disability leave. The Democratic Congress was able to pass a weaker version of the bill that exempted all businesses with less than fifty employees (the vast majority) and steered away from the question of paid leave. Nevertheless, it was vetoed by Republican President George Bush. The 103rd Congress passed the bill again, and the newly elected Democratic President, Bill Clinton, signed the Family and Medical Leave Act into law in 1993 (Burrell 1994).

Even without a change in the law, changes in partisan control have meant dramatic changes in the enforcement of existing programs and policies. The election of a Democratic president in 1992, for example, effected a virtual reversal of a number of pro-life federal policies established by his Republican predecessors. On his third day as president, Clinton issued memorandum lifting the gag rule prohibiting abortion counseling in clinics that receive federal financing, allowing fetal tissue research, and requesting a reassessment of the French abortion drug, RU 486 (Toner 1993). The consequences of partisan turnover extend to the judicial branch as well, effects that can be considerably long-lasting. Presidents appoint federal judges who, because of lifetime tenure, maintain their seats, and thus impact the law, long after the appointing president has left office. In recent years, appointees' views on abortion have garnered particular attention. While often decried as an inappropriate litmus test, inquiries into judges' views on abortion are entirely consistent with partisan positioning on the issue; the Republican platform has explicitly pledged the appointment of pro-life judges since 1980. The effects of partisanship on the judicial branch are not necessarily limited to appointments and abortion; Democratic judges have been shown to be more supportive of accusers in sex discrimination cases, for example (Gryski and Main 1986).

In short, party issue positions matter because parties do. Political parties provide cues, manage competition and debate, control resources, structure government, and shape policy making. As a result, their positions are ultimately consequential for the lives of the women, and men, who live in that political system. In the case of women's rights, their ability to fulfill these functions in the face of widespread social upheaval and transition is quite remarkable. As debate over the role of parties in the modern American political system continues, the capacity of parties to absorb and channel an issue of this scale and divisiveness stands as testament to the continuing relevance and importance of parties in the functioning of American democracy.

CONCLUSION

This book began with the dramatic events of 1980: the Republican reversal on the ERA and the concomitant Democratic embrace of feminism. In the 1950s and early 1960s, partisan alignment on women's rights was both different and less polarized. The events of 1980 reflect the culmination of developments tracing back several decades and signaled the emergence of a new partisan equilibrium in which Democrats and Republicans now stand on opposite sides of the women's rights debate. In examining this transformation, I have sought to answer two central questions. First, what has been the nature of the parties' evolving positions on women's rights issues? This research suggests that the transformation indicated by the events of 1980 reflects a long-term process in which Republicans, once the party slightly more likely to advocate women's rights, have ceded that claim to Democrats, who became far more active than Republicans in supporting women's rights. Second, why have the parties realigned themselves as they have? This research has answered that question by focusing on the process of equilibrium disruption and the role of changes in the issue, the parties' coalitions, and the party elites themselves.

When Republicans took both the House and Senate following the 1994 elections, the Republican leadership held an orientation weekend attended exclusively by incoming Republicans. The featured speaker, who was given credit for the Republican Revolution by many in attendance, was radio talk show personality Rush Limbaugh, a man who coined the derisive phrase "femiNazi" and actively criticized what he termed the feminist agenda (Rosentiel 1994; Merida 1994). In light of such events, it is perhaps not surprising that from our present standpoint it can be difficult to conceive that, compared to the Democratic party, the Republican party was once the champion of women's rights. Yet it is the very fact that we find that possibility so odd that makes the puzzle of the realignment of the parties on women's rights issues so compelling. For many years, Republicans were more active for women's rights than were Democrats, but almost two decades after the GOP backed away from the ERA, the present women's rights cleavage between the parties, and the sides that they have chosen, have become part of the political landscape that citizens and social scientists alike recognize and accept.

Appendix

Z-TEST FOR BINOMIAL DATA

THE Z-TEST for binomial data indicates whether the rates of behavior of two groups are significantly different. Specifically, the Z-test for binomial data allows us to compare two discrete random variables. Where n and m are the sample sizes for two independent groups (such as Democratic and Republican House members) and x and y are the number of successes (members cosponsoring any pro-women's rights bills, for example) experienced by each, respectively, we can reject the null hypothesis (H_0: $p_x = p_y$) if

$$\frac{\dfrac{x}{n} - \dfrac{y}{m}}{\sqrt{\dfrac{\left(\dfrac{x+y}{n+m}\right)\left(1 - \dfrac{x+y}{n+m}\right)(n+m)}{nm}}} \leq -z_{\propto/2} \quad \text{or} \quad \geq +z_{\propto/2}$$

where α is the level of significance (Larsen and Marx 1986, 378–82).

MEDIA COVERAGE

The *New York Times* index is employed to derive a measure of the level of public attention to women's rights as reflected in media coverage, employing a methodology loosely adopted from Baumgartner and Jones (1993). To track changes in the level of press coverage of varying issues over an extended period of time, I code all items listed under the heading of "women" in the annual *New York Times* index. Baumgartner and Jones replicate the process with the index to the *Reader's Guide* and report strikingly similar findings across the two sources. I am thus confident in limiting data collection to the *New York Times*.

The *New York Times* index provides a brief abstract of each item listed, in addition to basic descriptive information (data and placement). Using that abstract, I determine whether each story involved women's rights. Consistent with the definition of women's rights employed in this research, a story was coded as relevant to the women's rights debate if it involved questions of women's social, economic, or political role; referenced a women's rights policy concern (as defined in chapter 1); or involved feminism, the women's movement, or opposition to either. I include only national-level stories in this analysis, meaning that those stories specific to New York City or state, and not of more general interest to the nation as a whole, are not included. While the *New York Times* is a local paper for New York citizens, it is also clearly a national paper, read by a large number of people outside of the region and providing a source of information for numerous regional and local newspapers and other press throughout the United States. It is because of the national import and reach of the *New York Times* that it provides a useful indicator for my purposes.

CONGRESSIONAL HEARINGS

Congressional hearings data are derived from the Congressional Information Service's *Congressional Masterfile 1* and *2* available on CD-ROM. These computer files, which replicate data also available in paper format, contain detailed information on Congressional activity from 1789 to the present in machine-readable and searchable format. Under hearings, I searched for the subject words women, woman, female, or sex. Based on the hearing titles and text abstracts, I coded all hearings that concerned women's rights (as defined in this research) for Congressional session, chamber (House, Senate, or Joint), hearing date(s), committee and subcommittee, and a short description of the hearing topic. If a hearing focused on a broad topic that included, but was not limited to, a women's rights issue, it is included in the analysis.

MOVEMENT EVENT SERIES

The procedures for coding women's rights events data were adopted from Costain's (1992; see also Rosenfeld and Ward 1996) study of the women's movement (1950–1986). Costain, in turn, based her coding on McAdam's (1982) work on the civil rights movement (1930–1970). Because I seek a less detailed picture of movement activity than either of these authors, for whom their respective movements were the focus of research, I have not coded the data for the 1952–1992 time period with as great as detail. As a result, while the time series constructed can be considered similar, they are not entirely comparable to those created by Costain or McAdam.

The following basic guidelines were followed. All synopses of stories in the annual index of the *New York Times* under the heading "Women:

United States"[1] were read and coded if they meet the following guidelines. Only those events relevant to women's rights were coded. Stories or articles that did not directly concern women's rights, such as profiles of female athletes or the like, were not coded. Only *events* were coded. Events include protest activities, press conferences, meetings, announcements of positions (again, formal announcements, not interview statements), lecture series, passage of legislation, proclamations, launching of campaigns, and so on. Interviews with movement leaders or other individuals are not events and thus were not coded. When two (or more) different and discrete events are covered in one story, two (or more) separate events were coded. Alternatively, more than one story reporting on the same event was coded as only one event.

Each event was coded for direction (pro–women's rights or anti–women's rights), type of event (protest/agitation, lobbying, advocacy, organizational or membership activities, government action, or assistance/ education/entertainment), and level (local, state, national, or international). The women's movement event series is an annual count of national-level pro–women's rights events, not including those events involving government action or strictly educational or entertaining in nature. The opposition event series is an annual count of national level anti–women's rights events, not including those events that involve government action or are strictly educational or entertaining in nature.

[1] In 1984 the *New York Times* index changed its organization slightly and ceased to provide separate categories for different countries, but instead included all synopses under a general heading. Examination of the subsequent years' synopses suggests that they contain similar information to that included under the subheading "United States," in addition to a small number of synopses of stories which concern other countries. Synopses of stories on other countries were not coded unless they concerned events that affected or were related to the women's movement in the United States, such as the U.N. Conference on the Decade of the Woman.

References

Abramowitz, Alan I. 1995. "It's Abortion, Stupid: Policy Voting in the 1992 Presidential Election." *Journal of Politics* 57:176–86.

Abzug, Bella with Mim Keller. 1984. *Gender Gap: Bella Abzug's Guide to Political Power for Women.* Boston: Houghton Mifflin.

Adams, Greg. 1997. "Abortion: Evidence of Issue Evolution." *American Journal of Political Science* 41:718–37.

Aldrich, John. 1983. "A Downsian Spatial Model with Party Activism." *American Political Science Review* 77:974–90.

Alesina, Alberto. 1988. "Credibility and Policy Convergence in a Two-Party System with Rational Voters." *American Economic Review* 78:796–805.

Andersen, Kristi. 1979. *The Creation of a Democratic Majority, 1928–1936.* Chicago: The University of Chicago Press.

———. 1996. *After Suffrage: Women in Partisan and Electoral Politics before the New Deal.* Chicago: The University of Chicago Press.

Aranson, Peter H. and Peter C. Ordeshook. 1972. "Spatial Strategies for Sequential Elections." In *Probability Models of Collective Decision Making,* ed. Richard G. Niemi and Herbert F. Weisberg. Columbus, OH: Charles E. Merrill.

Asher, Herbert B. and Herbert F. Weisberg. 1978. "Voting Change in Congress: Some Dynamic Perspectives on an Evolutionary Process." *American Journal of Political Science* 22:391–425.

Baer, Denise L. 1993. "Political Parties: The Missing Variable in Women and Politics Research." *Political Research Quarterly* 46:547–76.

Baer, Denise L. and David A. Bositis. 1988. *Elite Cadres and Party Coalitions: Representing the Public in Party Politics.* New York: Greenwood Press.

Baker, James N. with Howard Fineman and Timothy Noah. 1988. "Closing the Gender Gap: How Dukakis Squandered His Lead among Women." *Newsweek,* October 24, p. 22.

Basler, Barbara. 1984. "G.O.P. Starting Campaign to Show 'Reagan Is Terrific on Women's Issues.'" *New York Times,* April 6, p. A24.

Bass, Harold F., Jr. 1991. "Background to Debate: A Reader's Guide and Bibliography." In *The End of Realignment? Interpreting America's Electoral Eras,* ed. Byron E. Shafer. Madison: The University of Wisconsin Press.

Baumgartner, Frank R. and Bryan D. Jones. 1993. *Agendas and Instability in American Politics.* Chicago: The University of Chicago Press.

Beck, Nathaniel. 1982. "Parties, Administrations, and American Macroeconomic Outcomes." *American Political Science Review* 76 (March):83–93.

Beck, Paul Allen. 1997. *Party Politics in America.* Eighth Edition. New York: Longman.

Bennett, Linda L. M. 1986. "The Gender Gap: When an Opinion Gap Is Not a Voting Bloc." *Social Science Quarterly* 67:613–25.

Bennetts, Leslie. 1980a. "Rights and Abortion Planks Are Achieved by Feminists." *New York Times*, August 13, p. 3.

———. 1980b. "Republicans and Women's Issues: For Some, a Painful Conflict." *New York Times*, September 2, p. B12.

———. 1980c. "NOW Rejects All 3 for President, Condemns Reagan as 'Medieval.'" *New York Times*, October 6, p. 20.

Bernhardt, M. Daniel and Daniel E. Ingberman. 1985. "Candidate Reputations and the 'Incumbency Effect.'" *Journal of Public Economics* 27:47–67.

Biersack, Robert and Paul S. Herrnson. 1994. "Political Parties and the Year of the Woman." In *The Year of the Woman: Myths and Realities*, ed. Elizabeth Adell Cook, Sue Thomas, and Clyde Wilcox. Boulder, CO: Westview Press.

Bird, Caroline and the Members and Staff of the National Commission on the Observance of International Women's Year, eds. 1979. *What Women Want: From the Official Report to the President, The Congress and the People of the United States*. New York: Simon & Schuster.

Black, Earl and Merle Black. 1992. *The Vital South: How Presidents Are Elected*. Cambridge, MA: Harvard University Press.

Blair, Emily Newell. 1929. "Women in the Political Parties." *The Annals of the American Academy* 143:217–29.

Blumenthal, Sidney. 1996. "A Doll's House: Not So Long Ago, the G.O.P. Still Had Room for Suffragettes." *The New Yorker* (August 19):30–33.

Boles, Janet K. 1979. *The Politics of the Equal Rights Amendment: Conflict and the Decision Process*. New York: Longman.

Bonk, Kathy. 1988. "The Selling of the Gender Gap." In *The Politics of the Gender Gap: The Social Construction of Political Influence*, ed. Carol M. Mueller. Newbury Park, CA: Sage.

Brady, David W. and Naomi B. Lynn. 1973. "Switched-Seat Congressional Districts: Their Effect on Party Voting and Public Policy." *American Journal of Political Science* 17 (August):528–43.

Brennan, Mary C. 1995. *Turning Right in the Sixties: The Conservative Capture of the GOP*. Chapel Hill: The University of North Carolina Press.

Brown, Robert D. 1995. "Party Cleavages and Welfare Effort in the American States." *American Political Science Review* 89:22–33.

Bruce, John M., John A. Clark, and John H. Kessel. 1991. "Advocacy Politics in Presidential Parties." *American Political Science Review* 85:1089–1105.

Budge, Ian, and Richard I. Hofferbert. 1990. "Mandates and Policy Outputs: U.S. Party Platforms and Federal Expenditures." *American Political Science Review* 84 (March):111–31.

Burkett, Elinor. 1996. "In the Land of Conservative Women." *The Atlantic Monthly* (September):19–29.

Burnham, Walter Dean. 1970. *Critical Elections and the Mainsprings of American Politics*. New York: W. W. Norton.

Burns, John W. 1997. "Party Policy Change: The Case of the Democrats and Taxes, 1956–68." *Party Politics* 3:513–32.

Burns, John W. and Andrew J. Taylor. 1996. "The Positions Parties Take: Congressional Republicans and the Individual Income Tax, 1969–1994." Paper presented at the 1996 Annual Meeting of the American Political Science Association, San Francisco, August 29–September 1.

Burrell, Barbara. 1994. *A Woman's Place Is in the House: Campaigning for Congress in the Feminist Era.* Ann Arbor: University of Michigan Press.

Calvert, Randall L. 1985. "Robustness of the Multidimensional Model: Candidate Motivations, Uncertainty, and Convergence." *American Journal of Political Science* 29:69–95.

Campbell, Angus, Philip E. Converse, Warren E. Miller, and Donald E. Stokes. 1960. *The American Voter.* New York: Wiley.

Campbell, James E. 1982. "Cosponsoring Legislation in the U.S. Congress." *Legislative Studies Quarterly* 7:415–22.

Carmines, Edward G. and J. David Gopoian. 1981. "Issue Coalitions, Issueless Campaigns: The Paradox of Rationality in American Presidential Elections." *Journal of Politics* 43:1170–89.

Carmines, Edward G. and James A. Stimson. 1986. "On the Structure and Sequence of Issue Evolution." *American Political Science Review* 80:901–20.

———. 1989. *Issue Evolution: Race and the Transformation of American Politics.* Princeton, NJ: Princeton University Press.

Carroll, Susan J. 1985. *Women as Candidates in American Politics.* Bloomington: Indiana University Press.

———. 1988. "Women's Autonomy and the Gender Gap: 1980 and 1982." In *The Politics of the Gender Gap: The Social Construction of Political Influence,* ed. Carol M. Mueller. Newbury Park, CA: Sage.

Cater, Douglas. 1964. *Power in Washington.* New York: Random House.

Chafe, William H. 1972. *The American Woman: Her Changing Social, Economic, and Political Roles, 1920–1970.* London: Oxford University Press.

Clark, Cal and Janet Clark. 1999. "The Gender Gap in 1996: More Meaning Than a 'Revenge of the Soccer Moms.'" In *Women in Politics: Outsiders or Insiders?* Third Edition, ed. Lois Duke Whitaker. Upper Saddle River, NJ: Prentice Hall.

Clausen, Aage. 1973. *How Congressmen Decide: A Policy Focus.* New York: St. Martins.

Clines, Francis X. 1984. "Reagan Defends His Record on Women." *New York Times,* April 6, p. A24.

Clymer, Adam. 1979. "Board of NOW to Oppose Carter, Charging Lag on Women's Issues." *New York Times,* December 11, p. 1.

———. 1982. "Subtle Shifts in G.O.P. Appeals Aimed at Women." *New York Times,* August 5, p. A16.

———. 1983. "G.O.P. Women Ask For President's Help On Equity Measure." *New York Times,* March 11, p. A13.

Clubb, Jerome M., William H. Flanigan, and Nancy H. Zingale. 1980. *Partisan Realignment: Voters, Parties, and Government in American History.* Beverly Hills, CA: Sage.

Cobb, Roger W. and Charles D. Elder. 1983. *Participation in American Politics: The Dynamics of Agenda-Building.* Second Edition. Baltimore: The Johns Hopkins University Press.

Coleman, James S. 1972. "The Positions of Political Parties in Elections." In *Prob-*

ability Models of Collective Decision Making, ed. Richard G. Niemi and Herbert F. Weisberg. Columbus, OH: Charles E. Merrill.

Congressional Record Index. 1953–1988. Washington, DC: United States Government Printing Office.

Conover, Pamela Johnston. 1988. "Feminists and the Gender Gap." *Journal of Politics* 50:985–1010.

Conover, Pamela Johnston and Virginia Gray. 1983. *Feminism and the New Right: Conflict over the American Family.* New York: Praeger.

Converse, Philip E., Angus Campbell, Warren E. Miller, and Donald E. Stokes. 1961. "Stability and Change in 1960: A Reinstating Election." *American Political Science Review* 55:269–80.

Converse, Philip E., Aage R. Clausen, and Warren E. Miller. 1965. "Electoral Myth and Reality: The 1964 Election." *American Political Science Review* 59:321–36.

Cook, Elizabeth Adell. 1989. "Measuring Feminist Consciousness." *Women and Politics* 9:71–88.

Cook, Elizabeth Adell and Clyde Wilcox. 1991. "Feminism and the Gender Gap— a Second Look." *Journal of Politics* 53:1111–22.

Costain, Anne N. 1988. "Women's Claims as a Special Interest." In *The Politics of the Gender Gap: The Social Construction of Political Influence*, ed. Carol M. Mueller. Newbury Park, CA: Sage.

———. 1991. "After Reagan: New Party Attitudes toward Gender." *Annals of the American Academy* 515:114–25.

———. 1992. *Inviting Women's Rebellion: A Political Process Interpretation of the Women's Movement.* Baltimore: Johns Hopkins University Press.

Costain, Anne N. and W. Douglas Costain. 1987. "Strategies and Tactics of the Women's Movement in the United States: The Role of Political Parties." In *The Women's Movements of the United States and Western Europe: Consciousness, Political Opportunity, and Public Policy*, ed. Mary Fainsod Katzenstein and Carol M. Mueller. Philadelphia: Temple University Press.

Costain, Anne N. and Steven Majstorovic. 1994. "Congress, Social Movements, and Public Opinion: The Multiple Origins of Women's Rights Legislation." *Political Research Quarterly* 47:111–35.

Cott, Nancy F. 1987. *The Grounding of Modern Feminism.* New Haven, CT: Yale University Press.

Cox, Gary W. and Mathew D. McCubbins. 1993. *Legislative Leviathan: Party Government in the House.* Berkeley: University of California Press.

Cummings, Judith. 1983. "Several Republican Women in Legislatures Urge Party to Shift on Rights." *New York Times*, December 4, p. 30.

Curtis, Charlotte. 1972. "Draft Abortion-Reform Plank Being Written at White House." *New York Times*, August 6, p. 40.

Dales, Douglas. 1960. "Candidates Urge End to Bias in U.S." *New York Times*, October 13, p. 26.

Davis, Flora. 1991. *Moving the Mountain: The Women's Movement in America since 1960.* New York: Simon & Schuster.

Deckard, Barbara Sinclair. 1979. *The Women's Movement: Political, Socioeconomic, and Psychological Issues.* Second Edition. New York: Harper & Row.

Dowd, Maureen. 1984. "Women Assess Impact of Mondale Loss." *New York Times*, November 14, p. A22.

Downs, Anthony. 1957. *An Economic Theory of Democracy*. New York: Harper-Collins.

Drew, Elizabeth. 1981. *Portrait of an Election: The 1980 Presidential Campaign*. New York: Simon & Schuster.

————. 1989. *Election Journal: Political Events of 1987–1988*. New York: W. Morrow.

The Economist. 1997. "Wimmin Are from Mars, Women Are from Venus." June 21, pp. 87–89.

Edelman, Murray. 1964. *The Symbolic Uses of Politics*. Urbana: University of Illinois Press.

Edsall, Thomas Byrne with Mary D. Edsall. 1991. *Chain Reaction: The Impact of Race, Rights, and Taxes on American Politics*. New York: W. W. Norton.

Eldersveld, Samuel J. 1981. *Political Parties in American Society*. New York: Basic Books.

Epstein, Lee and Thomas G. Walker. 1995. *Constitutional Law for a Changing America: Rights, Liberties, and Justice*. Second Edition. Washington, DC: CQ Press.

Erie, Steven P. 1988. *Rainbow's End: Irish-Americans and the Dilemmas of Urban Machine Politics, 1840–1985*. Berkeley: University of California Press.

Erie, Steven P. and Martin Rein. 1988. "Women and the Welfare State." In *The Politics of the Gender Gap: The Social Construction of Political Influence*, ed. Carol M. Mueller. Newbury Park, CA: Sage.

Erikson, Robert S. 1971. "The Relationship between Party Control and Civil Rights Legislation in the American States." *Western Political Quarterly* 24: 178–82.

Erikson, Robert S., Gerald C. Wright, Jr., and John P. McIver. 1989. "Political Parties, Public Opinion, and State Policy in the United States." *American Political Science Review* 83 (September):729–50.

Evans, Sara. 1979. *Personal Politics: The Roots of Women's Liberation in the Civil Rights Movement and the New Left*. New York: Random House.

Evans, Sara M. 1989. *Born for Liberty: A History of Women in America*. New York: The Free Press.

Felsenthal, Carol. 1981. *The Sweetheart of the Silent Majority: The Biography of Phyllis Schlafly*. Garden City, NY: Doubleday & Company.

Fenno, Richard F., Jr. 1973. *Congressmen in Committees*. Boston: Little, Brown, and Co.

Ferree, Myra Marx and Beth B. Hess. 1985. *Controversy and Coalition: The New Feminist Movement*. Boston: Twayne Publishers.

Fiorina, Morris P. 1974. *Representatives, Roll Calls, and Constituencies*. Lexington, KY: Lexington Books.

Flexner, Eleanor. 1959, 1970. *Century of Struggle: The Woman's Rights Movement in the United States*. Cambridge, MA: Harvard University Press.

Franklin, Charles H. and John E. Jackson. 1983. "The Dynamics of Party Identification." *American Political Science Review* 77:957–73.

Frankovic, Kathleen A. 1988. "The Ferraro Factor: The Women's Movement, the Polls, and the Press." In *The Politics of the Gender Gap: The Social Construction of Political Influence*, ed. Carol M. Mueller. Newbury Park, CA: Sage.

Freeman, J. Leiper. 1965. *The Political Process.* New York: Random House.

Freeman, Jo. 1975. *The Politics of Women's Liberation: A Case Study of an Emerging Social Movement and Its Relation to the Policy Process.* New York: David McKay Company.

———. 1986. "The Political Culture of the Democratic and Republican Parties." *Political Science Quarterly* 101:327–56.

———. 1987. "Whom You Know Versus Whom You Represent: Feminist Influence in the Democratic and Republican Parties." In *The Women's Movements of the United States and Western Europe: Consciousness, Political Opportunity, and Public Policy*, ed. Mary Fainsod Katzenstein and Carol M. Mueller. Philadelphia: Temple University Press.

———. 1988. "Women at the 1988 Democratic Convention." *PS: Political Science and Politics* 21:875–81.

———. 1989. "Feminist Activities at the 1988 Republican Convention." *PS: Political Science and Politics* 22:39–47.

———. 1993. "Feminism vs. Family Values: Women at the 1992 Democratic and Republican Conventions." *PS: Political Science and Politics* 26:21–28.

———. 1999. "Gender Gaps in Presidential Elections" (Forum). *PS: Political Science and Politics* 32:191–92.

Gerber, Elisabeth R. and John E. Jackson. 1993. "Endogenous Preferences and the Study of Institutions." *American Political Science Review* 87:639–56.

Germond, Jack W. and Jules Whitcover. 1981. *Blue Smoke and Mirrors: How Reagan Won and Why Carter Lost the Election of 1980.* New York: Viking Press.

———. 1985. *Wake Us When It's Over: Presidential Politics of 1984.* New York: Macmillan.

Gertzog, Irwin N. 1995. *Congressional Women: Their Recruitment, Integration, and Behavior.* Second Edition. Westport, CT: Praeger.

Ginsberg, Benjamin. 1976. "Elections and Public Policy." *American Political Science Review* 70:41–49.

Grofman, Bernard, Robert Griffin, and Amihai Glazer. 1990. "Identical Geography, Different Party: a Natural Experiment on the Magnitude of Party Differences in the U.S. Senate, 1960–84." In *Developments in Electoral Geography*, ed. R. J. Johnston, F. M. Shelley, and P. J. Taylor. New York: Routledge.

Gryski, Gerard S. and Eleanor C. Main. 1986. "Social Backgrounds as Predictors of Votes on State Courts of Last Resort: The Case of Sex Discrimination." *Western Political Quarterly* 39:528–37.

Harrison, Cynthia. 1988. *On Account of Sex: The Politics of Women's Issues, 1945–1968.* Berkeley: University of California Press.

Hartmann, Susan M. 1989. *From Margin to Mainstream: American Women and Politics since 1960.* New York: Alfred A. Knopf.

Harvey, Anna L. 1998. *Votes without Leverage: Women in American Electoral Politics, 1920–1970.* New York: Cambridge University Press.

Heclo, Hugh. 1978. "Issue Networks and the Executive Establishment" In *The*

New American Political System, ed. Anthony King. Washington, DC: American Enterprise Institute.

Hedlund, Ronald D. and Keith E. Hamm. 1996. "Political Parties as Vehicles for Organizing U.S. State Legislative Committees." *Legislative Studies Quarterly* 21:383–408.

Heinz, John P., Edward O. Laumann, Robert L. Nelson, and Robert H. Salisbury. 1993. *The Hollow Core: Private Interests in National Policy Making.* Cambridge, MA: Harvard University Press.

Heywood, Leslie and Jennifer Drake, eds. 1997. *Third Wave Agenda: Being Feminist, Doing Feminism.* Minneapolis: University of Minnesota Press.

Hibbs, Douglas A., Jr. 1977. "Political Parties and Macroeconomic Policy." *American Political Science Review* 71:1467–87.

Hill, Kim Quaile and Jan E. Leighley. 1996. "Political Parties and Class Mobilization in Contemporary United States Elections." *American Journal of Political Science* 40:787–804.

Himmelstein, Jerome L. 1990. *To the Right: The Transformation of American Conservatism.* Berkeley: University of California Press.

Huckfeldt, Robert and John Sprague. 1992. "Political Parties and Electoral Mobilization: Political Structure, Social Structure, and the Party Canvass." *American Political Science Review* 86:70–86.

Hunter, Marjorie. 1963. "U.S. Panel Urges Women to Sue for Equal Rights." *New York Times*, October 12, p. 1.

———. 1984. "Reagan Defends Record on Women." *New York Times*, February 18, p. A7.

Jackson, John E. 1975. "Issues, Party Choices, and Presidential Votes." *American Journal of Political Science* 19 (May):161–85.

———. 1996. "Electoral Competition with Endogenous Voter Preferences." Paper presented at the Annual Meeting of the Midwest Political Science Association, April 18–20, Chicago.

Jacoby, William G. 1988. "The Impact of Party Identification on Issue Attitudes." *American Journal of Political Science* 32:643–61.

Jennings, Edward T., Jr. 1979. "Competition, Constituencies, and Welfare Policies in American States." *American Political Science Review* 73:414–29.

Jennings, M. Kent. 1990. "Women in Party Politics." In *Women, Politics, and Change*, ed. Louise A. Tilly and Patricia Gurin. New York: Russell Sage Foundation.

Jewell, Malcolm E. 1955. "Party Voting in American State Legislatures." *American Political Science Review* 49:773–91.

Jewell, Malcolm E. and David M. Olson. 1988. *Political Parties and Elections in American States.* Third Edition. Chicago: The Dorsey Press.

Johnson, Donald Bruce. 1973. *National Party Platforms, 1840–1972.* Urbana: University of Illinois Press.

Katzenstein, Mary Fainsod. 1998. *Faithful and Fearless: Moving Feminist Protest inside the Church and Military.* Princeton, NJ: Princeton University Press.

Kessel, John. 1988. *Presidential Campaign Politics.* Fourth Edition. Pacific Grove, CA: Brooks/Cole.

Kessler, Daniel and Keith Krehbiel. 1996. "Dynamics of Cosponsorship." *American Political Science Review* 90:555–66.

Kessler-Harris, Alice. 1982. *Out to Work: A History of Wage-Earning Women in the United States.* New York: Oxford University Press.

Key, V. O., Jr. 1955. "A Theory of Critical Elections." *Journal of Politics* 17:3–18.

———. 1959. "Secular Realignment and the Party System." *Journal of Politics* 21:198–210.

———. 1964. *Politics, Parties, and Pressure Groups.* Fifth Edition. New York: Crowell.

———. 1967. *Public Opinion and American Democracy.* New York: Knopf.

King, Gary, and Michael Laver. 1993. "Party Platforms, Mandates, and Government Spending." *American Political Science Review* 87:744–50.

King, Martin Luther, Jr. 1963. "Letter from the Birmingham Jail." In *The American Intellectual Tradition, Volume II: 1865 to the Present,* ed. David A. Hollinger and Charles Capper. 1989. New York: Oxford University Press.

Kingdon, John W. 1973. *Congressmen's Voting Decisions.* New York: Harper & Row.

———. 1984. *Agendas, Alternatives, and Public Policies.* New York: Harper-Collins.

Klatch, Rebecca E. 1987. *Women of the New Right.* Philadelphia: Temple University Press.

Klein, Ethel. 1984. *Gender Politics: From Consciousness to Mass Politics.* Cambridge, MA: Harvard University Press.

Kollman, Ken, John H. Miller, and Scott E. Page. 1992. "Adaptive Parties in Spatial Elections." *American Political Science Review* 86:929–37.

Krehbiel, Keith. 1995. "Cosponsors and Wafflers from A to Z." *American Journal of Political Science* 39:906–23.

Krukones, Michael G. 1984. *Promises and Performances: Presidential Campaigns as Policy Predictor.* Lanham, MD: University Press of America.

Ladd, Everett Carll. 1991. "Like Waiting for Godot: The Uselessness of 'Realignment' for Understanding Change in Contemporary American Politics." In *The End of Realignment? Interpreting America's Electoral Eras,* ed. Byron E. Shafer. Madison: The University of Wisconsin Press.

Larsen, Richard J. and Morris L. Marx. 1986. *An Introduction to Mathematical Statistics and Its Applications.* Englewood Cliffs, NJ: Prentice Hall.

Leader, Shelah Gilbert. 1977. "The Policy Impact of Elected Women Officials." In *The Impact of the Electoral Process,* ed. Louis Maisel and Joseph Cooper. Beverly Hills, CA: Sage.

Leege, David C. and Kenneth D. Wald. n.d. *The Politics of Cultural Differences: Social Change and Voter Mobilization Strategies in the Post-New Deal Period.* Notre Dame, IN: draft manuscript.

Lelyveld, Joseph. 1976. "Normally Proper G.O.P. Women Come Out Fighting Over E.R.A.." *New York Times,* August 17, p. 36.

Luker, Kristin. 1984. *Abortion and the Politics of Motherhood.* Berkeley: University of California Press.

Lydon, Christopher. 1976. "Abortion Plank Is Fought By Republican Feminists." *New York Times,* August 8, p. 23.

Lynn, Frank. 1982. "Women's Issues Given Strong Support by Democrats in Philadelphia." *New York Times*, June 28, p. B7.

MacDonald, Stuart Elaine and George Rabinowitz. 1987. "The Dynamics of Structural Realignment." *American Political Science Review* 81:775–96.

Madden, Richard L. 1976a. "G.O.P. Platform Unit Votes, 8–7, Not to Take Stand on Equal Rights." *New York Times*, August 12, p. 16.

———. 1976b. "Platform Panel Votes to Endorse Equal Rights Plan." *New York Times*, August 13, p. 1.

Mansbridge, Jane J. 1985. "Myth and Reality: The ERA and the Gender Gap in the 1980 Election." *Public Opinion Quarterly* 49:164–78.

———. 1986. *Why We Lost the ERA*. Chicago: The University of Chicago Press.

Mathews, Donald G. and Jane Sherron De Hart. 1990. *Sex, Gender, and the Politics of the ERA: A State and the Nation*. New York: Oxford University Press.

Mayhew, David R. 1974. *Congress: The Electoral Connection*. New Haven, CT: Yale University Press.

McAdam, Doug. 1982. *Political Process and the Development of Black Insurgency, 1930–1970*. Princeton, NJ: Princeton University Press.

McClosky, Herbert, Paul J. Hoffman, and Rosemary O'Hara. 1960. "Issue Conflict and Consensus Among Party Leaders and Followers." *American Political Science Review* 54:406–27.

McGlen, Nancy E. and Karen O'Connor. 1995. *Women, Politics, and American Society*. Englewood Cliffs, NJ: Prentice Hall.

———. 1998. *Women, Politics, and American Society*. Second Edition. Englewood Cliffs, NJ: Prentice Hall.

Melich, Tanya. 1996. *The Republican War against Women: An Insider's Report from Behind the Lines*. New York: Bantam Books.

Merida, Kevin. 1994. "Rush Limbaugh Saluted as a 'Majority Maker.'" *The Washington Post*, December 11, p. A30.

Mezey, Susan Gluck. 1978. "Women and Representation: the Case of Hawaii." *Journal of Politics* 40:369–85.

———. 1994. "Increasing the Number of Women in Office: Does It Matter?" In *The Year of the Woman: Myths and Realities*, ed. Elizabeth Adell Cook, Sue Thomas, and Clyde Wilcox. Boulder, CO: Westview Press.

Miller, Arthur H., Warren E. Miller, Alden S. Raine, and Thad A. Browne. 1976. "A Majority Party in Disarray: Policy Polarization in the 1972 Election." *American Political Science Review* 70:753–78.

Miller, Judith. 1980. "An Unrepentant Mary Crisp Departs." *New York Times*, July 11, p. 14.

Miller, Warren E. 1988. "Gender and the Vote, 1984." In *The Politics of the Gender Gap: The Social Construction of Political Influence*, ed. Carol M. Mueller. Newbury Park, CA: Sage.

Miller, Warren E. and M. Kent Jennings in association with Barbara G. Farah. 1986. *Parties in Transition: A Longitudinal Study of Party Elites and Party Supporters*. New York: Russell Sage Foundation.

Miller, Warren E. and Teresa E. Levitin. 1984. *Leadership and Change: Presidential Elections from 1952 to 1976*. New York: University Press of America.

Monroe, Alan D. 1983. "American Party Platforms and Public Opinion." *American Journal of Political Science* 27:27–42.

Morehouse, Sarah McCally. 1973. "The State Political Party and the Policy-Making Process." *American Political Science Review* 57:55–72.

Morgan, Robin, ed. 1970. *Sisterhood Is Powerful: An Anthology of Writings from the Women's Liberation Movement.* New York: Random House.

Morton, Rebecca. 1993. "Incomplete Information and Ideological Explanations of Platform Divergence." *American Political Science Review* 87 (June):382–92.

Mueller, Carol M. 1988a. "The Empowerment of Women: Polling and the Women's Voting Bloc." In *The Politics of the Gender Gap: The Social Construction of Political Influence,* ed. Carol M. Mueller. Newbury Park, CA: Sage.

———. 1988b. "Continuity and Change in Women's Political Agenda." In *The Politics of the Gender Gap: The Social Construction of Political Influence,* ed. Carol M. Mueller. Newbury Park, CA: Sage.

———. 1991. "The Gender Gap and Women's Political Influence." *Annals of the American Academy* 515:23–37.

Nelson, Candice J. 1994. "Women's PACs and the Year of the Woman." In *The Year of the Woman: Myths and Realities,* ed. Elizabeth Adell Cook, Sue Thomas, and Clyde Wilcox. Boulder, CO: Westview Press.

Neustadt, Richard E. 1990. *Presidential Power and the Modern Presidents: The Politics of Leadership from Roosevelt to Reagan.* New York: The Free Press.

Nexon, David. 1971. "Asymmetry in the Political System: Occasional Activists in the Republican and Democratic Parties, 1956–1964." *American Political Science Review* 65:716–30.

O'Neill, William L. 1969. *Everyone Was Brave: A History of Feminism in America.* New York: Quadrangle/The New York Times Book Co.

Orfield, Gary. 1975. *Congressional Power: Congress and Social Change.* New York: Harcourt Brace Jovanovich.

Page, Benjamin I. 1978. *Choices and Echoes in Presidential Elections: Rational Man and Electoral Democracy.* Chicago: The University of Chicago Press.

Palfrey, Thomas R. 1984. "Spatial Equilibrium with Entry." *Review of Economic Studies* 21:139–56.

Perlez, Jane. 1984. "Plan to Omit Rights Amendment From Platform Brings Objections." *New York Times,* May 17, p. B14.

Petrocik, John R. 1981. *Party Coalitions: Realignments and the Decline of the New Deal Party System.* Chicago: The University of Chicago Press.

Phillips, Kevin. 1969. *The Emerging Republican Majority.* New Rochelle, NY: Arlington House.

Plutzer, Eric. 1988. "Work Life, Family Life, and Women's Support for Feminism." *American Sociological Review* 53:640–49.

Polsby, Nelson W. and Aaron Wildavsky. 1991. *Presidential Elections: Contemporary Strategies of American Electoral Politics.* Eighth Edition. New York: The Free Press.

Pomper, Gerald M. with Susan S. Lederman. 1980. *Elections in America: Control and Influence in Democratic Politics.* Second Edition. New York: Longman.

Poole, Keith T. 1997. "Changing Minds? Not in Congress!" GSIA Working Paper 1997–22, Carnegie-Mellon University.

Poole, Keith T. and Howard Rosenthal. 1991. "Patterns in Congressional Voting." *American Journal of Political Science* 35:228–78.
———. 1997. *Congress: A Political-Economic History of Roll Call Voting*. New York: Oxford University Press.
Raines, Howell. 1980. "Reagan Implies He Wants Platform To Drop Equal Rights Endorsement." *New York Times*, June 21, p. 8.
———. 1983a. "President Is Assailed By Women's Leader; 2d Term Is Opposed." *New York Times*, July 10, p. A1.
———. 1983b. "Democrats Line Up on Feminist Issues." *New York Times*, July 11, p. A1.
Ranney, Austin. 1968. "The Concept of 'Party.'" In *Political Research and Political Theory*, ed. Oliver Garceau. Cambridge, MA: Harvard University Press.
Ranney, Austin and Willmoore Kendall. 1956. *Democracy and the American Party System*. New York: Harcourt, Brace and Company.
Redford, Emmette S. 1969. *Democracy in the Administrative State*. New York: Oxford University Press.
Regens, James L. 1989. "Congressional Cosponsorship of Acid Rain Controls." *Social Sciences Quarterly* 70:505–12.
Reingold, Beth. 1992. "Concepts of Representation among Female and Male State Legislators." *Legislative Studies Quarterly* 17:509–37.
Reinhold, Robert. 1978. "Government Expands 'Minority' Definition; Some Groups Protest." *New York Times*, July 30, 1978, p. A1.
Reiter, Howard L. 1993. *Parties and Elections in Corporate America*. Second Edition. New York: Longman.
Riker, William H. 1986. *The Art of Political Manipulation*. New Haven, CT: Yale University Press.
Ripley, Randall B. and Grace A. Franklin. 1976. *Congress, the Bureaucracy, and Public Policy*. Homewood, IL: Dorsey Press.
Robertson, Nan. 1965. "Johnson Discerns Crisis in Families." *New York Times*, July 30, p. 29.
Rohde, David W. 1991. *Parties and Leaders in the Postreform House*. Chicago: The University of Chicago Press.
Rosenfeld, Rachel A. and Kathryn B. Ward. 1996. "Evolution of the Contemporary Women's Movement." *Research in Social Movements, Conflict and Change* 19:51–73.
Rosentiel, Thomas B. 1994. "It's Rush Night for GOP's Lawmakers-in-Waiting." *Los Angeles Times*, December 11, p. A41.
Rossi, Alice S., ed. 1973. *The Feminist Papers: From Adams to de Beauvoir*. New York: Columbia University Press.
Saint-Germain, Michelle A. 1989. "Does Their Difference Make a Difference? The Impact of Women on Public Policy in the Arizona Legislature." *Social Science Quarterly* 70:956–68.
Salisbury, Robert H. and Michael MacKuen. 1981. "On the Study of Party Realignment." *Journal of Politics* 43:523–30.
Sanbonmatsu, Kira. 1996. "Gender Issues: Challenge to the Party System, 1968–1996." Paper presented at the 1996 American Political Science Association Meeting, August 29–September 1, San Francisco.

Sapiro, Virginia. 1981. "Research Frontier Essay: When Are Interests Interesting? The Problem of Political Representation of Women." *American Political Science Review* 75:701–16.

Scammon, Richard S., Alice V. McGillivray, and Rhodes Cook. 1998. *America Votes 22: A Handbook of Contemporary American Election Statistics.* Washington, DC: Congressional Quarterly.

Schattschneider, E. E. 1942. *Party Government.* New York: Holt, Rinehart and Winston.

———. 1960. *The Semi-Sovereign People: A Realist's View of Democracy in America.* New York: Holt, Rinehart and Winston.

Schiller, Wendy J. 1995. "Senators as Political Entrepreneurs: Bills Sponsorship to Shape Legislative Agendas." *American Journal of Political Science* 39:186–203.

Schlafly, Phyllis. 1964. *A Choice Not an Echo.* Alton, IL: Pere Marquette Press.

Schlesinger, Joseph A. 1975. "The Primary Goals of Political Parties: A Clarification of Positive Theory." *American Political Science Review* 69:840–49.

———. 1984. "On the Theory of Party Organization." *Journal of Politics* 46:369–400.

———. 1985. "The New American Political Party." *American Political Science Review* 79:1152–69.

Schlozman, Kay Lehman. 1984. "What Accent the Heavenly Chorus? Political Equality and the American Pressure System." *Journal of Politics* 46:1006–32.

Schlozman, Kay Lehman and John T. Tierney. 1986. *Organized Interests and American Democracy.* New York: Harper & Row.

Shafer, Byron. 1988. *Bifurcated Politics: Evolution and Reform in the National Party Convention.* Cambridge, MA: Harvard University Press.

———, ed. 1991. *The End of Realignment? Interpreting America's Electoral Eras.* Madison: The University of Wisconsin Press.

Shafer, Byron E. and William J.M. Claggett. 1995. *The Two Majorities: The Issue Context of Modern American Politics.* Washington, DC: The Brookings Institution.

Shanahan, Eileen. 1972. "Feminists Rate Democratic Vote Record in House over G.O.P.'s." *New York Times,* January 20, p. 54.

———. 1973. "Women's Group Vows Poverty Fight." *New York Times,* February 20, p. 38.

———. 1975. "Democratic Women Form an Alliance and Will Seek Woman Vice President." *New York Times,* October 14, p. 18.

———. 1976. "G.O.P. Feminists Angry at Party." *New York Times,* July 28, p. 9.

Shepsle, Kenneth A. 1972a. "The Strategy of Ambiguity: Uncertainty and Electoral Competition." *American Political Science Review* 66:555–68.

———. 1972b. "Parties, Voters, and the Risk Environment: A Mathematical Treatment of Electoral Competition Under Uncertainty." In *Probability Models of Collective Decision Making,* ed. Richard G. Niemi and Herbert F. Weisberg. Columbus, OH: Charles E. Merrill.

Sinclair, Barbara. 1982. *Congressional Realignment, 1925–1978.* Austin: University of Texas Press.

Smeal, Eleanor. 1984. *Why and How Women Will Elect the Next President.* New York: Harper & Row.

Smith, Mark A. 1997. "The Nature of Party Governance: Connecting Conceptualization and Measurement." *American Journal of Political Science* 41:1042–56.

Sorauf, Frank. 1992. *Inside Campaign Finance: Myths and Realities.* New Haven, CT: Yale University Press.

Spiegel, Irving. 1967. "'Under-Realized Resource.'" *New York Times*, April 14, p. 34.

Stanley, Alessandra. 1992. "'Family Values' and Women: Is G.O.P. a House Divided?" *New York Times*, August 21, p. A1.

Sullivan, Denis G., Jeffrey L. Pressman, Benjamin I. Page, and John J. Lyons. 1974. *The Politics of Representation: The Democratic Convention 1972.* New York: St. Martin's Press.

Sundquist, James L. 1973. *Dynamics of the Party System: Alignment and Realignment in the United States.* Washington, DC: The Brookings Institution.

Tabor, Mary B.W. and Peter Applebome. 1992. "Voices of Women in the 'Family Values' Debate: a Sampling, North and South." *New York Times*, August 21, p. A13.

Taeuber, Cynthia M. 1996. *Statistical Handbook on Women in America.* Second Edition. Phoenix: The Oryx Press.

Taylor, Stuart, Jr. 1983. "Justice Aide Resigns, Denouncing Reagan Views on Women's Rights." *New York Times*, August 22.

Thomas, Sue. 1989. "Voting Patterns in the California Assembly: The Role of Gender." *Women and Politics* 9:43–53.

———. 1991. "The Impact of Women on State Legislative Policies." *Journal of Politics* 53:958–76.

———. 1994. "Women in State Legislatures: One Step at a Time." In *The Year of the Woman: Myths and Realities*, ed. Elizabeth Adell Cook, Sue Thomas, and Clyde Wilcox. Boulder, CO: Westview Press.

Thomas, Sue and Susan Welch. 1991. "The Impact of Gender on Activities and Priorities of State Legislators." *Western Political Quarterly* 44:445–56.

Thompson, Hunter S. 1973. *Fear and Loathing: On the Campaign Trail '72.* New York: Warner Books.

Tolchin, Susan and Martin Tolchin. 1976. *Clout: Womanpower and Politics.* New York: G.P. Putnam's Sons.

Toner, Robin. 1987a. "NOW Head Criticizes Democrats As Being Aloof on Women's Issues." *New York Times*, July 9, 1987, p. A23.

———. 1987b. "Democrats and Women: Party Shifts Approach." *New York Times*, July 11, 1987, p. 10.

———. 1993. "Easing Abortion Policy: Clinton Orders Reversal of Abortion Restrictions Left by Reagan and Bush." *New York Times*, January 23, p. 1.

Wald, Kenneth D. 1987. *Religion and Politics in the United States.* New York: St. Martin's Press.

Weaver, Warren, Jr. 1980a. "Equal Rights Plan Splits Republicans Drafting Platform." *New York Times*, July 8, p. 1.

———. 1980b. "Foes of Equal Rights Plank Win: Republicans Also Back Proposed Amendment to Prohibit Abortions." *New York Times*, July 9, p. 1.

———. 1980c. "Full G.O.P. Platform Panel Votes to Abandon Rights Amendment." *New York Times*, July 10, p. 1.

Weisman, Steven R. 1983a. "Reagan's Joke Sours His Apology to Women." *New York Times*, August 4.

———. 1983b. "President Defends Policies On Women and Economy." *New York Times*, August 27, p. A5.

Wielhouwer, Peter W. and Brad Lockerbie. 1994. "Party Contacting and Political Participation, 1952–90." *American Journal of Political Science* 38:211–29.

Wilcox, Clyde. 1994. "Why Was 1992 the 'Year of the Woman'? Explaining Women's Gains in 1992." In *The Year of the Woman: Myths and Realities*, ed. Elizabeth Adell Cook, Sue Thomas, and Clyde Wilcox. Boulder, CO: Westview Press.

Wilson, Rick K. and Cheryl D. Young. 1997. "Cosponsorship in the United States Congress." *Legislative Studies Quarterly* 22:25–43.

Winters, Richard. 1976. "Party Control and Policy Change." *American Journal of Political Science* 20:597–636.

Witt, Evan. 1985. "What the Republicans Have Learned about Women." *Public Opinion* 8:49–52.

Wittman, Donald A. 1973. "Parties as Utility Maximizers." *American Political Science Review* 67:490–98.

———. 1977. "Candidates with Policy Preferences: A Dynamic Model." *Journal of Economic Theory* 14:180–89.

———. 1983. "Candidate Mobilization: A Synthesis of Alternative Theories." *American Political Science Review* 77:142–57.

———. 1990. "Spatial Strategies When Candidates Have Policy Preferences." In *Advances in the Spatial Theory of Voting*, ed. James M. Enelow and Melvin J. Hinich. Cambridge: Cambridge University Press.

Wolbrecht, Christina and Andrew D. Martin. n.d. "Cosponsoring, Waffling, and Bandwagoning on the ERA: Pre-Floor Decision Making in the House of Representatives." Unpublished Manuscript, University of Notre Dame.

Women's Bureau of the U.S. Department of Labor. 1976. *The Role and Status of Women Workers in the United States and Japan*. Washington, D.C.: U.S. Government Printing Office.

———. 1985. *The United Nations Decade for Women, 1976–1985: Employment in the United States*. Washington, DC: U.S. Government Printing Office.

Zaller, John R. 1992. *The Nature and Origins of Mass Opinion*. New York: Cambridge University Press.

New York Times Articles

By Date (No Author)

'President Says Women Qualify for His Position." *New York Times*, January 14, 1954, p. 16.

"Equal Rights for Women Stir a Distaff Argument." *New York Times*, August 12, 1956, p. 61.

"Equal Rights Mentioned in Message First Time." *New York Times*, January 17, 1957, p. 17.

"'Mere Man' Might Think Women Have Equality." *New York Times*, August 8, 1957, p. 6.

"President Vetoes the 'Woman Angle,'" *New York Times*, June 19, 1958, p. 35.

"Backs Women's Rights: Nixon Favors Amendment to Guarantee Sex Equality." *New York Times*, September 3, 1960, p. 18.

"Careers for Women Pushed by Johnson." *New York Times*, March 1, 1966, p. 42.

"Republican Feminists Prepare to Fight for Convention Delegates, Rights Amendment and Abortion." *New York Times*, February 19, 1976, p. 25.

"AFL-CIO Convention Moved at Women's Request." *New York Times*, January 6, 1979, p. 6.

"44 G.O.P. Lawmakers Urge Party to Retain Its Equal Rights Plank." *New York Times*, July 2, 1980, p. 16.

"The Storm over Women's Rights." *New York Times*, August 20, 1980, p. A18.

"G.O.P. Women Assail Stand of Reagan on Equal Rights." *New York Times*, October 13, 1981, p. 8.

"NOW, a Tactical Change." *New York Times*, February 12, 1982, p. A20.

"Miss Reagan Is Hired As Advisor on Women." *New York Times*, August 24, 1983, p. A21.

women (*cont.*)
126, 151, 175, 177; as workers, 12, 42,
100, 127, 154–55, 176, 177
Women's Bureau (of the Department of
Labor), 100; and the ERA, 30, 32, 153,
167; as nexus of women's rights debate,
67, 135, 226
Women's Campaign Fund (WCF), 57–58,
61
Women's Caucus (Democratic Party), 36–
37, 45, 56, 63
Women's Division (Democratic Party), 27,
29
Women's Equity Action League (WEAL),
34, 163, 165
women's movement, 21, 33, 35, 54, 136–
37, 140, 153, 158, 215, 227; first wave,
21, 25, 159, 161–62; effect on women's
rights debate, 124–25, 144, 161–68, 175

women's rights, 133, 137; definition of,
19–21, 79, 100, 105, 239–40; elite
attention to, 139–43; party realignment
on, 4–6, 66, 92, 94–96; public attention
to, 136–39; redefinition of, 123–24,
135–36, 144, 151–52, 157–59, 161,
164, 170. *See also* specific policy issues;
agenda, political; ideological spectrum;
issue equilibrium disruption
Women's Strike for Equality (1970), 35,
140, 229
Women's Trade Union League (WTUL),
155
women-owned business, 47, 165

Yard, Molly, 56
Young Republicans, 40
Young Women's Christian Association
(YWCA), 153